*The World
of Mary O'Connell*

for my grandmothers,
Florence Bishop and Isabel McCormick

The World
of Mary O'Connell

[1778 – 1836]

ERIN I. BISHOP

The Lilliput Press, Dublin

First published 1999 by
THE LILLIPUT PRESS LTD
62–63 Sitric Road, Arbour Hill,
Dublin 7, Ireland.

A CIP record for this
title is available from
The British Library.

ISBN 1 901866 19 x

The Lilliput Press receives financial assistance from
An Chomhairle Ealaíon/The Arts Council of Ireland.

Set in 11 on 14 Elegant Garamond
Index by John Bergin
Printed and bound in England by Biddles Ltd

Contents

Acknowledgments

This book was originally written as a doctoral thesis for the National University of Ireland, University College Dublin. I owe a great deal of thanks to my post-graduate advisor, Donal McCartney, for encouraging me to pursue a dissertation on a virtually unknown woman. I am also extremely grateful for the support, guidance and encouragement of my doctoral advisor, Professor Mary E. Daly. In addition, I am indebted to the many staff persons, librarians and archivists who aided my research, most especially those at the National Library of Ireland. I also owe thanks to the staff at the UCD Archives and the UCD Computing Services. The Southern Illinois University School of Medicine at Springfield, especially Barbara Moran, provided invaluable help in relation to the chapter on sickness and health. The staff of the Tralee Library and Derrynane National Historic Park also aided my research, as did many other individuals, among them Dr Tim O'Neill, Professor Ingrid Scobie, Professor Maurice R. O'Connell, Dr Maurice Bric, Anne Quinlan, Katherine O'Sullivan, Jeffrey Connor and Gerry Lyne. I wish to express my gratitude to Antony Farrell for taking an interest in Mary O'Connell and to Brendan Barrington for his diligence, patience and attention to detail in editing the manuscript. It is a better piece of work thanks to his expertise. And to my parents, my friends and my family, who patiently listened and, even after five years, still managed to look somewhat interested, I am eternally grateful.

Introduction

The surviving correspondence of the O'Connell family is staggering in size and content. A large part of the correspondence is made up of letters between Mary and Daniel O'Connell. There are 315 extant letters written by Mary O'Connell between the years 1800 and 1836, 262 of which were written to her husband. When added to the 764 surviving letters she received from him, they make an astounding collection. In addition to the correspondence between husband and wife for these years, letters between them and their children still exist, as do letters amongst the siblings. The family papers also include the reminiscences of Ellen O'Connell-FitzSimon, a journal of Kate O'Connell and a small diary of Daniel O'Connell, Jr.[1]

My research on Mary O'Connell began with the letters published in *The Correspondence of Daniel O'Connell* (8 vols, Shannon, 1972), edited by Professor M.R. O'Connell. I owe a debt to Professor O'Connell for his accurate transcriptions and careful annotations. Due to deadlines and constraints of space, Professor O'Connell was forced to edit the letters, and he notes that what was taken out (all carefully marked by ellipses) included any material he found 'tedious' or 'repetitious', much of which dealt with family matters. Therefore, upon concluding my analysis of all the published letters (including the correspondence published by W.J. Fitzpatrick in 1888[2]), it was necessary to look at the originals as well in order to glean information lost in those ellipses.

Professor O'Connell estimated that there were 660 extant letters from O'Connell to Mary.[3] To my surprise and delight, I found over one hundred more, making a total of 1026 letters between the couple. Of these, 176 had never been published. The material that previous scholars thought to be irrelevant proved to be the heart of my research, for it is in this mass of seemingly extraneous detail that the private lives of Mary and Daniel emerge. From the 'trivial' accounts of family matters emerge many stories, each shedding light on the virtually unexamined world of Mary O'Connell.

Historians generally agree that Mary was a good match for O'Connell. Robin Dudley Edwards wrote that despite Mary's lack of fortune, her

> gifts were, however, far more necessary to him [O'Connell]. She had no brilliance, could in no way outshine him, but was an admirable recipient for all his confidences. She provided, in addition to their substantial family, a wealth of common sense and down-to-earth devotion to his family, to his interests, to his career.

She was, in short, 'probably the most stabilizing influence on his career'.[4] Michael MacDonagh depicts O'Connell in his domestic life as 'supremely happy … at home there was always peace and sunshine, the love of a most devoted wife, and the endearing voices of children'.[5] Fergus O'Ferrall writes of Mary, 'She was intelligent, perceptive and understanding, and she and her children gave O'Connell enormous praise and support … Mary was crucial for O'Connell in being perhaps the only human being in whom he could confide, almost totally, his misgivings, vanities, triumphs and defeats.' While generous in his depiction of Mary as a wife, O'Ferrall is less than kind in his assessment of Mary as a mother, stating that 'due to O'Connell's lengthy and frequent absences [the children] were probably more influenced by her. The tremendous O'Connell life-force displayed by [Daniel's uncle] Hunting Cap and Daniel O'Connell was not transmitted through Mary O'Connell to the next generation, which was characterised by bourgeois mediocrity.'[6]

Each of these historians views Mary in relation to how O'Connell perceived her or how she affected his life. None view her in her own right, as a person, a woman. In these few phrases of O'Connell's biographers she is flat and lifeless, the many sides to her personality hidden by O'Connell's massive shadow.

Helen Mulvey's treatment of the O'Connell correspondence, specifically the letters between Mary and Daniel, was the first to intimate that Mary O'Connell was 'a more complicated, interesting and forceful woman than any of O'Connell's biographers have suggested'.[7] Oliver MacDonagh, in his biography of O'Connell, has painted perhaps the most rounded and sensitive portrait of Mary O'Connell to date.[8] Still, in both these works, Mary is portrayed only in relation to the Liberator: her influence on O'Connell is exaggerated, while her private domestic concerns are trivialized and even criticized. O'Connell's biographers make Mary over to mirror his public persona—be it as a subordinate wife or an intellectual companion.

In order to place Mary at the centre of this study and to explore the complexity of her experience as a middle-class Catholic woman in nineteenth-century Ireland, I have opted against the chronological format of the traditional biography. A strict adherence to chronology in telling Mary's tale would bring the political events of the day to the fore of my narrative. Daniel O'Connell would once again take centre stage, leaving Mary hidden in the background. Instead I have taken a thematic approach. After the opening chapter, which gives a biographical overview of Mary's life, each chapter addresses a specific issue in her life and allows a glimpse into the lives of middle-class Catholic women in the early decades of the nineteenth century.[9]

While the primary source material for this project is extensive, it does leave many gaps. In the first place, material pertaining to Mary before her marriage to O'Connell is non-existent. Secondly, letters between Mary and her mother, daughters, sisters and female friends are also no longer extant. Thirdly, many of the letters Mary wrote to her husband were destroyed or are missing. This is especially true of any chastising or 'scolding' letters O'Connell may have received from his wife, which he himself destroyed. Finally, because Mary and Daniel were rarely separated after 1830 (she followed him to London during the parliamentary sessions, leaving her grown children in Ireland), little is known of Mary's life in the years preceding her death in 1836 at the age of fifty-eight.

These gaps notwithstanding, the surviving letters are enormously valuable and open several relevant topics worthy of discussion. Most obviously, a portrayal of Mary O'Connell must include an analysis of marriage, domesticity and mothering—for these were central to her world. In addition, I have investigated the role Mary played with regard to her family's religious practices, the importance of health and well-being in nineteenth-century Ireland and the many aspects of 'kin work'—letter writing, gossip and visiting—through which Mary retained and strengthened her family's extended kin network.

Mary's story will help to fill a gap in the history of women in Ireland. There is very little source material available to document the experiences of Irish women of any rank, religion or era. Little scholarly study has been carried out on the scant source material in existence, although increased interest and research in the field of women's history is beginning to fill this void.[10] L.A. Clarkson and L.M. Cullen have both utilized the memoirs of Dorothea Herbert to ascertain patterns of 'love, labour and life' in and around late-eighteenth-century Carrick-on-Suir; Stella Tillyard's research on the Lennox sisters provides further insight into the social and cultural history of female members of the Ascendancy in Ireland in the late eighteenth and early nineteenth centuries; the diary of Mary Shackleton furnished Kevin O'Neill with the source material for his analysis of gender and adolescence in rural areas during the same period; Mary McNeill's biography of Mary Ann McCracken tells the story of a Belfast woman in the tumultuous 1790s and after; and the letters between Bishop Edward Synge and his daughter Alicia, recently published in full and edited by Marie-Louise Legg, are a valuable source for women's and social history.[11] The experience of Mary O'Connell—the only Catholic among the women listed above and, besides McCracken, the only member of the middle class—will add to this small pool of knowledge. This biographical account, then, also stands as a social and cultural history of Ireland from 1800 to 1836, a period in which great change took place—the Industrial Revolution in England, the fall of the *ancien régime* in France, unprecedented population growth in Ireland, the collapse of ancient Gaelic culture and language, the Act of Union and Catholic Emancipation.

Daniel Corkery coined the term 'the hidden Ireland' in his work of the same title first published in 1925. The concept has long since been established as a means of interpreting the eighteenth- and early nineteenth-century economic and social history of Ireland. The problem with Corkery's theory is that it depends on the existence of two opposing cultural worlds: the ruling élite and the common people. For Corkery, the worlds of the Protestant Ascendancy and the Gaelic peasantry were wholly separate ones, between which no interaction could take place. While few historians today would entirely accept Corkery's concept of Ireland, his underlying image of a culturally divided society remains influential.[12]

S.J. Connolly, though critical of Corkery's over-simplified view of Irish society, recognizes the 'vertical' lines of division that separated ethnic and religious groups and the 'horizontal' lines that divided social classes. Connolly argues that 'it still remains possible to speak of a popular culture, distinguished from that of the élite by being, not necessarily illiterate, but dependent on the spoken word, governed by custom and ritual, localistic, community-minded and conservative'.[13] Drawing on Peter Burke's work,

Connolly adds that the various groups standing apart from either the élites or the commoners could be considered as 'mediators, persons with a foot in both cultural worlds that acted as channels of communication between them'.[14] Kevin Whelan, in his analysis of Catholic middlemen in eighteenth-century Ireland, has identified an 'underground gentry'—descendants of the old, Catholic, landowning families who became middlemen and farmers. 'As the *de facto* leaders of Catholic society,' Whelan writes, 'in a situation where vertical attachments persisted after their landed power was broken, such families had a pivotal brokerage role to play in the articulation of political and popular culture.'[15]

It is within this group that we find the old, landowning O'Connell family of County Kerry. The family had been a 'minor but persistent force' in the county for two centuries. More than any other factor, it was their geographic location—the western portion of the main peninsula of Kerry, also known as Iveragh—that allowed them to survive and indeed advance as small gentry. The rugged terrain of their ancestral home was not conducive to Anglicization, while the extensive Kerry coastline allowed for the smuggling of contraband which was sold to the gentry for profit and legal immunity.[16]

Like other members of the 'underground gentry', the O'Connells considered themselves—and more importantly were considered—to be part of a parallel aristocracy with a more authentic claim to the land than the surrounding Protestant gentry. In political terms, the community's acceptance and acknowledgment of the self-image of these gentlemen farmers facilitated the generation of 'a residual respect, which cushioned their decline and allowed these families to replicate their traditional status and leadership role'.[17]

The lifestyle of this underground gentry had many facets. They were obsessive about their ancestry. They became extremely influential within the Catholic Church. They enjoyed social prestige within their community and held responsibilities to local families to act as sponsors, to settle disputes and to set moral standards. In addition, these families acted as 'brokers' across political, social, cultural and economic boundaries. At ease with both gentry and common traditions and cultures, they effectively 'bridged two worlds. They were the hubs around which Catholic society revolved, the solid backbone of the emerging Catholic nation in the eighteenth and early nineteenth centuries.'[18]

This is the milieu from which Daniel O'Connell emerged, and which he never wholly abandoned. O'Connell was steeped in the Gaelic culture of his native Kerry, and, as an adult, visited Iveragh twice yearly for a vacation. These visits allowed him to regain a sense of his own identity; Oliver MacDonagh says they were 'literally recreative: they restored his harmony'.[19] Like other members of his class, O'Connell enthusiastically followed the leisurely pursuits of a gentleman while on vacation. Hunting and horse racing were some of his favourite pastimes while in Kerry. He regularly attended festivals and patterns. Furthermore, his extravagant hospitality and generous attention to kinship obligations exemplified the Gaelic ideal of gentility and breeding.

Fostered until the age of four, O'Connell's first world was that of the Gaelic peasant. His removal as a young boy to his uncle's home at Derrynane, however, also signalled his removal from this Gaelic world. The house itself, the first slated building in Iveragh, stands as a symbol of social change and modernization. Still, the process of de-Gaelicization was hardly complete. Gradually, a more formal and distant relationship developed between members of the peasantry and the Catholic gentry. As the gap widened, traditional Gaelic culture, measured in part by the use of the Irish language, fell into decline. Corkery attributes this almost entirely to political defeats, but economics was also a factor. The increased circulation of bills of exchange and bank notes in English encouraged learning that language. Economic expansion brought more extensive means of communication and increased mobility, which resulted in many Irish leaving home or entering the military. Mobility in turn exposed more people to new customs, assumptions, languages and cultures, all of which facilitated change.[20] O'Connell himself firmly believed that 'the superior utility of the English tongue, as the medium of all modern communication, is so great that I can witness without a sigh the gradual disuse of Irish'.[21] The rationale behind this view went beyond the superior utility of the English language. The Gaelic way of life was generally viewed as less advanced than the English. As Gerard Murphy puts it:

> A natural tendency to choose what is economically advantageous in preference to what is economically disadvantageous, to choose the mature in preference to the immature, to choose civilization in preference to barbarism, and to choose what is vital and growing in preference to what is decaying, is doubtless, then, what has all along been at the root of the gradual yet consistent abandonment of Gaelicism by those born into it.[22]

Gradually, then, Irish society in the late eighteenth century became increasingly complex and unstable. The Penal Laws had been in place in Ireland since the seventeenth century.[23] Despite these restrictions, Catholicism was widely practised without much government interference. As the eighteenth century progressed the penal codes were relaxed. By the 1790s Catholic priests were being trained at Maynooth, Catholics could buy and sell land, intermarriage between Catholics and Protestants was allowed, and, in 1792–3, the franchise was granted. In 1792 Catholics were allowed to sit at the bar, prompting O'Connell's uncle 'Hunting Cap' to direct his nephew into the legal profession.

The patriarchal bond which joined the Gaelic lord and his followers no longer existed by the late eighteenth century. The money economy of the new world was fast replacing the trade and service system that had characterized Gaelic life. This new system eroded the affectionate bond between the patriarchal lord and his follower. As a result, the breach between Catholic peasantry and Catholic gentry grew.[24]

Another important development was the emergence of a Catholic middle class. The penal laws having effectively wiped out Catholic land-owning, Catholics took up different pursuits. Their representation within the professions gradually increased throughout the early nineteenth century. As they rose to affluence through professions such as medicine, commerce and, later, law, the new middle class rebelled against their exclusion from political life and societal influence. Gradually, they replaced the Catholic landowners as the representatives of Catholic interests, with Daniel O'Connell at their head.[25]

O'Connell's healthy earnings at the bar placed his family in the upper ranks of the middle class. The year O'Connell married Mary he made approximately £500. By 1807, his work at the bar, coupled with an increase in special engagements, earned him £2000. This increased to £3000 within four years and was probably £6000 or £7000 by 1815. In addition, from 1809 on O'Connell, as a Kerry landowner, took in upwards of £1000 per annum in rent.[26]

As a member of a growing middle class, Mary O'Connell lived a life marked by the overlaps that accompanied the social, political, philosophical and economic changes of her era. Ideas and practices that were at once traditional and modern, patriarchal and domestic, superstitious and scientific, pagan and orthodox, public and private, combined to influence the ways in which she and her contemporaries lived out their lives.

In 1778, the year Mary O'Connell was born, the Irish language was still widely used in Ireland. The life of the Catholic gentry was 'largely Gaelic in tone', although most members of this class were bilingual, speaking English amongst themselves and with the Protestant Ascendancy, while using Irish with the local tenantry and servants. Mary, however, was far removed from this Gaelic heritage. Born and bred in the Kerry town of Tralee, the product of a mixed marriage, she had very little exposure to the Gaelic background in which her husband was so immersed. She had little or no Irish. When discussing the wet-nurse engaged for her first-born son, Maurice, she told her husband, '[S]he does not speak a word of English which to me you know is unpleasant.' Still, she would make do with the woman, who had been chosen because she was the wife of O'Connell's foster brother.[27] Elevated in rank by her marriage into the old landowning O'Connell family, she embarked with her new husband on a path towards modernization. Although she clung to some traditional practices, in every aspect of her life, be it her ideas on domesticity, her religious practices or her theories on child-rearing, Mary embraced the new and progressive ideals of her class and era, perhaps more so than her learned husband. The King of the Beggars was in fact married to a Queen of the Bourgeoisie.

A NOTE ON THE TEXT

Mary O'Connell used punctuation sparingly and sometimes eccentrically in her letters, and she did not bother to capitalize initial letters of sentences. To aid the reader I have capitalized these initial letters and added a modicum of punctuation, although missing apostrophes have not been restored. Mary often underlined and capitalized words for no apparent reason, and these quirks have been retained, with underlined words appearing in italics. While Mary's spelling was relatively good, she often used alternate spellings of names, even for her own children—Betsey or Betsy, Ricarda or Rickarda—and I have not interfered with this either. In all the letters quoted, archaic words and spellings have been retained without comment; only misspellings and incomprehensible phrases have been marked [sic].

1

MARY O'CONNELL

Mary O'Connell was born in Tralee, Co. Kerry, on 25 September 1778. Her father, Thomas O'Connell, was a physician there. Dr O'Connell, a member of the Church of Ireland, was a widower with three children when he married Mary's mother, Ellen Tuohy. Ellen was a Catholic, and thus, as was the fashion, all the girls of this union, including Mary, were raised as Catholics, and the boys as Protestants. The family was a large one—eleven children, counting the three from the first marriage. Thomas's death in 1785, and the subsequent loss of his income, brought financial difficulty to the family. The large number of children and the family's relative poverty meant that Mary would have no dowry, an extreme handicap for any woman wishing to make a good marriage. Little is known of Mary's early life, but after her father died she remained in her mother's home in Tralee.

Tralee was a thriving town in the late eighteenth century. Its location at the head of Tralee Bay and the lack of any rival towns in Kerry made it the focal point of economic activity in the south-west of Ireland. The booming grain trade brought wealth and prosperity to the town, which in turn spurred vast urban renewal projects. Main Street was extended and the river, which originally flowed past the Great Castle, was diverted so as to pass through the Mall and Bridge Street instead. The town hub, known as the Square, was also substantially reorganized. New assembly rooms replaced the market house, county court-house and gaol located on the Square's northern side; and soon the Square became the social centre of the county. Other projects included the construction of several housing blocks for the growing middle class. Stoughton's Row, Godfrew Place, James's Street and Prince's Quay all followed the 1805 construction of Day Place. Financed by the local judge, Robert Day, Day Place was a successful speculative venture of ten houses, all boasting cut-stone steps and ornamental railings. It was here that Mary's sister Betsey and her husband James Connor made their home.[1]

In 1800, Mary entered into a secret discourse with Daniel O'Connell of Derrynane, Co. Kerry. The two probably met at one of the many social functions surrounding the circuit court session. As a young barrister, O'Connell rode the circuit twice every year, travelling from assize town to assize town with the other attorneys and judges, taking on cases upon arrival. Since O'Connell hailed from Kerry, it was only logical that he travel the Munster circuit, which incorporated Cork and Limerick cities, Ennis and Tralee. Here his many friends and relatives provided ample business for the ambitious young lawyer.

For the residents of Tralee, the assizes were a welcome diversion. The session was as popular as, and even more accessible than, the theatre. Perhaps Mary observed the young barrister as he defended a case; perhaps they met at one of the many social events surrounding the assizes. Or the two may have known each other even earlier than this, as Mary, through her father, was a distant cousin of Daniel's. Moreover, Daniel's friend and sometimes co-counsel James Connor was married to Mary's sister Betsey. It is likely that O'Connell lodged with the Connors, which would have put him directly in Mary's path. In any event, in the autumn months of 1800, Mary and Daniel's relationship blossomed into intimacy and before long the two were secretly engaged. Secrecy was necessary due to the fact that Daniel stood to inherit a significant sum of money from his uncle Maurice O'Connell, familiarly known as Hunting Cap. A marriage on the part of his young nephew, without gain of a dowry, was not to be tolerated by the domineering 'old gentleman',[2] and thus a public attachment to Miss Mary O'Connell would not do.

Faced with such a dilemma, O'Connell considered the matter carefully—he claimed he loved her long before he ever spoke to her on the subject—and decided he had found in Mary a potential partner unlike any woman he had known before. He confessed that while he had spoken of love to other women, she was the only woman he had ever addressed as his intended wife and partner. Though his letters seemed almost excessively impassioned, he assured Mary that his was not 'the idle love of a romantick boy'; rather, he regarded her with 'the affection of a man'.[3] Still, O'Connell was fully aware of the inappropriateness of addressing the young Miss O'Connell under such unusual circumstances and he spoke sensitively on the subject in the earliest surviving letter between the two:

> You will I hope, my dear Mary excuse me for not having written to you sooner. If it were a mere letter of ceremony or any matter of form I certainly should not have remained a week in town without having done that which Politeness requires; but when I write to you my heart and my affections are too deeply engaged to permit me lightly to put pen to paper, or to write with my usual rapidity ... Believe me My sweet Mary, that I really and truly love you and that I anxiously await the moment of convincing you how sincere and how fixt my regard is for you. You have I hope a sufficient reliance on my honor to be convinced that I write but what I think. There certainly is a great delicacy in my addressing you. I mean that I feel my situation is peculiarly distressing and delicate. I know that my attachment for you is of the most pure and honorable kind, I have but one motive and that is to make you happy.—Yet my sweet love, you know that it is not in my power to publish my situation or to call on you in the face of the world for a return of regard. I feel that I do not merit your affection. I have not had it in my power to show you how much I desire to do so. But if you will take the word for the deed until I am able to give stronger proof you will believe that your happiness is dearer to me than any earthly object. If you concur with me in Sentiment. If I am happy enough to hold the first place in your affections. Then I conjure you by the sincerity of my love not to risk all my hopes of happiness by communicating to any person whatsoever our— shall I call it our attachment. You know as well as I do how much we have at stake in keeping the business secret. I have certainly more at stake than ever I had before or I really believe if I fail at present I shall ever have again. Secrecy is therefore a favour I earnestly beg of you.[4]

Mary willingly agreed to his request. She confirmed that she reciprocated his feelings and happily entered into the secret attachment he suggested. It was not, of course, easy to maintain such secrecy as was necessary. Immediately O'Connell saw the benefits of bringing Mary up to Dublin, where 'I would have many more opportunities of seeing and conversing with you than in that prying, curious, busy town of Tralee'.[5] While this plan was being realized, however, a secret and discreet correspondence would have to suffice.

In the beginning, O'Connell relied upon a mutual friend, named Daniel O'Connell but known as Splinter, to convey his letters to Mary. Yet this was not always the most expedient method, especially if Splinter left Tralee. Even when in Tralee the dedicated, but unappreciated, intermediary sometimes could not be found—at least not where he was supposed to be. 'I was obliged to direct [my last letter] myself as that damned Splinter was at the play,' O'Connell fumed. This problem occurred on more than one occasion and left O'Connell enraged. 'He is not to be found,' he complained to Mary. 'He is very inconsiderate.'[6] Moreover, the frequency of Splinter's letters to Mary was bound to raise suspicion, and finally did so when Mary's brother Rickard intercepted one of the letters. Rickard was extremely displeased and thought it highly improper that Mary should hold a correspondence with any young man.[7]

Gradually, then, the circle of those in the know expanded. O'Connell himself wrote to Mary's mother because he 'felt that mentioning it to her was a compliment which I justly owed to your delicacy'.[8] Ellen O'Connell was delighted with the news. According to Mary, O'Connell had made her mother 'the happiest of women' by letting her in on the secret.[9] Once Ellen O'Connell was in the circle, she helped in furthering the couple's attachment. When Rickard O'Connell protested Mary's receipt of letters from a young admirer, Ellen intervened on Mary's behalf, saying she sanctioned the correspondence and found no impropriety in the letters. Lying to Rickard, she claimed she had read the letters and found them to be 'of the most innocent nature'. Rickard would not be appeased, however, until he wrote to Mary on the subject himself. The incident provoked a letter from Ellen O'Connell to Daniel, begging that he desist with the correspondence to spare Mary any more remarks from her brother.[10]

The lengths to which O'Connell went in diverting attention from his new romance knew no bounds. Following Mary's mother's plea to desist from writing, O'Connell sent Mary a 'mock' letter regarding a lottery ticket. By discussing a trivial and impersonal topic he was able to write to her directly 'without risk of my letter being seen or spoken of if it were so seen as to render it necessary for you to tell a slight fib about it'.[11]

Of course, tricks like these were impractical for two young lovers bent on regular correspondence. Therefore, James Connor, O'Connell's law partner and Mary's brother-in-law, was also let in on the secret, and O'Connell began to direct his letters through James. While more reliable than Splinter, James had his shortcomings as a courier as well. One of the first letters Mary received via James had James's handwriting on the envelope. His wife Betsey, present when the letter was delivered, recognized the writing and for some reason was convinced that her husband had fallen ill. She could not be persuaded otherwise until Mary told her the truth. Now four individuals besides Mary and Daniel knew of their secret.[12]

Worries that news of their attachment might spread further filled the pages of O'Connell's early letters to his love. 'For the world I would not have Rick[ard]'s wife know anything about it least [*sic*] it should reach the rest of her family who are proverbially indiscreet,' he cautioned.[13] Another real fear was the irregularity of the post, which might allow letters to fall into the wrong hands. Mails were sometimes robbed and rumours circulated that the postmaster's wife often took it upon herself to inspect Dublin letters before delivering them.[14] Moreover, letters were not always the best means by which to express matters of the heart.

Despite these many obstacles, O'Connell was not to be deterred. 'It is the ceremony that remains to be performed that should by its forced omission weaken the claims I have on you or you on me in the sight of God and Man. That ceremony is, my love, necessary I do admit for the sake of society and order as well as for conscience and honour.'[15] On 24 July 1802, with the aid of James and Betsey Connor and the complicity of Mary's mother, the couple were secretly married in Dublin, by a Rev. Finn of Irishtown. Within a few days, Mary returned to lodgings in Tralee while Daniel continued to move between Dublin, his circuit practice and the family home in Kerry. Letters continued to be the sole means by which the couple developed their relationship.

In these early days, letters from her husband, addressed to 'Miss Maria O'Connell', were Mary's only source of satisfaction. By early November, Mary was suffering not only from loneliness but also from the side-effects of her first pregnancy. So began several months of anxious worry as Daniel mustered the courage to face his uncle with the news of his secret marriage and pending fatherhood. In the end, his courage failed him and it was left to his brother John to inform Hunting Cap of his nephew's betrayal. 'My uncle is more grieved and exasperated than we were aware of,' John confided to his brother. 'I trust in God before many months elapse that [he] will overcome his disapprobation.'[16]

During the dreadful period of waiting for Hunting Cap's response, husband and wife attempted to reassure each other of their future happiness together. While O'Connell strove to convince Mary of his indifference to the real possibility of losing his fortune, Mary sought to assure O'Connell that his choice of her was not a wrong one. 'His [Hunting Cap's] displeasure my

Darling will I know give you more real sorrow than the loss of his fortune,' she commiserated. Still, she assured him, 'we will yet love be happy together. Depend on it.'[17]

The days of waiting must have been particularly difficult for Mary. She felt keenly the burden of being the cause of the falling out between her husband and his uncle. The episode caused a depression and uneasiness of spirits which in turn affected her physically. Through this illness, O'Connell continued to profess his undying love and disregard for fortune, his letters taking on a nearly wild tone. 'If you were well I care not for uncle, relative, or fortune. I would accept poverty, tortures and death to give you either happiness or even a single proof of the unceasing and consuming passion which devours whilst it consumes this anguished heart of mine,' he avowed.[18] He begged her to keep her spirits up. 'If you have any confidence in me surely you will take care of your health and not let the anger of my uncle ... prey upon your mind.'[19] Reassured, Mary seemed to recover. She reiterated her assurances that Hunting Cap's displeasure would soon pass and that all would be well. 'At all event he can't prevent us from being happy together,' she consoled. 'I declare to you most solemnly that if he altered his will tomorrow it would not give me a moment's unhappiness. It was not your fortune but yourself, my dearest heart, that I married. If you were possessed of but fifty pounds a year, I would be happy.'[20]

As time passed with no word from Hunting Cap, the couple lulled themselves into believing that no news was good news.[21] When Hunting Cap finally handed down his 'punishment' nearly a year later—effectively disinheriting his nephew—O'Connell, now more secure in his marriage and in his bar earnings, wrote to Mary:

> I really am surprised that I was so long a favourite of his and indeed I am almost ashamed of it. He could not but perceive that in every action my mind scorned the narrow bound of his. Darling, instead of vexing, it has amused me much and pleased me not a little. It surely in itself affords a vindication of my quarrel with him. How completely will he be despised ... I have more happiness in thinking of my wife—the wife of my soul—than these wretches suppose can be found on earth. How little does this man know the delight I experience in calling you mine.[22]

Despite the circumstances of the marriage, O'Connell's parents had no real objection to Mary, as John O'Connell assured his brother. 'My father disapproves of your marriage only as far as he thinks it will hurt you with your uncle. At any moment you please, he is satisfied to receive Mary at Carhen.'[23] O'Connell, however, did not immediately take his family up on the offer. In February 1803 he revealed to his wife that he had been house-hunting in Dublin and had every hope of finding a home that pleased her. 'You know my plan of domestic felicity,' he wrote. 'You approve of it too and upon that account it is doubly dear to me. I cannot enjoy happiness out of your sweet society.'[24] The search continued in April, with the help of James Connor, but to no avail. In truth, O'Connell's precarious financial situation would not allow him the luxury of a family home for some time.[25]

In June 1803 Mary gave birth to her first son, Maurice, named after Hunting Cap. By August it was determined that Mary should leave Tralee and take up residence with her in-laws in Caherciveen. The farmhouse at Carhen was of moderate size, located just outside Caherciveen on the banks of an estuary. Surrounded by low mountains and lush countryside, the home allowed for breathtaking views in all directions. 'How highly flattering to me my dearest love is the affection and kind attention I experience from all your dear family here,' Mary wrote to O'Connell upon her arrival at Carhen. '[Y]our dear Father and Mother in particular who seem to vie with each other in giving me proofs of their affection. As for our dear little Maurice, he is already a favourite with all his acquaintances.'[26] Yet a letter to her mother two months later had a different tone. O'Connell, who saw the letter, penned off a note to his upset wife. 'I am sorry to perceive … that you have not the feel of being happy. Indeed … it grieves me most sincerely to think that there exist circumstances which I cannot control to give you uneasiness.'[27]

Although the letters are not explicit, it would appear Mary's unhappiness was a result of loneliness. Married for over a year, she had never properly lived with her husband, who was now away on the circuit. To make matters worse, she had no real home of her own. Alone with her in-laws in the small house at Carhen, aware that her position as O'Connell's wife was not altogether a welcome one and had in fact caused his disinheritance, with no clear prospects of what the future held, it is understandable that she should have been on edge. The situation created tension among all involved, including O'Connell's parents, Morgan and Catherine O'Connell. Although in no way openly hostile to Mary, it is clear that they lacked enthusiasm for the union; and, as Mary and her children moved in, her parents-in-law were highly inconvenienced. 'Your father came to the gate to meet me and welcomed me in the kindest manner,' Mary told

O'Connell upon her return to Carhen in 1805. 'Your mother was out walking but soon came in and received me rather stiffly. However, I don't mind that as she is coming off of it this day.'[28] Despite this report, O'Connell's parents provided much-needed support to the young couple. Not only did they house Mary, but they also kept Maurice for nearly a year.

By March 1804 Mary was pregnant again, this time with Morgan, the couple's second son. O'Connell had taken lodgings in Dublin in November 1803. Located on Upper Ormond Quay, the accommodation consisted of three rooms on the first floor and two on the second. 'An admirably good kitchen and two servant rooms with coal cellar and a small wine vault,' O'Connell related.[29] Leaving Maurice behind in Carhen under the care of his grandparents and wet-nurse, Mary joined O'Connell in Dublin during the spring of 1804. In August, however, Mary once again made the long trek to Carhen. Reunited with Maurice, Mary waited out the end of her second pregnancy. She delivered Morgan in November, having removed to her mother's home in Tralee for the birth.

Mary remained in Tralee with Morgan until O'Connell joined her there in late December. Together the couple and their child journeyed on to Carhen, where they celebrated the holidays. Mary remained until early May 1805, at which time she and O'Connell departed together for Dublin. By this stage Mary was about two months pregnant. Once in Dublin, the couple settled themselves into their newly purchased home on Westland Row, 'a simple house, but a large one of its kind'.[30] Happily 'regulating matters', Mary wrote to O'Connell that her only cause of distress was 'taking possession without you and not having the happiness of seeing you in your own house, the day three years we were married'.[31] Yet Mary did not remain there long either. By the end of July she was back on the road to Carhen where she stayed until after the birth of her third child, Ellen, on 12 November 1805. Early in 1806 she returned to her Dublin home with Maurice and Ellen in tow. Morgan, wet-nursed on Valentia Island, remained in Kerry. Joined by O'Connell's sister Kitty, Mary finally was able to establish herself in her own residence.

Gradually the pattern of Mary and Daniel's life together was established. Every March, O'Connell left for six or eight weeks on the Munster circuit. The letters flowed between the couple nearly every day. Once the sessions had ended, O'Connell usually travelled to Carhen and Derrynane to visit his family and take care of any business that might need attending. While there, he also enjoyed a holiday of hunting and riding. Then he returned home to Mary—or she joined him somewhere along the way—only to repeat the cycle again the following autumn.

By summer 1806 Mary was pregnant again. Kate, born in March 1807, was the first O'Connell child to be born in Dublin. Mary became pregnant again in November of the same year. The early months of 1808 proved to be difficult for Mary. Her brother Edward fell ill in Tralee. The doctor 'holds out not the smallest hope of his recovery', Mary informed O'Connell, who was away in Ennis.[32] Every post brought further news of the young man's illness. At the same time, O'Connell's father was taken with 'a severe fit'. Although he was later much improved, Mary's letters continued to report on the health of both loved ones. So concerned was she over her brother's imminent death that she confined herself to her room for two days, suffering from 'grief and affliction'. O'Connell, alarmed by her behaviour, considered returning directly to Dublin. His letters continually chastised her for giving way to such grief. He asked a colleague, William Bernard, to watch over her, and, 'if it be impossible to give you sufficient fortitude to bear this calamity in my absence, I will consider my professional sacrifice of course as nothing compared with the duty and the desire of giving you support'.[33]

Fortunately Edward's condition stabilized and O'Connell remained in Munster. Mary, however, was given little relief, for shortly thereafter her housekeeper, Mrs Ryan, became sick. For nearly three weeks the woman suffered through an agonizing illness before dying late in April. Although highly sympathetic to the woman's plight, Mary was left greatly inconvenienced with four small children, one on the way, a household to run and a husband away. Luckily her sister-in-law, Betsey O'Connell, was able to lend her a hand. 'I can't tell you how glad I was to see her,' Mary confided to her husband the morning after Betsey's arrival.[34]

In July 1808 Mary delivered her third son, Edward O'Connell. Within weeks, she again moved her family to Tralee for their yearly holiday. Considering the difficulties in travel during the early nineteenth century, the frequency with which the O'Connells and their family and friends travelled is notable. Riding was the fastest, cheapest and least troublesome manner of getting around Ireland in the eighteenth and nineteenth centuries. It was the means by which most travellers, including most members of the Irish Bar, journeyed about the country. Another option for the traveller who did not own a horse or carriage was to hire a post-chaise. Although giving some shelter from the elements, the post-chaise covered only twenty to twenty-five miles a day. When travelling to areas off the beaten path, the jaunting car, particular to Ireland, was a cheap if uncomfortable alternative. Finally, the stagecoach brought great advancements in travel options. When, in 1784, a separate post office was established for Ireland, mail coach services were soon offered in addition to the stagecoach. In the early years, these coaches could carry only five passengers; as time passed they became larger, providing seating for as many as twenty. The southern mail coach left Dublin every night for Cork, taking passengers as well as post. As traffic increased, new and improved inns cropped up on roadsides, even in the most isolated places. These provided food, shelter and post horses to the weary or hurried traveller.

In general, the roads in Ireland were good. The absence of heavy-goods traffic helped to preserve road surfaces, and since few trees or hedges lined the roads, the wind and sun could more easily dry them after each rain. Moreover, immense sums of money were spent annually on their repair. Yet, despite the absence of deep ruts and potholes, road travel could be dangerous. Bandits and highwaymen plagued travellers for the first twenty years or so of the nineteenth century. Unsafe drivers and inclement weather also proved hazardous to passengers' health. Furthermore, travel by coach was slow and expensive. The journey from Dublin to Cork, for example, could take up to eighteen hours; to Limerick, twenty-one. And of course, not all roads were good. Many were only ruts or narrow laneways. Travel through the mountains could be especially perilous, with steep inclines, falling rocks and dangerous precipices. It was this type of road which wound through most of Iveragh.[35]

Nearly every summer the family set out from Dublin to holiday in the country. Visiting family and friends in Kerry was one object of these trips. In addition, the pursuit of health and well-being motivated city-dwellers like the O'Connells to seek the cleansing and beneficial air of the country. Especially in the summer, the intense heat and cramped quarters of the city created extremely unhygienic conditions in which disease could easily spread. Those of means evacuated the city in search of healthier environs. Often the destination was one of the many spas in Ireland where one could take the waters.

The 'Irish Bath' at Mallow was perhaps the best-known spa in Ireland. Mary visited Mallow every summer between the years 1812 and 1814 to partake of the spa in the hope of improving her health.[36] Located on the river Blackwater, the sleepy little town with its barracks and market-place had little to offer besides its warm springs, which were thought to cure consumption. In the summer, Mallow became a social venue for the fashionable and well-to-do. Here they drank the waters, meandered down the pleasant walks along the canals and cascades, bet on the races or attended the many dances and concerts held in the Assembly Room.[37]

In the beginning, Mary enjoyed herself at Mallow. Her letters to O'Connell described the bustling goings-on about the town as members of society arrived for the races. As long as the weather was good she found it pleasant, but 'in bad weather it is a horrid place, the house comfortless and cold'.[38] Gradually, she grew bored with the spa town. In 1814 she told O'Connell, 'This place is as stupid as the village of Cahcr[civeen?] could possibly be. I read a good deal and Ellen now and then reads a Novel. We play cards every Night which is a great indulgence to the girls.'[39] As the weather turned foul, so too did her temper: 'In all my life I never saw such a wretched place as this Town.' Indeed, she had had enough; the summer of 1814 was to be the family's last in Mallow.[40]

In 1809 Mary's son Edward O'Connell, only six months old, died from an unidentified illness. Then, in March, Mary appears to have suffered a miscarriage, and in May O'Connell's father died. By July, Mary was pregnant again and once more on the road to Tralee. As summer progressed, O'Connell began negotiations for a house in Merrion Square in Dublin, which he finally purchased despite Mary's objection to its cost. 'I wish to God you could get the house in the Square off your hands,' she implored O'Connell. 'I can't tell you, love, how unhappy I am about this business as I do not see the smallest chance of you ever getting it settled to your satisfaction … For God's sake, darling love, let me entreat of you to give up this house in the Square if it is in your power as I see no other way for you to get out of difficulties.'[41]

The house was clearly an extravagant purchase, made solely to promote O'Connell's growing social and political reputation. O'Connell had made his entrance into politics in 1800 during the union debate. Like his professional colleagues, he opposed the Act of Union, which united Britain and Ireland under one parliament located at Westminster. In 1804 he had become a member of the newly formed Catholic Committee. Among peers and baronets, he took his place as a representative of the increasingly vocal middle-class lawyers and merchants. As the composition and style of the

Catholic Committee began to change, these young and energetic middle-class members moved to seize leadership. O'Connell's aggressive politics and his reputation and talents as a lawyer propelled him to a position of power in the organization. The Catholic Committees of each county usually held their meetings during the spring assizes. O'Connell's attendance at these county meetings allowed him to reach more Catholics over a broader area, and thereby to increase his support and promote his political advancement. By 1809, the appointment of the 'notoriously unsympathetic' William Wellesley-Pole as the chief secretary further stirred agitation amongst Catholics, leaving O'Connell poised on the verge of national leadership.[42]

Sitting on the south side of Merrion Square, O'Connell's new house was a tall and stately brick structure, entirely Georgian in design. Black wrought-iron fencing and ornamental railings adorned its front steps and walk. Merrion Square was first laid out in 1762, and although it was not finished until well into the nineteenth century, its construction can be seen as marking the beginning of modern Dublin. Already, the city had been laid out on its basic north-south axis, along which, during the late eighteenth and early nineteenth centuries, the emphasis of the city shifted from Capel and Henrietta Streets, on the north side of the river Liffey, to Grafton Street on the south side. The dissolution of the Irish parliament in 1801 saw the evacuation of the many peers who had previously occupied Dublin's large urban mansions. As a result of this exodus, the professional classes moved to prominence in Dublin society. Between 1798 and 1841 the population of Dublin increased from 170,000 to 232,000. As the new century progressed, leading business and professional men moved their family homes from the city centre to the suburbs.[43] Gradually, the south-east portion of the city, including St Stephen's Green, Merrion Square and Fitzwilliam Square, became home to 'the nobility, the gentry and members of the liberal professions' while the merchant and 'official' class remained on the north side.[44]

In February 1810 Mary gave birth to Elizabeth Mary, known as Betsey, the first O'Connell child to be born at Merrion Square. Mary almost immediately became pregnant again, delivering John in December of the same year. Following this, the birth of her seventh child, Mary had her first pregnancy-free year since her marriage in 1802. Between 1812 and 1816, Mary gave birth to five more children, only one of whom survived to adulthood.[45] It was during these same years that O'Connell's activities in Irish politics began to compete with both his legal practice and his family for his time and energies.

Throughout 1812, O'Connell redoubled his efforts for Catholic Emancipation. In order to involve larger numbers in the Emancipation movement, Catholic leaders began to hold aggregate or county meetings across the countryside, and O'Connell spoke at nearly every such meeting held during the summer circuit. By the winter of 1813, he had adopted a new, populist style.[46] Consequently, the letters between Mary and Daniel became increasingly concerned with politics and political issues. Mingled with reports on health, children, gossip and social activities, Mary's political comments took no precedence in her writings or in her life; they were merely one facet of her world, arising simply from the fact that she was married to a public figure. She was well read on political subjects, combing several different newspapers. This interest was magnified as her children grew older and her husband was away even more. 'When I have not the happiness of hearing from you, my own love, it is the greatest delight to me to read of you,' she confessed.[47] An active understanding in politics was her only hold upon a husband who clearly placed his career and country over his wife and family.

Mary considered political issues in relation to their impact upon those closest to her. She wished for Emancipation, for example, because its achievement would rid her husband 'of the troublesome life you lead and leave you with your family more than you are'.[48] Above any of her religious or political affiliations, she was a woman connected to those around her. Her primary function in life was caring about others. Her opinions were formed out of concern for the people involved, not from any abstract idea of justice or human rights. 'Were I in your place I would not go a step to the Carlow meeting and, what is more, I would give up Catholic politics and leave the nasty ungrateful lot to sink into insignificance. Leave them all there and you in a short time make a fortune without sacrificing your time and your health,' she raged when O'Connell's position as leader of the Catholic Association was attacked in 1825.[49] She continued in a further letter on the subject:

> How cruelly and ungratefully the Catholics are acting by you. Is it not enough to make you retire with disgust from their service? It seems in vain to serve Ireland ... They will succeed, I fear, in setting to rest for ever the question of Emancipation. They deserve to be slaves and such they ought to be left. It only surprises me, heart, that you should persevere ... I could almost cry when I reflect for a moment on the many sacrifices you made to

21

> be of service to your Catholic countrymen and the return you met with. It is foul ingratitude and base duplicity.[50]

Moreover, when Mary voiced her opinions she often took on an apologetic tone, aware, as she wrote, that she crossed the boundary of her sphere. 'As to politics I am indeed a very bad judge,' she began in one letter to O'Connell, 'but I much fear there is little chance for Emancipation. Every thing seems to be against it and surely, while the Catholics continue to disagree among themselves, what can they expect?'[51]

As politics took on an increasingly important role within the O'Connell household, it brought with it some negative side-effects. One of these was O'Connell's propensity to engage himself in duels over political issues. In February 1815, O'Connell was called out by John D'Esterre for describing the Dublin Corporation, which was protesting against Emancipation, as 'beggarly'. D'Esterre, a member of the common council, took the epithet personally and soon the entire incident was converted into a Protestant-versus-Catholic encounter. After drawn-out preliminaries, O'Connell's shot fatally wounded his opponent, and O'Connell was forced into hiding at the home of Denys Scully. Mary was left alone at home with the firm instructions that 'If any suspicious person should come do not send *here* at all.'[52]

Scarcely had the dust settled from this affair when O'Connell found himself involved in another dispute, this time with the Chief Secretary, Robert Peel. The event—or non-event, as it turned out—was the result of 'ludicrous blunderings and misunderstandings', which probably would never have amounted to anything 'had not Peel and O'Connell been designated as champions by their respective factions'.[53] In any event, it was Mary O'Connell who, in taking matters into her own hands, effectively foiled the opponents' carefully laid plans.

O'Connell's uncle, Count Daniel O'Connell, was visiting Merrion Square at the time of O'Connell's falling-out with Peel. The General, as he was known, favoured O'Connell's taking up Peel's challenge. According to Kate O'Connell's recollections, Mary became worried and exasperated over the long conversations between her husband and his uncle, conversations carried out in French and then in Irish if a French-speaking person entered the room. Mary had neither Irish nor French and found her exclusion from such monumental deliberations intolerable. Once O'Connell had gone to bed, Mary, acting on her own initiative, alerted the sheriff to the upcoming duel and had her husband placed under house arrest. When the General voiced his stern objections at her behaviour, Mary was said to have replied, 'I am sorry to have annoyed you, uncle, but I'd much sooner vex you than let my husband be killed.'[54]

Despite the embarrassment her actions caused to her husband, Mary's decision can be easily understood. She and her husband were parents to seven children, including a three-month-old infant. Recent financial difficulties had left the family in serious debt. Moreover, the Catholic Church held that duelling was a mortal sin and Mary was the ever-vigilant protector of her loved ones' souls. As Oliver MacDonagh notes, a real gentlewoman might have turned a blind eye to these events, refraining from taking part in such obviously male matters. 'But Mary had not been bred a real gentlewoman. She was merely clear-headed and afraid.'[55]

In the end, O'Connell resorted to lying and circumvention in an attempt to engage Peel in a duel at a later date. Never, in any of the letters, did he chastise Mary for her action, which clearly had crossed the established boundaries of men's and women's spheres, and proved highly damaging to O'Connell's reputation. Instead, he begged her forgiveness. Again, Oliver MacDonagh offers the most obvious reason why. Within their relationship, Mary always held moral dominance. Although she in no way ruled her husband, she played the role of 'the perpetual forgiver; it was she who took up and held the strong positions ... as the virtual pronouncer of judgment on such ethical questions as arose between them.' O'Connell, on the other hand, time and again appeared to acquiesce before relying on duplicity to do as he pleased. Rather than confront her in anger, he opted to deceive her and then beg forgiveness when caught out.[56]

Complicating matters during these years was the near financial ruin of the O'Connell family due to the bankruptcy in 1815 of James O'Leary, a Killarney merchant for whom O'Connell stood as surety. This calamity heightened the need to economize, which would plague the family continually until 1829.[57] All of the above external stresses, coupled with the difficulties of almost continual pregnancy, childbirth and child-rearing—not to mention the loss of several children and close family members—took its toll on Mary's health. Drastic measures were necessary to restore her. In the spring of 1817, therefore, Mary removed to Clifton, England, with her daughters, son John, niece Ricarda, the governess Miss Gaghran and a few servants, in the hope that a summer spent in the spa town would revive her health and spirits. For a time it did. Yet, by autumn she had relapsed and a proposed trip to France for the winter was postponed. Mary returned to Dublin with her husband where she remained for the winter.

The trip to France finally came in the year 1822. Although the reasons for the journey were given out to others as being health-related, the correspondence clearly indicates that the journey was a financial necessity. On 2 May 1822, Mary, Ellen, Kate, Betsey, Morgan, John, Daniel Jr, O'Connell's sister Alicia Finn, and two servants, Hannah and Julia, sailed on the *Dorset*, bound for Pau via Bordeaux. Ellen O'Connell recorded their departure in her journal: 'The day was beautiful—the sea like a sheet of glass, and the air perfectly clear. My father and the others remained for a long time waving handkerchiefs on the pier, until we lost sight of them. I never felt such a chocking [*sic*] sensation as when I could see them no more.'[58]

O'Connell, too, was emotional at seeing his beloved family leave Ireland. 'How my heart travels with you and my children in your packet-boat—seasick and crowded in that small sloop a speck on the ocean,' he wrote to Mary the day after they sailed. He continued:

> I fancy myself present and blame myself for all you suffer. My sweet boy, my darling little prater complaining to his Mud who can give him no relief. My girls, my own sweet girls, suffering themselves and double sufferers by seeing their mother in torture. I do not forget my John and Morgan but they are able to bear it … I watched the wind all day yesterday. With us it was mild and fair. At night it blew fresh and I could not sleep because it blew our windows. I called them *our* but they are *my* melancholy windows.[59]

O'Connell wallowed in misery at the thought of their journey. As days passed and no word of their arrival reached Dublin, he began to fear the worst. He cursed himself for sending them all on the same packet and worried over every storm that blew through the city.[60]

The *Dorset* was a 'small but exceedingly neat and well fitted up vessel and a very good sailor'. The journey, though long and tedious, was in no way as dreadful as O'Connell had imagined. Mary suffered no sea-sickness at all, although the rest had intervals of illness, despite taking the home remedy of gingerbread to prevent it. Several times, the wind died out and the packet drifted quietly, making very little headway. Bored—'as Mama brought no books'—the children amused themselves by reading Goldsmith's *Essays*, telling stories and fishing. They arrived in Bordeaux nine days after leaving Dublin, settling in to await the arrival of Alicia's husband, William Finn.[61]

In Bordeaux, the family took lodgings with a Mrs Harrison, an Englishwoman. Formerly wealthy, she had married an American who had squandered all her money and then abandoned her. Their apartment consisted of three large rooms, two bedrooms and a dining and drawing room which was common to all boarders. Other Dubliners lodged in the house as well. On their first Sunday in Bordeaux, the family rose at six to attend mass at the Church of St Louis. 'I did not at all relish the fashion of kneeling on straw bottomed chairs,' recorded Ellen in her journal, 'it is very tiresome, and I think it very wrong to have the woman who hires them go about to collect the money a little before the Elevation. The people do not seem to have the least religion. I do not think there were *three* saying their prayers.'[62]

By 26 May, William Finn had yet to arrive and so, taking two carriages, the family departed for Pau. They travelled only fourteen miles the first day as the motion of the carriage greatly fatigued Mary. Upon arriving in Pau three days later, they met with the disappointing news that the woman who was to have arranged their accommodation had gone to the country for several days without securing them a place. And so began an extensive search for suitable lodgings. It was not an easy task. Locations were discarded for being too far out of town, too small, in poor repair, too expensive or unfurnished. Finally, on 8 June, Mary settled on an old, large, 'very handsome' house situated in the rue de Préfecture. On 10 June, however, Ellen recorded in her journal, 'A revolution in our affairs! Mama was at [the house] this morning where she found the beds in a most filthy state the agent refused to change them on which she has given up the house and is looking out for another.'[63] Eventually, on 13 June, they found suitable lodgings at 5, Cote du Moulin, Basses Ville.

The time in France proved difficult for the family. On Sunday, 11 May 1823, Ellen O'Connell began her journal, 'Exactly a year ago this day we landed in France and I do not think it contains British Subjects more heartily tired of it.'[64] The excessive heat of Pau was the worst enemy of the family, confining them to their lodgings and causing intermittent illnesses. Furthermore, Mary disliked the idea of wintering in a city where no English-speaking priest could be found. Therefore, in October, they moved to Tours where they rented a furnished house. It was hoped that the climate would be more agreeable to them all. O'Connell joined his family and helped in their relocation before returning to Dublin in November.[65]

Tours proved little better than Pau. '[O]nly that my father has bound us to this horrid house we should have gone to Paris the 1st of June—for Mama is sick of Tours, which does not agree with any of us,' recorded Ellen O'Connell.[66] As war between France and Spain became more and more likely, French soldiers quartered in the city, and only by a special reprieve was the O'Connell family exempt from housing them. Consequently, O'Connell began a plan to bring his family closer to home. England was the destination decided upon; which city in England was an issue in the letters between Mary and Daniel throughout the spring of 1823.

By autumn 1823 the family, minus John who was enrolled at Clongowes Wood College in Co. Kildare, was settled in Southampton. For Mary, life in England was little better than in France, as the lonely separation from her husband proved increasingly difficult to bear. The social scene in Southampton did not impress her: 'This is a most horrid stupid place for young People. The stiff starched proud English will not visit without letters of introduction. We shall not regret much our departure from England, but when we meet, Love, we must talk and consider well upon our future place of residence.'[67] She continually derided English manners, claiming, 'They are to be sure the coldest people in the world.' In many cases she felt snubbed, complaining to O'Connell, 'Not one of *those* introduced to us ... have as yet paid us a visit. We are Irish Catholics. This is against us.'[68]

O'Connell's visit over the holidays and the subsequent sorrow over his return to Ireland led the couple to discuss again the possibilities of reunion. O'Connell wanted her in Ireland but believed Dublin would prove too expensive; a place in the country, perhaps Killarney, might be just the thing. Mary, on the other hand, objected on many grounds to living anywhere outside of Dublin and she carefully laid these out in a letter to her husband. In the first place, she worried over her health, which she felt benefited from a dry climate. Killarney was certainly not a healthy environment, she insisted, and Dublin was the only place in Ireland where she really enjoyed good health. Mary's second objection was based on her daughters who, she told her husband, 'should not appear in Ireland until they can do so as your daughters ought'. The society of a country town in Ireland, she felt, was 'not the most advantageous for young girls educated as they have been'. Moreover, after discussing the situation with the girls themselves, Mary reached the conclusion that 'they would rather live in the greatest obscurity anywhere than live in any of the country parts of Ireland in our present circumstances'.[69]

Finally, Mary could see no money saved by living in Kerry. Well aware of her husband's ways, she reminded him that 'Your doors could not be kept shut to your connections or to mine. There would be an eternal *relay* of *cousins*.' Besides, Mary concluded, O'Connell had 'a respectability to keep up', and should he fail, '*they* would delight to think your embarrassments were such as to oblige you to send your family to live separate from you in the same kingdom with you.' No, they must keep up appearances, and her poor health and Maurice's studies in England were sufficient excuses to keep them there without inviting public speculation or ridicule.[70]

As Mary and Daniel debated the issue, James O'Connell, acting as the family financial advisor, wrote to O'Connell with his own opinion on the subject: 'I now have little doubt a few years of persevering prudence will not only enable you to do so [become free from debt] but also to provide for the junior members of your family. As you must bring your family to Ireland, I really think Dublin, where you have a house, is after all the cheapest place they can be in.'[71] Mary yielded, allowing herself to be swayed by her dislike of England, her loneliness for her husband, and a sense that all these enforced separations were making very little dent in their mounting debts.

Mary returned to Ireland in May 1824 with O'Connell's strict assurances that a rigid economy would be followed in order to clear their debts. Upon Hunting Cap's death in February 1825, the couple decided the best means of accomplishing this was by installing the family at Derrynane. It is interesting to note that there is no evidence of Mary's ever having visited Derrynane before Hunting Cap's demise and O'Connell's subsequent inheritance of the house and grounds. Nor does it appear she ever met her husband's uncle. Perhaps Mary's 'dislike' of Kerry can be traced to a general discomfort and guilt associated with her part in O'Connell's falling out with Hunting Cap. Perhaps she never felt truly welcome there. Whatever the case, Mary had very little objection to life as mistress of Derrynane Abbey. 'Every day I get more pleased with Derrynane,' she wrote to her husband in September 1825. 'I always like Iveragh but now I like it extremely. A *home* endears the most solitary place to those who have everything in this world to make them happy.'[72] In fact, Mary seems to have found something of a mission in taking up residence in Kerry. She told O'Connell, warming to the idea of settling in Iveragh, 'Beside the delight of being with you I think I should be able to do a great deal of good for the poor people about Derrynane.'[73]

Even the 'air' in Kerry no longer seemed to afflict Mary. 'Rest assured,' she wrote, 'the air of Derrynane was not the cause of my illness … If the air of this place disagreed with me my chest would never be free.'[74] Still, it was not the ideal place to spend the winter. 'This house with all our precautions is miserably cold, wind blowing from every direction, but I believe it is the case in every other house in such weather,' Mary informed her husband. Moreover, Mary felt it unfair to keep her daughters isolated in Kerry during Dublin's Season, especially now that they had approached marriageable age. 'Derrynane at this season of year is a dreary place for young people.'[75]

The years between 1825 and 1829 passed in a flurry as Mary, moving between Dublin and Kerry, oversaw renovations and room extensions at Derrynane, married off her eldest daughter and applauded her husband's election to Parliament. From 1830 Mary and Daniel were hardly ever separated, though when they were, daily missives flowed between them. Still, the number of letters is slight compared with previous years. As a result, information regarding Mary's activities and private life during her later years is lacking.

In the public arena, as political pressures increased, O'Connell found in Mary a well-informed and sympathetic listener in whom he could confide his inner fears. According to Oliver MacDonagh, 'By her intelligent sympathy, she took some of the incessant strain off O'Connell's shoulders, and in return his self-revelation and dependence on her approval and applause warmed her by the assurance of her own indispensability and filled her with a sense of vicarious achievement.'[76]

Their love was ever apparent in the letters between them. In 1825 O'Connell wrote to his wife from London, 'You are the solace and sweetness of my existence and my heart feels widowed and solitary at being long separated from you, whilst in absence when you do condescend to write to me in terms of love you cannot imagine what *a drink of honey* these tender expressions are to me.' He continued, 'I have come to a time of life when it is not [?possible] that I should have a woman's love.'[77] To this Mary replied with some consternation:

> What reason have you to suppose you are not the idol of my heart? Oh Dan, it is impossible for me to give you the smallest notion how beloved you are by me. Why should you speak of your age or allude to it? Surely,

my own heart, I am for a woman much older. If I had not real love for you, would not my pride make me love you? By real love I mean loving you for yourself alone. Do not, my own heart, vex me by ever writing or speaking in this manner again.[78]

When O'Connell took his seat in Parliament, Mary joined him and their son Maurice in London for the session, accompanied by her youngest daughters, Kate and Betsey. Morgan, now an officer in the Austrian service, had been stationed on the Continent but returned home that spring. Meanwhile, John remained in Dublin to finish his studies at Trinity College. Ellen O'Connell, the eldest daughter, having married Christopher FitzSimon in 1825, was comfortably established in Ireland with two children and one on the way. And Daniel Jr, following in the footsteps of his three older brothers, had been enrolled at Clongowes Wood College.

In London, Mary was 'anxious to make a good appearance' in order to show off her still unattached daughters. She found the city 'a wonderful place', but conceded that Dublin, too, 'would be handsomer if we had some of the english wealth'. She attended the opera on occasion as well as the theatre. As the session progressed, however, she wrote to Daniel Jr of their desire to be gone from London. 'It is becoming so stupid [i.e. dull],' she complained.[79]

The close of 1832 saw the O'Connell family 'flush with funds, if not altogether free from debt', due to the workings of O'Connell's political manager and financial agent P.V. Fitzpatrick, who had set out to raise £1000 per month for the O'Connell Tribute. O'Connell supporters began this subscription fund in 1829 in order to support the Liberator once he gave up his legal practice to pursue politics full-time. Fitzpatrick's goal was easily exceeded and the correspondence between Mary and Daniel ceased, after all these years, to be laden with references to money—or lack thereof. As the years passed Mary and Daniel attempted to settle their children into suitable marriages. Some of their aspirations were easily met, as in the case of Betsey, who married the prosperous Nicholas Ffrench, and Kate, who happily married her kinsman Charles O'Connell. Maurice, however, disappointed them when he eloped with a Protestant woman of less fortune than they would have hoped. Still, they looked on with delight as their grandchildren were born.[80]

The year 1832 also brought scandal, when Ellen Courtenay published a pamphlet accusing O'Connell of fathering her illegitimate son. O'Connell maintained public silence, and there is nothing in the correspondence regarding the incident, which seemed to fade away entirely by summer's end. O'Connell emerged with his reputation intact, the matter seemingly behind him. The scandal resurfaced, however, in March 1836, when O'Connell was confronted by the woman and child while walking with his son John. John, in attempts to drive the boy away, hit him several times with his umbrella, an act which landed him in court on charges of assault. Again O'Connell maintained his silence, allowing his son-in-law Christopher FitzSimon to appear for him before the judge. This time the affair was widely publicized, and gossip regarding the woman's story was rampant. To counter such tattle, Mary joined her husband in his political tour of the English midlands in April 1836, despite her declining health.

Gradually, Mary's ill health caught up with her. The letters trace the beginnings of her decline back to September 1835. However, for the next year she travelled between Kerry, Dublin and London, which in some measure suggests a recovery. In May 1836 she began taking the waters at Tunbridge Wells in Kent, which were believed to be the best for her 'complaint'. By August, Mary and Daniel had returned to Derrynane, where Mary's health continued to deteriorate. In September, O'Connell wrote to his political ally Richard Barrett in a confidential letter, 'God help me! my ever beloved is in a state of much suffering and daily losing ground. I do most potently fear she cannot recover. She may linger weeks. One week may—Oh God help me—!'[81]

In an attempt to improve her health, Mary was moved to John Primrose's home, outside Cahersiveen, on 19 September, but to no avail. She was soon returned to Derrynane where she lingered in a state of delirium until her death on 31 October 1836. She was buried in Hunting Cap's tomb on the Abbey Island at Derrynane.

2

'partner of my soul'

— LOVE AND MARRIAGE —

Love and marriage in nineteenth-century Ireland did not necessarily go hand in hand. Traditional notions of patriarchy deemed that the head of the household owned his wife, children and servants in the same way he held his property. Therefore, he chose a spouse who was best suited to increase the wealth and prestige of his family. Traditional marriages, especially in the middle and upper classes, were accompanied by financial negotiations. Because these detailed accounts were put onto paper and saved, the historian is left with the view that at the middle and upper levels, marriage was a commercial transaction. Indeed, the marriage settlement was extremely important for it had serious implications for the financial future of the family and all of its members. In all sectors of society there were established standards about 'fitting unions'. A fitting union was one economically strong enough to sustain the couple and to ensure the survival of their family according to the standards of their class. It must be remembered, however, that the parties entering into the marriage settlement generally met on equal footing. Neither side was willing to give more than it received, and the bride's portion had to be matched by the groom's wealth, position and potential to earn. Thus, while a satisfactory settlement was important, it was a precondition to the marriage, not the sole end to be attained.[1]

According to historians of England, during the late eighteenth and early nineteenth centuries this patriarchal system gradually gave way to domesticity—that is, a system of household interaction based upon companionate marriages, romantic notions, nurturing environments and a more egalitarian relationship between husband and wife.[2] Until recently, little research has been conducted regarding the rationale for marriage in pre-Famine Ireland. Scholars hold that while peasants tended to marry for love, with little regard to economic interests, élites sought property and position as well as love and affection.[3] Indeed, the high number of clandestine marriages in Ireland during the nineteenth century reveals the means by which many couples subverted family pressures.[4] Although romantic matches became more common, the pool from which partners were drawn was still strictly limited. Occasions at which young women and men could meet were arranged and monitored so that only those of the same social class might mix. While a woman was allowed more freedom to choose her own partner, she was still limited by the fact that she was introduced only to those men who found approval within the social group. Moreover, many parents still held a veto power over their offspring's choice.[5]

In the case of the bourgeoisie, marriage arrangements were used to gain social status. The marriage of a middle-class daughter into a great family required a substantial dowry or marriage portion to mark the rising social standing of the bride's family, which would in turn attract eligible suitors to the remaining unmarried daughters of the family. An eldest son was expected to marry, to produce an heir and to act as an administrator over all family settlements. This last task required securing the interests of his siblings and, in some cases, paying off his father's debts. Family obligations, therefore, often interfered with an eldest son's personal preference.[6]

Little is known about the courtship patterns of the emerging Irish middle class, but it is clear enough that Daniel O'Connell's decision to take a dowerless bride without family sanction, thereby risking disinheritance, was a blatant dismissal of those factors which might conventionally be expected to lead to his personal success. In an era when a political career required large financial resources, young men with an eye towards politics were well aware that they could not, in most cases, 'afford' a poor wife. As O'Connell's uncle, Count Daniel O'Connell, observed of his nephew's situation in 1804, 'The bare prerequisites [sic] of his profession are probably very inadequate to the support of a wife and family, besides his personal expenses. Much will depend on his Professional Abilities, but, great as they might be, I conceive it will require time and labour to bring them under notice.'[7] Moreover, O'Connell's shirking of familial responsibilities as a first son and heir is even more striking, for the primary function of marriage was to enhance the economic, political or social interests of the extended family.[8] O'Connell's choice of Mary O'Connell as a marriage partner, then, is remarkable when we consider that he willingly forewent a dowry and jeopardized his own inheritance. As a result of the union between Mary and Daniel, O'Connell's uncle Hunting Cap divided his fortune between the three O'Connell brothers, leaving Daniel only one-third of his fortune instead of the entirety as had been originally anticipated.[9]

Though O'Connell acted as an individual, marrying Mary to fulfil his own ideal of happiness, he was still keenly aware of his familial duties. Writing to Mary about her brother Rickard's marriage to Betsey Tuohy in January 1801, he commented:

> … their worldly prospects are not so very flattering. And though you know I am an advocate for the heart, yet I oftentimes think a man cannot love truly without preferring the happiness of the beloved object to his own, and therefore do I blame those who precipitantly marry without considering how their future family is to be provided for.[10]

Moreover, his attempts at settling his own children reveal his desire to further the family interest despite the personal wishes of his offspring.[11]

Even to Mary, who came to her marriage dowerless, money was an important consideration in approving a marriage partner for others. Perhaps her situation made her even more aware of the benefits of a 'good match'. She was extremely sensitive to the lack of fortune granted to O'Connell as a result of his unsanctioned marriage to her. When O'Connell's father changed his will to favour his son James, Mary begged her husband to harbour no ill feelings towards his family. 'It grieves me,' she confided, '… more particularly as I feel myself unintentionally the cause of your present quarrel with James.' She continued by reassuring him that his own prospects for an independent fortune were favourable and that he had a wife who loved him no matter his wealth.[12] Still, she did not hesitate to judge the benefits, or lack thereof, of other unions. For example, Mary opined of one couple's upcoming nuptials, 'she has the worst of the bargain for he is of mere Rank without a shilling and she has a good fortune'.[13] Of another impending match, Mary found the young man to have the worst end of the deal for the widow he married had very little money.[14] Yet, fortune was not everything. Of Peter Hussey's marriage to a Miss Hickson, Mary remarked, 'What a lucky fellow he is to get so nice a girl. God knows between you and me what a sacrifice it is notwithstanding all his money.'[15]

The correspondence between Mary and Daniel O'Connell holds a wealth of information regarding how the couple viewed marriage in general and their own marriage in particular, as well as how they defined their respective roles and functioned within them. The letters between the couple in the months following their wedding reveal a long-distance exercise in redefining their relationship as husband and wife. Each assured the other of their commitment to their vows and outlined their expectations of their spouse's conduct. O'Connell considered his wife a 'friend and companion through life'. He would do anything to make her happy—anything, that is, except give up his 'rights' on her.[16] He believed that neither money nor fame was the way to make him happy. 'I am, it is true, attached to them and in the soberness of my soul I seek for them, but it is not there that real pleasure is to be found,' he assured Mary. 'No, my dear wife they are my *business* only.'[17]

In O'Connell's eyes marriage was a partnership, and he often used the term 'partner' when referring to Mary. 'I am proud of you,' he wrote to her on one occasion, 'I am as proud as I am pleased that I have secured to myself a partner for life of such qualities as you possess.'[18] He reiterated the need for truthfulness and sincerity between them, convinced he would only receive 'the utmost candour' from her, and he declared 'most solemnly to God *I do not wish* to have one thought concealed from you' [emphasis added].[19] This was hardly a firm commitment to honesty, and O'Connell revealed on more than one occasion—notably in cases of finances and of duels—how willing he was to keep Mary uninformed of his actions.

As to fidelity, O'Connell pledged, 'I do solemnly assure you that my fidelity is not only as sincere as yours but that it is also as chaste.' Still, honour and loyalty were not the reason for his faithfulness, he conceded. 'I have not and I do not claim any merit for this because in truth and in fact I have no eyes for any other woman but you. It is no sacrifice that I make in keeping [? this] vow.'[20] While O'Connell vowed fidelity, Mary pledged to obey his will. O'Connell accepted her pledge that 'my will shall be a law to you'. However, he hoped he need not rely merely on his rights as a husband to guarantee her compliance. 'It will be my study to require nothing from your *duty*, everything from your *gratitude*.'[21]

The first year of their marriage proved difficult for Mary, sitting alone in Tralee and unable to reveal her married status. Her future with O'Connell dominated her thoughts. 'I can't, as I see other women do, enjoy themselves in their husbands' absence,' she confessed. 'When you are away my wish is never to stir out. I could sit forever alone thinking of you and embracing your dear resemblance. Do not, my darling, be angry with me when I own to you that hardly a day passes that I do not shed tears on your picture. You will not, I know, be angry with me as it is a kind of indulgence I give myself. I always feel my spirits lighter after doing so, and therefore it must be of use to me to cry.'[22] Such pledges of devotion thrilled O'Connell. He responded: 'I am not unrewarded for having placed all my solicitude and all my ambition with you—for you confer on me more serene and unclouded happiness than I ever tasted before. Even the evil of absence is softened by the certainty of your love, by the knowledge of your heart—by your being mine.'[23]

Though preoccupied with business, O'Connell too found their separation difficult. 'Oh God what would I not at this moment give to have an opportunity now to press your lips to squeeze to my bosom my adored Girl ... Oh how my fond heart longs again to feel the pressure of my love's sweet sweet bosom,' he wrote.[24] 'Sweet Mary,' he confessed a week later, 'I rave of you! I think only of you! I sigh for you, I weep for you! I almost pray to you! Darling, I do not—indeed I do not—exaggerate.'[25]

O'Connell's devotion to Mary in the early years of their marriage was flamboyant and exuberant. 'Indeed my angel, my love for you has a species of religious enthusiasm in it that makes it more resemble devotion than mortal doating,' he wrote to his new bride shortly after their wedding in July 1802.[26] Marriage only enriched their feelings in O'Connell's eyes, and he determined that he had never truly loved her until after the wedding. 'What I now experience is so infinitely beyond my former sentiments for you that I could not call those sentiments *love* because the present so secede [*sic*] them.'[27]

As the years passed, the couple's love remained ardent. 'Mary,' O'Connell wrote earnestly in 1809, 'it never entered into the heart of man to love more tenderly or indeed with half the affection with which I *doat, doat* of you.'[28] Six years later he confirmed, 'no man ever loved with more constant and unremitting tenderness than I love you'.[29] On 1 January 1820, after some eighteen years of marriage, O'Connell reflected on his past life with Mary:

There is a kindliness in my own Mary which renders her society most endearing to her husband ... I can well say that you have constituted the sweetness and happiness of the past. The season of compliments is over between us, but I can say in perfect sincerity that during this last year as during many preceding ones there was not a single action, word or thought of yours but what was directed to the comfort and happiness of your husband and children ... I prize and cherish you with all the fondness and the pride of one, who has made the best of all human selections ... Indeed, darling, I love you with more of tenderness and truth than ever woman was loved before.[30]

Moved by her husband's words, Mary replied, 'To you, darling, I owe everything. It would be quite impossible for any woman married to you not to be happy, but never could a woman love you as well or as truly as I do. You are dearer to me than existence.'[31]

Disagreements between the couple—at least in their letters—were rare. Small disagreements were usually handled in a light-hearted or teasing manner. O'Connell would tease Mary for her 'scoldings'. He wrote to her from the circuit regularly in 1810, for he 'should dread a *scolding* if I missed a single day. See what it is to be too indulgent to a saucy cocknosed woman. But I doat of you, darling, and I love even your passion.'[32] In response to a letter from Mary in Dublin in which she complained of his long stay in Kerry, O'Connell wrote teasingly upon further delays, 'This annoys me for a thousand reasons, one of which is that I owe you a pulling by the *cock nose* for your *saucy* letter. Dearest love, the fact is that I ought rather to make my peace with you than to *threaten* you, but I believe you are not much afraid of my threatenings.'[33]

O'Connell begged of Mary to do as she pleased with regard to most decisions, whether it be renovating the house, raising the children, allocating funds or managing servants. Yet he always managed to urge her in the direction he favoured. After insisting she depart at once for Derrynane in the summer of 1811, he concluded by saying, 'I know how much pleasure it gives the best and sweetest of wives to comply with my request and I should be more than sorry to urge you to any thing that was not perfectly consistent with your own wishes—Do therefore my sweet love precisely as you please on this subject.' His next two letters, however, urged her to depart at once.[34]

While O'Connell seemed partial to compromise, diplomacy and gentle persuasion in settling disputes, Mary resorted to bursts of temper and guilt to get her way. In August 1819 O'Connell debated about coming home before going to Kerry for his yearly business trip/vacation. The incident is revealing as to the means by which the O'Connells settled their differences. O'Connell listed for Mary the pros and cons of his coming home as opposed to going directly to Kerry. Travelling up to Dublin would put him through a good deal of trouble and cut into his vacation time; at the same time, however, he wanted to see his family. He asked her to decide the matter for him, 'but there is no use in putting the question to the poll in the house as I believe all votes would concur in deciding for my return'.[35] Mary had little choice in her reply. Telling him to come home would appear selfish and put him at a great inconvenience. Thus she wrote back: 'After maturely considering everything for and against my wishes on the subject I think you had better go on to Kerry.' O'Connell succeeded in getting his wish free from any argument or anger. Still, Mary could not resist adding to her reply her own emotional blackmail: '*It* would be impossible for me to give you an idea of the gloom that spread o'er the face of your family when I communicated the subject of your letter … My poor Nell and Kate wept and wished Iveragh was out of the world.' The girls had complained that 'every barrister returns to stay with his family (but our father) when circuit ends'. It was they who would suffer most in his absence, she informed him.[36] While O'Connell stuck to his plan of going directly to Kerry, Mary's ploy worked in securing a promise from him that he would not linger there any longer than necessary to complete his business. Mary's following letters made certain it was a promise he could not forget.[37]

Frequent separations were one of the main causes of unhappiness between Mary and Daniel throughout their married life. O'Connell's circuit practice took him away from home for five or six weeks between March and May and again between July and September. Furthermore, he attended special assizes and arbitrations as well as working as a legal officer for parliamentary elections, all of which combined to keep him away from home for substantial periods of time.[38] In the later years of their marriage, political success and financial difficulties brought about even more extended separations.

Mary found these separations particularly difficult. 'Your society is all I want,' she told her husband. 'Even when you are engaged writing or reading, it is company to me to be looking at you.'[39] While the couple continually cursed the circumstances which required that they be parted, they also accepted them as necessary and inevitable. As Mary once wrote, 'I wish to God it were possible for us never to be separated but there is no such thing as perfect happiness in this life.'[40] O'Connell likened their time apart to widowhood and even quoted a poem on the subject to Mary when she was 'banished' to France: 'All this they bear but not the less/Have moments rich in happiness/Blest meetings after many a day/Of widowhood past far away/When the loved fair again is seen.' He concluded, 'This is what your husband looks to as the recompense of this his solitary widowhood.'[41]

The passage of time did not make the separations any easier to bear. In 1810 Mary wrote to O'Connell, 'I thought my heart would break when I saw you drive from the door last Thursday and your Doats gathered round me to know when you would come again.'[42] O'Connell too found that separations never became any easier. 'I feel lonely and weary at being so long absent from you and as to these assizes, they will never be over,' he complained from Cork in 1817.[43] Homecomings and reunions were always looked forward to and the days were counted down. Plans that might bring the couple together sooner were made, discarded and remade. 'I hope heart you will not give up your intention of coming up to see us from Cork, it will help to make the three months pass away quicker than they otherwise would.'[44]

Delays which kept O'Connell from his family were usually business-related and were a constant source of disappointment to all involved. 'Just when my Babes and I had proposed to ourselves the happiness of seeing you tomorrow our hopes were crushed by that *abominable* Darly Leahy. Oh then Darling if you dont make him pay you well for this delay you deserve to be punished still more than you are at present.'[45] At times Mary could not contain her anger, as in 1814 when she wrote to O'Connell from Mallow, 'Have we any chance of seeing you here on Saturday? The *traversing* of some *shabby* presentment will I suppose, deprive us of that happiness. I am so angry I can scarcely write with *patience to you.*' And she signed her letter, 'Your affectionate though *angry* Mary O'Connell.'[46] Another delay in Cork brought this missive from Mary:

> Surely, darling, you must certainly have made a mistake when you say the
> business of Cork will not be over until tomorrow week. I never knew the

assizes business to hold longer than a fortnight and you were scarcely ever delayed beyond three or four days after … I should be sorry you lost any business by quitting Cork, nor would I say a word on the subject if I was not quite convinced the business you would get here would amply compensate you for any you may lose in Cork beside the happiness to your family of having you at home with them—Realy [*sic*] Darling the Idea of your being delayed so much longer than I could expect has frightened me so much I fear I write exactly as if I thought arguments were necessary to induce you to return to us. But my Dearest Dan you know me too well to think me capable of forming any such opinion. I know there is not that man in existence [who] feels half the happiness you do in the society of your family.[47]

Repeated separations required repeated reassurances of love and affection, and the two were happy to oblige each other. Upon receipt of one such avowal from Mary, O'Connell replied, 'your letter so full of love overpowers my heart with delight'.[48] Since the separations were borne only with frequent 'affectionate and cheerful letters',[49] many of the couple's quarrels revolved around miscommunications caused by lapses in correspondence. Both were aware of the limits of letter-writing in maintaining a relationship, especially when difficulties arose. Mary had piqued her husband's anger on occasion by neglecting to write. Just as often, the fault was his. On one occasion, after not hearing from him for several days, she wrote to a third party to inquire as to her husband's well-being. When O'Connell heard of this he was furious. A letter to another person indicated that he had been lax in his marital obligations, and for Mary to air such a complaint in public was intolerable. The 'scolding letter' he sent to her on the subject no longer exists, but Mary's reply defending her actions reveals her hurt feelings and includes a humble request for forgiveness.

I made no *complaint of you. God* forbid I should (If I ever had cause) to those more interested for me than Mr. Mahony possibly could be—but as it has given you pain to have me write at all to him from my heart I regret it but love when I did write I was in such a state of anxiety and uneasiness at not hearing from you for so long a time that twenty things occurred to my imagination and I thought he was the only person in Carhen who could let me know if any thing serious had happened to prevent your arrival in Cork … Surely then heart it was no wonder I should be alarmed at a silence so uncommon but forgive me.[50]

A short time later, as O'Connell waited four days to receive her response, he admitted in his next letter, 'I in my turn experience all the anxiety you felt.'[51] Quarrels such as these greatly upset the two. On one occasion O'Connell confided to Mary, 'I was so fretted at being scolded by my own Love that I went to bed in *a rage* and dreamt of nothing but quarrels and battles all night.'[52] The two usually were able to make up their differences fairly quickly. Until both were reassured that all was forgiven, however, letters flew fast and furious between them.

In the end, O'Connell consoled himself with the idea that 'These short absences serve only to make us know the Value of each other's society' and 'it is only in absence one knows the strength of affection'.[53] He further resolved during almost every separation that it would be the last. As he told his wife in 1804 and on many other occasions, 'nothing shall again seperate [*sic*] us in this manner'.[54] Unfortunately, it was a promise he was never able (or willing) to keep.

Both Mary and her husband were prone to jealousy. O'Connell fell prey to envy while Mary was away in the spa town of Clifton, near Bristol, during the summer of 1817. There she made the acquaintance of a Captain John O'Connell, who regularly called to their home and even took the children on outings. Aware that his suspicions were baseless, Daniel revealed his sentiments to Mary, laughing at his own behaviour. 'I have been making myself very miserable about *your friend*,' he told her. Mary had described the man as 'respectful and kind'. 'Now what train of thought was it that could put the word *respectful*?' O'Connell asked. 'How could it be necessary to think of that! Thus, my own darling Mary, did I torture myself asking foolish questions ... It has completely cured me to see how absurd my fears appear when written.'[55]

This is the only evidence in the correspondence of Mary having developed a friendship with a gentleman; O'Connell, on the other hand, was a known flirt. 'A lady just called for your address but not a young one. I therefore gave it to her ... . Take care, heart, and don't be so liberal to Julia Blake [unidentified] as you were this time twelvemonth,' Mary instructed her husband in 1809. 'I ought to lecture you well for being such a plague to young girls,' she again chided in 1818. 'Really, darling, it is a shame to annoy the poor girls so much.'[56]

O'Connell's flirtatious manner and charismatic charm are well documented, and these incidents appear harmless enough. It is the more serious charge of adultery, however, that has haunted O'Connell throughout history. Tradition holds that O'Connell was sexually promiscuous and fathered many illegitimate children. Recent historical works on O'Connell, however, go to great lengths to establish that he was a faithful husband; yet the arguments laid out in support of this theory are lacking in many respects. Research to date has unearthed no decisive evidence; on the matter of O'Connell's fidelity the jury is still out.

Most historians, struggling to prove O'Connell's faithfulness, have fallen upon two ready explanations to account for the lore surrounding the Liberator's supposed adulterous lifestyle. Helen Mulvey found that the affectionate letters between Mary and O'Connell 'are powerful evidence of O'Connell's fidelity and devotion to his wife and of his deep happiness in every aspect of his relationship with her'.[57] Unfortunately, Mulvey based her analysis on only those letters chosen and edited for publication. While Mulvey's line of reasoning has been accepted by many O'Connell historians,[58] the small number of excerpts on which Mulvey bases her argument, many of which were edited and taken out of context, cannot exonerate O'Connell from the charges of adultery.[59]

More recently, studies in Irish folk tradition have provided another possible explanation for the popular belief in O'Connell's sexual misconduct. Diarmaid Ó Muirithe has suggested that O'Connell, as a principal folk hero in Irish history, was destined to fall victim to 'a product of the folk-mind'. In short, Ó Muirithe argues that 'the heroes of old were ever famous for their sexual energy,' and that this tradition attached itself to O'Connell.[60] J.J. Lee goes one step further:

> Gaelic folk-heroes had rendered a psychic service to the vivid imagination of the plain people by having attributed to them tales of insatiable sexual prowess. It is a tribute to O'Connell's popular stature that he was the first in centuries to adequately service the popular imagination in this respect ... The stories of O'Connell's philandering tell us far more about the need of the popular imagination than they do about the historic O'Connell.[61]

Fergus O'Ferrall concurs that the popular lore concerning O'Connell's infidelity originates in the Irish folk tradition of attributing great sexual prowess to its heroes. Oliver MacDonagh agrees that this is 'a possible answer', but his treatment of the question of O'Connell's fidelity is inconclusive. M.R.

O'Connell, an O'Connell scholar and a descendant of the Liberator, writes, 'This combination of history, correspondence and folklore points to the (disappointing?) conclusion that O'Connell was a faithful husband.'[62]

The letters, not surprisingly, reveal little with regard to Mary and Daniel's sex life. Amidst the ardent and sometimes impassioned avowals of love lurks a smattering of spicy sexual rapport. Mary delighted in 'saucy chats' with her husband, claiming, 'All *pets* you *know* heart are impertinent'. Her impertinence would earn her a 'scolding', or at least the continued threat of one. Of course, these threats were not meant to make her uneasy; as O'Connell admitted, '*the above* [scolding] shall not be very severe'.[63] O'Connell too was often flirtatious. 'What a sweet bedfellow my darling will be before me if she takes care of herself,' he wrote on one occasion. 'And what a saucy wretch I am to talk to her in this way.'[64] O'Connell regularly teased his wife, extracting promises from her in return for unscheduled trips home from the circuit. '[Y]ou would tell me that,' he wrote, 'as I return at once to you from this, you will certainly do anything I ask you when I reach home. Promise me that, darling.' Mary was only too willing to comply, and O'Connell, thrilled at her affirmative response, replied, 'I can now impose upon my sweet—oh my sweet woman as much as I please.'[65] Sex and intimacy, then, appear to have played an important part in the couple's marriage. The number of children brought forth from their union, especially considering O'Connell's long and frequent absences from home, is certainly evidence that Mary and Daniel indulged themselves frequently.

The correspondence between Mary and Daniel O'Connell also includes some references to O'Connell's roving eye. O'Connell certainly had mistresses before his marriage.[66] In 1820 O'Connell made a vow to Mary, revealing that there was some cause for concern on Mary's part that her husband might not be entirely faithful. O'Connell, however, assured Mary, 'I would not darling *now* be unfaithful to you even by a look for the created universe' [emphasis added].[67] Still, in 1823, while living in France, Mary again voiced her doubts. The reproachful letter she wrote is no longer extant—O'Connell frequently destroyed any such letters he received from his wife—but her husband's reply is. The incident involved his visits the family's former governess Miss Gaghran, visits Mary felt were too familiar. This complaint was not the first she had made and O'Connell responded to her accusations angrily.

I own with some surprise that you should, after my former letter, continue another reproach on the subject of my visits to Miss Gaghran ... Surely I said enough on that subject—at least I think I did—to set your mind at ease ... I never in my life showed the slightest tinge of preference to any being above you, and why now, when I would not look at any other woman for a moment, you should thus persevere in an angry correspondence on a subject so trivial ... I have only to repeat my solemn promise of never again seeing her without your express permission ... .Can you for one moment doubt that, if I thought it would have given you the slightest pain, I never would have paid her a visit? If you think I would, you do indeed wrong me ... you whom both duty and tender affection bid me cherish ... I repeat that you shall never again have the slightest cause to reproach me ... Depend on it, you shall have no 'Lord or Master'—I know of course who you allude to—she always treated you I think with respect and affection—but at all events she certainly shall have nothing of interference with you of any kind save the mere exchange of friendly civilities.[68]

It is difficult to understand the exact substance of O'Connell's allusion without the benefit of Mary's letter. Moreover, the location of O'Connell's original letter is unknown; this excerpt was purportedly taken from a letter presented to Sean O'Faolain and published in the *Irish Times*. O'Connell's claims to love no other 'above' his wife can be viewed as meaning any of a number of things. If the letter is real then it is Mary's angry accusations that are so telling, especially coming in the twenty-first year of their marriage. Despite her husband's constant assurances of love and dedication, she obviously felt she had something to worry about. O'Connell, angry as he was at her accusations, agreed to her demands that he never visit the former governess again. In later letters he emphasized his caution in dealing with the woman. 'I *sent* to Miss Gaghran' the letters from Ellen, he expressly reported to Mary.[69]

It is Ellen Courtenay's account of her affair with O'Connell that stands as the most damaging 'evidence' against the Liberator's fidelity. In 1832, in Fleet Prison for debt, Courtenay published her tale in the laboriously entitled, *A Narrative by Miss Ellen Courtenay, of Most Extraordinary Cruelty, Perfidy & Depravity, Perpetrated Against Her by Daniel O'Connell, Esq. (M.P. for Kerry): and also A Faithful History of Many of the Circumstance of her Eventful Life, Which such Outrage immediately, collaterally or remotely influenced.* The pamphlet claimed that in the year 1817 Courtenay sought out O'Connell, a friend of her father, for legal advice. There in his study in the house on Merrion Square, the pamphlet claimed, O'Connell seduced the reluctant Courtenay, then aged fifteen, the result of which was the birth of a child. According to Courtenay, O'Connell refused to acknowledge the child and paid her only a paltry sum over the years for the boy's upkeep. Now, perishing in prison, Courtenay publicly confessed her story—a necessary act, she claimed, forced upon her by 'cruel circumstances'.[70]

Courtenay's story contains some major discrepancies. Never is she very clear about the exact duration of her affair with O'Connell. In some parts of her account the reader is left with the impression that a rape occurred in the summer of 1817, resulting in an unwanted pregnancy. Yet if this is the case, the dates do not add up, for she claims her son was born on 4 November 1818. In order for Henry Simpson to be O'Connell's son, relations between Courtenay and O'Connell had to have taken place in February or March of 1818.

Published at an important juncture in O'Connell's political career, the pamphlet proved exceedingly damaging. Indeed, the footnotes of the accusation contained harsh political rhetoric aimed directly at O'Connell, denouncing his public activities as an agitator for Ireland. O'Connell claimed it was an orchestrated attempt by his political enemies to discredit him,[71] and later historians have argued that the political nature of the pamphlet proves O'Connell's innocence in the whole affair, noting that the publisher of the work, Barnard Gregory, editor of the *Satirist*, was well known as a blackmailer of public figures.[72] Other historians have attempted to discredit the pamphlet by analysing O'Connell's lifestyle in the year 1817, when the affair was alleged to have occurred.[73] Some have cited the loving letters written between O'Connell and Mary that year as proof that O'Connell's marriage vows remained unbroken. Historians have continually attempted to refute the claims of Ellen Courtenay, and in many cases their arguments smack of a desperate need to clear O'Connell's name, as if this one whisper of immoral behaviour threatens to override completely the man's great deeds.

In the summer of 1817, Mary was thirty-eight years old. In the thirteen years between 1803 and 1816, she carried twelve children to term and most likely suffered some unknown miscarriages. Of those twelve children only seven survived, the youngest daughter having died very early that year. The difficult birth of Daniel Jr in 1816 taxed Mary's physical and emotional strength. Perhaps she was physically unable to bear any more children; perhaps she made a conscious decision not to do so. It is quite possible that

Mary would be at risk should she again become pregnant. Thus it is relevant that the first intimation of marital infidelity on the part of O'Connell comes in 1817, a year after the birth of their last child.

The year 1817 proved to be a difficult one for the O'Connell family. During this year, it was decided that Mary should move to Bristol for the betterment of her health. No discussion of the matter appears in the letters between Mary and O'Connell during the spring of that year. Mary was busy looking after her sick children, for Daniel Jr, then just eight months old, was recovering from measles and whooping cough. Presumably, the same illness took the life of his older sister Ricarda, for about this time her presence disappears from the correspondence altogether.[74] Perhaps the fragile state of the children's health precipitated the decision to move. Perhaps grief and fatigue had taken a toll upon their mother. Whatever the reason, the first inkling of the relocation comes in a letter to O'Connell from his brother James, dated 18 April, in which he wrote, 'Need I tell you how sincerely I regret the necessity of your dear Mary's going to Bristol. God grant the waters may have the desired effect.'[75] By 31 May, Mary was firmly established in Clifton, near Bristol, with Ellen, Kate, Betsey, John, her niece Ricarda, the governess and a few servants. Maurice and Morgan remained in Ireland, in boarding school at Clongowes, while Daniel Jr, still weak, stayed with Betsey O'Connell in Tralee.

Clifton agreed with Mary. Her letters to O'Connell during this period were particularly light-hearted and happy. She was improving rapidly. With only a few servants, Mary had to keep her own house, and she found the exertions therapeutic. She would often go to the Bristol market in a donkey gig with all the children in tow. 'On getting to town I discharged the gig, paying a shilling, and sallied forth to the market where I think I made for my first time some bargains,' she bragged. After sending her servant, Hannah, home with the groceries, 'Miss G[aghran], the children and myself went to execute commissions and will you believe it possible that I should be walking from 11 in the morning until four in the evening without once sitting down except a few moments in a shop. I was realy [*sic*] surprised at myself and this morning I feel as well, nay better than if I had not walked half so much.'[76]

Mary's letters continued to report improvement in her health. She was drinking the waters for some sort of eye ailment that plagued her. Though confined earlier on, she was now quite well. Still, in June, O'Connell began to encourage her to spend the winter in France. Mary baulked at this idea immediately, and her method of attempting to dissuade O'Connell proved interesting. She asked, 'And how, darling, do you feel? I often think, lonely enough. It is a new thing to you to be at home without your family but I hope this time will be the last we shall be so long separated.' Then, she appealed to his sense of practicality, presenting a rational argument: 'If I continue to improve in health as I have since I came here, a journey to France will be unnecessary until the time arrives when it will be an advantage to my boys and girls to spend some time in France. Then, darling, you will be on the Bench and a little more of your own master than you are at present.'[77] Failing all else, perhaps flattery would win her husband over. However, in July, O'Connell continued with his insistence that she go to France, arguing that 'if I could see you spend one winter without illness I should quiet all my alarms for you'. He would consult his uncle in Paris and Dr Leyne in Tralee for advice on how best to proceed.[78] Again Mary quickly responded in a long attempt, similar to her previous letter, to dissuade him from this course. Many O'Connell scholars quote the following passage to demonstrate Mary's heartfelt affection for her husband:

> I assure you my darling you are our continual subject. When a kind husband or Father is spoken of, Ellen and Kate will exclaim, "Mamma sure he is not so good a husband or Father as our Father", you may guess darling what my reply is. You know what you deserve—and you are aware that in existence, I dont think, there is such a Husband and Father as you are and always have been indeed … in truth, my own Dan, I am always at a loss for words to convey to you how I love and doat of you. Many and many a time I exclaim to Myself "what a happy creature am I. How grateful should I be to Providence for bestowing on me such a Husband." And so indeed I am—We will Love shortly be married fifteen years, and I can answer that I never had cause to regret it. I have darling experienced all the happiness of the married state without feeling any of *its* Misery thanks to a fine and indulgent Husband …

Helen Mulvey argues simply that the passage gives 'the impression of the happy and united family', and reveals 'Mary's unclouded delight' in receiving a letter from her husband.[79] Sean O'Faolain uses the passage to counter Ellen Courtenay's claim of having had an affair with O'Connell, for Mary wrote the endearing quotation in the same year as the supposed affair took place. Mary O'Connell would surely have been aware of her husband's infidelity, O'Faolain reasons, and she would be incapable of composing such a loving tribute to her husband if she knew he were having an affair.[80] W.J. Fitzpatrick cites the passage to a similar end. 'Composition', he notes, 'was not the *forte* of the little Kerry girl [she was thirty-eight at the time], whom he [O'Connell] was all but disinherited for marrying, but her words have an earnestness all the same.'[81]

They were earnest words all right, from a woman desperate to return to her husband and her home. Yet Fitzpatrick underrates Mary's letter-writing skill. Whereas he and subsequent historians give the impression that the passage was a spontaneous outburst of love and affection from a dutiful and smitten wife, when viewed in their full context the words come across as a strategic bit of flattery before a heartfelt plea that she be allowed to come back to Ireland rather than travel to France. Never do these authors present the rest of the letter in their arguments.[82] One must ask why Mary was so set on coming home and why Daniel was so insistent that she not do so.

Mary continued the letter by assuring O'Connell that his happiness was her only concern, claiming, 'that Woman whom you married must be lost to all feeling and affection if your happiness was not her first and only object'. Aware that their current separation had been particularly difficult for O'Connell, she then carefully reminded him that *his* happiness was at stake when they lived apart. When he was unhappy, Mary reasoned, she, whose only duty and desire was to see him in good spirits, became doubly sad as she believed herself to have failed in her marital obligations.

> It is a consolation to me that you will have left home before this reaches Dublin. The lonely life you led *there* often made me melancholy. How often Love I wished to be with you for three or four hours. I dont know any thing half so painful as a separation from those we love and to a Domestic Mind, separation is doubly painful. Yet still Darling you urge me to go to France for the Winter. The Idea of going so far from you and my Boys is quite dispiriting and when I write the words the tears roll down my face.

Mary concluded with a direct assertion that her health was improving and the trip was unnecessary.

> My health is not entirely so bad as to require a trip to France. My consti-
> tution will be always delicate but (as Doctor Barry of Mallow once told

me) I may expect to live to a good old age. Let us then, darling, hope for the best and when we meet, we shall settle all difference between us on this subject.[83]

Despite her impassioned argument, O'Connell refused to change his mind. By 5 August, the decision was made. 'I will write again this day to the General to settle about our journey to Toulouse. We will go, darling, early in September that you may have fine weather. I shall again enjoy the unrestrained society of my darling children.'[84] Ever obedient, Mary accepted his will gracefully. However, she could not resist one slight jibe when she responded, 'I must be content and look forward to the hope that this banishment (if I may call it so) from you and my darling children will give me health and length of years to enjoy the blessings the Almighty has conferred upon me.'[85]

On this occasion, however, Mary eventually won her hard-fought battle to avoid 'banishment'. For reasons that are not clear, the family did not remove to France in the winter of 1817. For nearly the entire month of September, Mary was ill and confined to her rooms in Clifton. When O'Connell joined her in October, the family removed to Bath. Perhaps in the end O'Connell could not afford the cost of moving his family. Perhaps he could not be away from his practice at this juncture. But Mary's sudden illness might also be called into question. It is not altogether implausible that she enhanced her malady and claimed she was too ill to travel in a final effort to remain with her husband that winter.

One cannot help but ask why O'Connell was so very keen to send his wife away despite her protests that she was in good health. Financial considerations, which led Mary and the children to relocate to France in 1822, are never mentioned in the 1817 correspondence. Mary's frantic opposition to her 'banishment' is suggestive. Was Mary suspicious that something was amiss and determined to return to her rightful place beside her husband to rectify it?

The last letter for the year 1817 between Daniel and Mary is dated 20 October. The lack of correspondence between the two suggests they were not separated again until March 1818, when O'Connell wrote from the circuit town of Ennis. He had left Mary quite unwell, a condition the bitter weather that spring did not improve. The letters reveal nothing unusual in the daily life of the couple during this, the time when Ellen Courtenay would, theoretically, have conceived O'Connell's child. No letters exist between Mary and Daniel for the month of November, when Henry Simpson, Courtenay's son, was allegedly born—again indicative of their being reunited in Kerry and then Dublin.

Did O'Connell have an affair with Ellen Courtenay? Did she bear his illegitimate child? Or was she merely a pawn in an intricate political manoeuvre to discredit the popular (and threatening) Irish leader? O'Connell certainly had the time and the freedom to engage in a dalliance with Ellen Courtenay, or with any woman for that matter. Throughout his long legal and political career he was separated from his wife and family for many months out of each year. At the time of the alleged affair with Ellen Courtenay, the summer of 1817, O'Connell was completely alone in Dublin while Mary lived in England. Moreover, O'Connell's determined efforts to send Mary to France and her even more determined refusal to go are circumstantial evidence in support of the theory that O'Connell had a new mistress. Likewise, in March 1818, the approximate time when Henry Simpson was conceived, O'Connell's legal practice took him away from home to the circuit, again allowing him the freedom and opportunity to be with Courtenay if he so chose.

But did Courtenay bear O'Connell's child? In answering this question we find perhaps the most convincing argument for O'Connell's innocence. Ellen Courtenay had legal recourse to obtain the money she thought to be her due, if she was in fact the mother of O'Connell's illegitimate child. Never once, however, did she bring O'Connell before a court of law in her attempts to redress her grievances. Surely, had there been any truth to her story, O'Connell's enemies would have seen legal acknowledgment of O'Connell's bastard as far more damning than mere gossip and would have sought it actively.[86]

Finally, was Courtenay's story merely an attempt to discredit O'Connell politically? Clearly Ellen Courtenay was used by O'Connell's political enemies to stain his good name. This motive is obvious in the very political nature of the footnotes in the pamphlet and the notorious reputation of its publisher as a blackmailer. Still, the possibility that she was a pawn or a profiteer, that she sold her story and that she first attempted blackmail, are not necessarily indicative of the falseness of her story, and the validity of Courtenay's accusations remains open to debate.

Evidence of jealous disagreements is rare in the existing correspondence between Mary and O'Connell. By far, the most common subject for dispute amongst the couple was money. As Helen Mulvey puts it in her article on the correspondence, 'Money, or rather O'Connell's misuse of it, was the great cloud over the happiness of Mary O'Connell.'[87]

Apparently O'Connell, even as a young unmarried man, was not inclined to thrift. Hunting Cap, who funded O'Connell's studies, often complained about his nephew's excessive spending.[88] Upon marriage, as the couple slowly settled into their domestic arrangements, O'Connell counselled Mary: 'I need not recommend a moderate and reasonable economy to you. But let me insist that you will not carry it too far in any instance whatsoever.'[89] By late 1803, he boasted to Mary that he expected to clear £1000 the following year. His letters consistently predicted rising fortunes and he regularly encouraged Mary to spare no expense. 'You will not allow yourself to want for either conveniences or luxuries … I entreat and even *command* you not to be in any degree sparing.'[90] In March 1807, O'Connell reported that he was making 'a load of money'. He was delighted with himself and with their prospects for the future. 'At this rate you shall soon have not only carriages but a country house. It is an infinite pleasure to me to succeed thus as it enables me to give my sweetest little woman all the luxuries of life. We loved each other, darling, when we were poor … And now that we are becoming rich it is the chief sweetener of life.'[91]

O'Connell left Mary a free hand to spend the money he sent her in the way that she saw fit.[92] In general the couple's manner of dealing with their domestic finances was frighteningly lax. O'Connell never seemed to know exactly how much money Mary had or what she spent. She had no set allowance or budget. O'Connell merely sent her money from each assize town if he had any left to spare after his own expenses. As a result of this haphazard system, Mary was on occasion left with no money. 'I *want money love*,' she would stress in her letters from Dublin.[93] At one time Mary was so desperate for money that she had to rely on the allowance the housekeeper received from her brother to see her through.[94] Of course much of this was due to the irregularity of O'Connell's own earnings, which varied from circuit town to circuit town, and debts continually ate into his income, in many cases leaving the money spent before it even reached his hands.[95]

The reality of O'Connell's financial situation, then, differed greatly from the boastful accounts he gave to Mary. He 'said goodbye to solvency' with the purchase of the house on Westland Row in 1805.[96] As time passed, Mary seemed more attuned than her husband to the precarious state of their finances. She had grown up poor and was well acquainted with living frugally. Unlike O'Connell, she did not feel herself bound by the Gaelic tradition of generous hospitality. The house on Merrion Square, an entirely extravagant purchase, proved a point of contention between the couple. Mary simply thought the cost would place them far too deeply in debt and she implored him not to buy.[97] He would not, however, be dissuaded. Furthermore, his constant reassurances of fortunes being made on the circuit and his own flamboyant spending lulled her into a false sense of security. She trusted him, believing the money was there—or at least would be very shortly.

Scholars have unfairly accused Mary of excessive spending. Granted, the yearly domestic expenditure for the O'Connell household was over £16 per week, twenty times the average contemporary labourer's wage.[98] Mary, however, was only living up to the appearance and standard that her husband believed proper for his upwardly mobile social and professional status. He continually sent visitors to Mary to be entertained, fed and housed for as long as they wished at his expense. The finest wines must grace his table, the best horses pull his carriage.[99] The house on Merrion Square, far above his means, was purchased as proof of his increased social standing. Naturally, then, Mary was required to dress herself and her children in a manner equal to the style of living upon which O'Connell insisted. The children were required to have drawing, dancing and music masters even while 'economising' in France.

O'Connell's willingness to lend money and to act as security on loans made to his many friends and relatives contributed to his money problems. On more than one occasion when the debt was called, the balance due fell to O'Connell. Mary was fully aware of this flaw in her husband's judgement and attempted to curb his generosity. Her disapproval is expressed clearly in the letters. For example, when O'Connell informed her that he had been repaid £100, a sum he 'never expected to have returned', Mary commented on his good fortune: 'I wish all those who owe you money would surprise you as he has done.' She then reminded him firmly, 'I expect you will bring a great purse home with you.'[100]

Tradition holds that Mary held a strong dislike for Kerry, finding it cold, backward and dull. In reality, Mary found the county disagreeable not in and of itself, but for the demands made upon her husband when he was there.[101] She recognized the pull of responsibility O'Connell felt towards his many kinfolk in Kerry. It often seemed every visit left him in greater debt than before. In 1808 she wrote to O'Connell before he departed for Kerry: 'I assure you I am very *prudent*, should you my darling not send me up the money as you earn it you will be *tempted* to distribute it when you go to Kerry. It is there all the claims are on you.' Apparently O'Connell obliged her, for she wrote a few days later, 'I can't tell you what pleasure it gave me to see so much of your earnings.' She concluded her lecture, 'So you see, heart, if you are sending me the money how fast I *am disposing* of it again, and how incumbent it is on you to be *prudent* with so large a family to support in Dublin where every article at present is as dear as dear can be.'[102]

O'Connell, however, continued in his errant ways, much to the distress of his wife. She wrote again on the subject in early 1813.

> With grief I perceive you still, my heart, persevere in accepting bills ... I shall say no more, my heart, on this subject until we meet, only to assure you with the truest sincerity that the only thing I have to make me unhappy is your accepting bills, and I am confident, were you aware of the constant uneasiness it gives me, you would entirely give it up ... In truth you think too little of yourself and allow every person to make too free with you but, heart, notwithstanding you have the respect and good wishes of every individual who knows you.[103]

Her pleas fell on deaf ears, and in late 1814 she discovered O'Connell was financially compromised when James Sugrue defaulted on a loan for which O'Connell had stood as surety. 'I cannot help feeling most acutely the danger you expose yourself to in accepting bills for every *schemer* that applies to you ... .why won't you put on a resolution on any account never to accept a bill, bond or note?' she implored upon learning of this latest crisis.[104] Unfortunately, this financial disaster was merely a practice run for the greater misfortune about to befall the O'Connell family when O'Connell was involved as security in the bankruptcy of James O'Leary.

The crisis led to one of the worst disputes between the couple documented in their surviving letters. In 1815 James O'Leary, a Limerick merchant for whom O'Connell had stood as security, went bankrupt, leaving O'Connell £8000 in debt. Mary only learned of the fiasco from O'Connell's brother James. Her ensuing fury prompted a letter to her husband so horrible that he destroyed it after having 'wept over it for two hours'. O'Connell blamed his brother for 'instilling this poison into your [Mary's] mind'. He continued, 'I know he did it for the best but it was a cruel experiment to render … the most beloved of wives and mothers unhappy on a loose and idle suspicion. Indeed … you have no cause of uneasiness … Do believe me, you have no cause for your misery. Did I ever deceive you.'[105] O'Connell was understating the seriousness of the matter, for the incident nearly ruined him financially and placed the family in a precarious economic position from which they never fully emerged. While damaging in the long run, the crisis, nevertheless, further strengthened the love and trust between Mary and her husband. Faced with the obvious misery her chastising letter had caused, Mary could do nothing but forgive her errant husband and beg forgiveness for her harsh words. O'Connell was only too happy to 'forget this momentary uneasiness or think of it only as proof of the lively sentiment of pure love which we reciprocally entertain for each other'.[106]

In March 1817 James O'Connell added up his brother's debts. The grand total was £18,699, which he believed to be rather low, expecting the debts in reality to be around £20,000.[107] A contributing factor to O'Connell's continued extravagance was his assumption that the death of his uncle with its resulting inheritance would see him clear of debt. In March 1818 he told Mary of Hunting Cap's declining health. 'The death of the old gentleman would give us, exclusive of profession, full £4000 a year between my present and *his* income,' O'Connell predicted.[108] When the man lingered on and O'Connell was forced to send his wife away to 'economise', he finally admitted that 'I always looked to the resources to come from my Uncle Maurice's succession as a means of paying off, and I went into debt on that speculation.'[109] When the old man finally died in 1825 O'Connell's inheritance amounted to only £20,000, not enough to see the family clear of all financial problems.[110]

O'Connell's reluctance to call in loans was a further obstacle to clearing his own debts. He worried lest he cause offence. Moreover, his upbringing had emphasized kin obligations. Traditional social pressures required that he be generous and helpful to those less fortunate. Mary, on the other hand, viewed matters in a much more practical light. 'I don't see why the gentleman should not be obliged to pay,' she opined of Miles McSwiney, who owed O'Connell between £400 and £600. 'I should be sorry you distressed him but you must consider for your own children and not throw such a sum away.'[111] By this stage, money had become so tight that only by intricate financial orchestrations could the family stay afloat. Money must be carefully allocated. 'Do not touch the bill money,' O'Connell instructed Mary. 'It would see me quite astray if you were to do that ... Say to me in your answer to this the exact balance of bill money which you have with a promise not to touch it and then I am quite safe.'[112] Unfortunately, miscommunications produced dire consequences, as O'Connell explained to his wife:

> I had determined that the bill you made James Sugrue take up should be protested in case John Hickson pressed it on me. I wrote to him to say that I could not take it up ... then, darling, I had with difficulty made some arrangements which would have brought me near the other outstanding bills all of which I am extremely desirous to take up. I had just got myself into a comfortable state of hope of being able to accomplish all this when you have disarranged me completely by taking up this bill. Indeed after my letter to Hickson, I did not think it would be called for at all and still less could I have imagined that you, my darling Mary, would have committed so large a share of my resources to take up a bill I did not mention especially as I had in the spirit, but without the intention of precaution, sent you a list of the frightful number of bills still remaining.[113]

Gradually money matters came to dominate the couple's correspondence. Whereas O'Connell had always been careless about keeping accounts, now he asked for precise lists of all the notes he sent to Mary. 'See what a woman of business I am making you,' O'Connell commented as he enclosed money and instructions in nearly every letter home.[114]

All these machinations were to no avail. A famine in Kerry in 1822 resulted in falling rents and further contributed to O'Connell's financial woes. Money became so tight that only extraordinary measures could secure the O'Connells' economic future. 'I trust you have made your entire family acquainted with your real situation,' James O'Connell wrote to his brother in the spring of 1822. 'If they and you are serious in wishing to conform yourselves to your embarrassed circumstances, the South of France would in my opinion be the place to fix them.'[115] Thus, Mary and the children were sent abroad where they could live more cheaply away from the prying eyes of Dublin society. Word was put out that Mary 'suffered from her chest, and was ordered to spend a couple of years out of Ireland'.[116] The house at Merrion Square was to be sold, as were the horses and carriage; the servants were to be let go except for those absolutely necessary. The family found 'banishment' the only means of clearing themselves financially. Though it would be difficult, O'Connell wrote, 'the advantages to our family are so great that we must endure it with resignation'.[117]

Once she was settled in France, O'Connell directed Mary to be 'in love with every farthing because the pence saved will hurry the reunion of family'. He insisted she keep strict accounts. 'Take first an account of how much money you have still in hands, and then at the other side begin to put down your expenses and Darling every monday morning deduct the expenditures from the sum in hands and ascertain how *the cash* stands, and once a month at least let me know how the balance is.' At last O'Connell saw the necessity of record-keeping, a lesson Mary, who had sent O'Connell details of her expenditures throughout their married life, had already learned.[118]

Mary's talent at making money last while in France surprised even her husband.[119] Unfortunately, the enforced separation and 'economising' of two years did little to ease their financial difficulties. In 1824, Mary and the children agreed to return to Dublin. Humbled by near financial ruin, O'Connell promised never again to conceal such troubles from his wife. He apologized profusely for the actions that had led to their separation, and blamed himself entirely. In the future he would be more frugal, he assured her.[120] Yet such was not the case. In the years that followed, O'Connell's continued references to economizing would seem almost comical if they did not reveal a man completely deluded with regard to his real financial situation. 'A couple of years is the utmost' necessary to see them clear, he told Mary in January 1824. By the end of February he believed one year of 'strict economy' would do the trick. At the close of 1825 he wrote, 'if I had but one or two years of strict economy I would be entirely out of debt'.[121]

O'Connell's problem seemed to be that he had no notion of what 'strict economy' meant. When he inherited Derrynane in 1825, he concluded that the family could live there more economically than in Dublin. The place, however, had to be made fit for their habitation. Improvements to Derrynane included the addition of several sitting-rooms and bedrooms and the turning of the back of the house into the front. Of course, the cost of all this renovation, not to mention the cost of additional furniture, ran far over the amount anticipated.[122] Eventually, and belatedly, O'Connell realized his folly. 'I laid out a foolish deal of money at Derrynane to practise the economy which we are now suffering under,' he confessed to Mary during yet another separation brought about by money troubles.[123] What money he had was further stretched when his daughter Ellen married in 1825 and was dowered with £5000, payable over four years. Moreover, O'Connell's absence from the circuit that same year, to participate in the push for Catholic Emancipation in London, meant a substantial loss of bar earnings.[124]

It was only the Catholic Emancipation Act of 1829 that brought O'Connell and his family any relief. A national testimonial was organized and presented to O'Connell in recognition of his efforts in getting the bill passed. With this money he was able to pay off all his debts, to leave his law practice and to devote himself entirely to politics. At last this cloud over Mary's happiness had dispersed.

Helen Mulvey, in her treatment of the couple's correspondence, points out that Mary 'learned over the years what peace of mind about herself meant to him [O'Connell], and at some cost to her own feelings would refrain from bringing up unpleasant subjects, such as money matters, on the eve of his departures'.[125] Ellen O'Connell's recollections of her parents' relationship uphold this view. Ellen wrote of her mother:

> She knew that it was necessary for the greatness of the affairs of both law and politics with which his mind was occupied continually that he should never be troubled about household affairs, and she therefore, while regulating hers with the greatest exactness, took care never to harass him with any of her domestic troubles, as so many unthinking women are in the habit of doing, and on the contrary endeavoured so to arrange matters so that he should never find anything but peace and repose at his own fireside![126]

While Mulvey admits this picture gives a distorted view of Mary as a paragon of selflessness who always put her husband first, she fails to see the deeper relevance of Ellen's comments in relation to O'Connell. O'Connell frequently requested good news from home. He longed for letters reporting on his happy and stable family, which would relieve his guilty conscience. Despite the many letters he composed expressing his desire to be reunited with his wife and children and the tension he felt between duty to family and to country, O'Connell made his choice. He wrote his comforting, loving and affectionate letters from the circuit, from Derrynane, from London, from wherever his public responsibilities took him—in short, away from Mary. In making choices, O'Connell considered his duty to his profession or to his country more important than personal happiness derived from being with his wife and family. He was willing and able to keep his political appointments but easily and often allowed business engagements to keep him away from his family, despite his promises to the contrary, and despite the deep disappointment and loneliness his choices caused his wife and children.[127]

O'Connell's behaviour followed the same pattern throughout his marriage to Mary. He continually wrote about undying love and a supreme wish to make his wife happy, yet he consistently managed to make her miserable. The couple's constant separation was only one example. His flagrant use and abuse of money was another. 'Oh, what a scoundrel I am to have made it necessary to separate from you,' he castigated himself. Self-reprobations and requests for forgiveness fill his letters, and yet he continued in his errant ways, fully aware that their unhappy separations were his 'own extravagant fault'.[128] Mary, however, bore all these failings with great patience—at least within the frame of her letters. And it was this trait in her personality which so endeared her to her husband. 'Into what bosom would I pour my sorrows but yours,' he asked her in 1827. 'To whom should I look for comfort consolation and assistance but you.'[129]

3

'angel mother'
— MOTHERHOOD —

Mary O'Connell delivered twelve healthy babies in thirteen years, suffering no tortuous or prolonged labours in the process. Her experiences of pregnancy and childbirth, as described in her correspondence, contradict the findings of scholars who have painted a bleak picture of the emotional and physical plight of childbearing women at this time.[1] Her pregnancies appear to have been happy and joyful events; the birth of each child was awaited with excitement, and the mundane ills of pregnancy borne without much comment. Indeed, the sparse references to her maternal health suggest that pregnancy and childbirth—aside from the extreme excitement of the first birth—were normal events, too common to be particularly noteworthy. Moreover, the routine hardships of childbearing appear to have accounted for most of Mary's ill health, which brings into question the conventional viewm that Mary had a weak constitution and poor health generally.

Mary's first pregnancy was indeed a difficult one, both physically and emotionally. Separated from her husband, her marriage still a secret, she suffered quietly from severe bouts of illness and low spirits. At first O'Connell dismissed her sickness as trifling, writing, 'The illness you feel is the natural consequence of having made me the happiest of men. It is the child of your Dan that gives you so much trouble. Let not your pains be increased by thinking of the pangs of seperation [sic] but rather look forward to the happy, happy hours we shall spend together.' He continued, counselling her about the harsh results of poor spirits at such an important time:

> They say, my heart, that the state of the mother's mind when pregnant much affects the health the temper and even the understanding of her progeny. I do not deceive you in this particular though I do not either attach much credit to notions of the kind. Yet they are not to be entirely despised. There may be something in it. And surely my Mary would not do any thing that could possibly [?hamper] the fond expectation her husband entertains of seeing her children resemble in mind and health [their] angel mother. For my part I will do all I can to soften the ills of seperation [*sic*]. I will write ... by almost every post ... Do not distress yourself to write to me—But write as often as you can with ease to yourself.[2]

O'Connell was delighted with the pregnancy and saw it as a symbol of his own masculine potency. He told his wife, 'Do you know that I treat myself with a kind of respect every time I recollect that you will make me the father of a being to which my heart, my soul and my every sentiment is attached.'[3] Later, however, when O'Connell realized the extent of his wife's illness, the tone of his letters changed from slightly chastising to frantically worrying.

> My heart bleeds for my love ... I fear much that I do very wrong in not flying to you at once ... You are so ill; so very ill that you even conceal your situation from your mother and Betsey. These cold perspirations, these shiverings, fill my heart with apprehension and horror ... sure you do not mean to leave your doating husband a prey to the tortures of knowing that through his fault you do not take sufficient precautions, that my foolish wish for secrecy prevents you from taking that regular exercise, those medical assistants which would render your situation so comparatively easy and trifling. I do most humbly but most fervently entreat that you will not again conceal your state of health from my mother [i.e. Mary's mother] and Betsey. Their experience, Darling, may at once point out means of affording you ease.

O'Connell was so distraught that he could no longer hide his anxiety from his partner James Connor and was thus forced to confess Mary's situation. He determined that he would write to her mother and have her send for Dr Leyne. He ended his letter begging that she conceal nothing of her illness from him, imploring that they must always tell each other the truth.[4] Mary's prolonged illness so frightened him that he actually sat down to read a treatise on midwifery in the hope of easing his worries.[5]

Mary's illness continued intermittently for several months. Although it appears the majority of her ill health was pregnancy-related, Mary attributed much to the 'uneasiness and grief' she felt over the row between Hunting Cap and her husband upon news of Daniel's secret and unsanctioned marriage.[6] Amid all this distress, however, the couple was able to find happiness in the thought of impending parenthood. O'Connell was thrilled at the prospect of a child and professed that he would 'fondly … cherish the little stranger coming'. Furthermore, he hoped for a daughter who would be just like his wife.[7]

Mary's second pregnancy was no less troublesome than the first. Again expressing his desire for a girl, O'Connell described the unborn child as 'impudent' and hoped that the Iveragh air—for Mary had travelled to Kerry to await her confinement—would provide a more gentle influence on the unruly baby. 'Indeed heart *she* ought to be fond of you,' he wrote to his wife from Cork, 'for you have suffered severely by her.'[8] The uncomfortable pregnancy resulted in the birth of Morgan on 31 October 1804. Expected early in the month, the baby was long overdue. Moreover, although her recovery period was fairly quick, Mary was confined for nearly two weeks before the child was born.[9]

Her 1805 pregnancy with Ellen proved no easier. Mary was again plagued with illness. This time, however, the veteran O'Connell was better able for it, writing, 'I should be long since with you if I had not the strong hope that your illness was merely the result of fatigue and of *your* situation.'[10] Morning sickness and other pregnancy-related inconveniences were viewed as a good sign, ensuring the health of the baby and the well-being of the mother.[11]

August 1806 saw Mary pregnant with her fourth child, Kate. Edward followed in July 1808. The pregnancy and delivery appear to have been relatively trouble-free. Mary came downstairs on the third of August, ending her confinement (which normally lasted one month). On 20 August she took the child out in the carriage. Her letters to O'Connell reported a healthy, thriving baby who gave his wet-nurse little rest. On or around 21 August Mary left Dublin to meet O'Connell in Tralee. Despite his robust start, however, little Edward lived only six months and died in January 1809.[12]

In early 1809 it would appear that Mary lost another child. Although the letters are not explicit it seems that Mary became pregnant again almost immediately following Edward's birth. In March O'Connell wrote to Mary imploring her to take care of herself as her 'situation requires'. He concluded by telling her, 'Indeed Mary you make me the happiest of men.'[13] By this stage, Aunt Nagle, who was frequently present for the births of the O'Connell children, had been corresponding with O'Connell in place of Mary, who was only able to write again on 13 March. The following day she received visitors and used the term 'confinement' in referring to her situation. No mention is made of a baby and it is not clear whether Mary had a miscarriage, a still birth, or a premature birth in which the baby died almost immediately. Although Mary recovered quickly, she confided in her husband, 'I went through this turn more than ever I did.'[14]

By June Mary was pregnant again. Betsey was born 21 February 1810, immediately followed by John in December of the same year. Between the years 1812 and 1816, Mary delivered a child every year: Daniel Stephen in December 1812; Gloriana in 1813; Mary in April 1814; Ricarda in May 1815; and Daniel Junior in August 1816. (Of these only Daniel Jr survived infancy.) It would appear that Mary and Daniel gave no serious thought to the frequency and spacing of their children. Morgan's birth, for example, proved highly inconvenient for O'Connell. While Mary awaited her confinement in Carhen, O'Connell wrote to her from the circuit, 'Do now dearest, contrive to get rid of your burden as early in October as possible for indeed I cannot possibly go to Dublin without you. The fact is, heart, that we arranged the matter badly.'[15] O'Connell was insensitive to the general fatigue, ill health and even dangers surrounding Mary's closely spaced pregnancies. His desire for children seemed to supersede any concern for his wife's health. Only a few weeks after the apparent miscarriage in March 1809 O'Connell wrote to his wife, 'What a sweet bedfellow my darling will be before me if she takes care of herself.'[16]

In order to secure the reproduction of healthy offspring, patients and doctors practised prenatal care from the first weeks of a pregnancy. Contrary to popular myth, there seems to have been no social taboo against appearing in public during pregnancy. Indeed, women were encouraged and expected to remain active even up to their ninth month. Using pregnancy too often as an excuse for inactivity was likely to be questioned and even ridiculed by one's social circle.[17] Mary herself socialized during her many pregnancies. She often called upon neighbours or dined out, even in her last months of pregnancy. When in Tralee or Mallow, she did not allow her condition to keep her from the town's races and balls.[18]

The new emphasis on the 'natural' state of pregnancy, which developed at the end of the eighteenth century, also brought about a change in the perception of childbirth. Due in part to the influence of progressive medical theories, traditions such as dark and stuffy lying-in rooms attended by crowds of onlookers gave way to more natural and private deliveries. Women were not generally made to take to their beds the moment labour came upon them. Instead they were encouraged to walk or stand and generally to pursue any interest that might distract them. Thus, Ellen O'Connell, upon the birth of her third child in five years, walked about the house until half past five; by seven o'clock she had delivered a healthy baby boy.[19]

Despite medical advances, the exact delivery date of a child remained difficult to predict and miscalculations could result in serious inconveniences for the entire family. On occasion Mary, and consequently her husband, were taken by surprise. For example, Kate was born in Dublin in March 1807. Although O'Connell promised to be with Mary during her lying-in, her early delivery prevented his attendance at this birth.[20]

False alarms were not uncommon. Mary wrote to O'Connell a week before her last child was born: 'I thought I was *going* to be *ill* last night but *it* was a *false* alarm for I was well enough this morning to go to my duty and hear three Masses. Would to God I was once well, but I must have *patience* and trust in the goodness of God for a happy time.' A week later she was predicting her delivery to be as far off as the next week, causing O'Connell to comment, 'This is almost the first time that you were *after* your calculation. I am indeed impatient.' In the event, Mary delivered a baby boy, Daniel Jr, that very day.[21]

Sometimes, miscalculations reached outrageous proportions. Maurice O'Connell's wife, Mary Frances, seriously underestimated the date of her confinement, much to her father-in-law's dismay. Mary had travelled to Derrynane to be with the young woman when she gave birth but found herself waiting interminably. 'I can not but think of Maurice's wife who would never lye in if it were possible for her to refrain,' complained O'Connell on 20 November 1834. Six days later he burst forth in agitation, 'How cruel of Mary O'C. to separate us thus! Surely she should have guessed better!' His complaints at the delay became more unkind to the poor woman as another week passed.[22] 'Perhaps after all she is not with child at all,' he speculated. 'That would be the ludicrous part of it. What a prize my unfortunate Maurice drew for himself in the lottery of life. But he clearly has nobody to blame but himself, which after all is but a poor consolation.' 'Is it certain she is with child at all for I have my doubts,' he further inquired the following day. 'She fell into such *fatness* which is a symptom of ceasing to breed.'[23] By mid-December, O'Connell was convinced Mary Frances was not pregnant at all. 'She could not mistake by so many months and her excessive corpulence and great appetite favour my opinion,' he reasoned. By this stage the woman was nearly three months off her mark. Her 'eternal' pregnancy, as O'Connell termed it, finally concluded around 18 December 1834 with the birth of a baby girl. Obviously, the child was conceived after the mother was already believed to be pregnant. The most important revelation of these seriously 'overdue' babies, then, is that the couple continued sexual activity during the supposed pregnancy.[24]

The period of confinement after the delivery of the child consisted of clearly defined stages of recovery. While the stages themselves were universal, the length of time for each depended upon the individual as well as the pregnancy, and allowed outsiders to assess the well-being of the new mother. 'I did not expect, my dear life,' O'Connell wrote to Mary after the birth of Morgan, 'that you could have attempted to write for many days to come.' A letter penned by the newly delivered mother was a sure sign of recovery.[25] Other stages consisted of moving from the bed to a sofa, and then, gradually, to the dressing room just outside the birth chamber, removing downstairs, and lastly, leaving the house for the first 'airing'.[26]

The length of confinement generally depended on the health of the mother and her economic situation. Amongst the middle and upper classes the period of confinement usually lasted for four to six weeks.[27] After the birth of each child Mary rested four weeks on average before going downstairs. Frequently there was an interval of a week before she was permitted to write to her husband. She then went to the drawing-room where she would receive callers. One week after Morgan was born O'Connell counselled his wife to remain at home for at least three weeks, then, 'If the sun should then permit take a chaise and air yourself in the middle of the day.'[28]

Traditionally no man was allowed to enter the lying-in chamber at any time until two weeks after the delivery. During the third week, ceremonial visits by close male relatives were accepted and in the fourth week all men were allowed. During the nineteenth century these rules began to change and men began to take a more active role in childbirth both physically and emotionally. It would appear that by 1830 allowing male relatives into the outer room of the lying-in chamber had become perfectly acceptable.[29]

Mary O'Connell used wet-nurses for nearly all her children. The reasons for using a wet-nurse were many and varied. Some mothers had an inadequate supply of milk, found breast-feeding painful or were too ill after the delivery to nurse their own child. In these cases, the lack of an alternative artificial source of nourishment meant that wet-nursing was the only solution. In the upper classes, the need to produce heirs would not allow for the contraceptive side-effect of maternal breast-feeding, not to mention the fact that nursing an infant also interfered with the mother's sleep and her social engagements. Moreover, as stated above, the unhygienic conditions of city living were believed to be detrimental not only to the child but also to the milk produced by the mother. Likewise, copulation during the period when a mother was nursing was considered harmful to the milk. Again, lacking an alternative food source, many husbands insisted children be wet-nursed so as not to hinder sexual relations between the couple. The taboo was not necessarily universal, as it does not appear to have been observed in seventeenth-century France, nor eighteenth-century Britain or America. Contrary to the doctrine of Protestant sects from the late sixteenth century, the Catholic Church did not condemn the practice of wet-nursing and even encouraged it as a means for couples to avoid the dangers associated with nursing and conjugal relations. This stance on the part of the Catholic Church may in some measure explain why wet-nursing remained widespread in Catholic France but not in England. Although no conclusive studies exist for Ireland, the experience of Mary O'Connell lends itself to this theory.[30]

Mary O'Connell's decision to wet-nurse her children in no way reveals a neglectful or selfish attitude towards her children. Often, the mother was not the only party involved in the decision of whether or not to nurse. In the case of her first-born, Mary told her husband, 'I have got a nurse for him as they [O'Connell's parents] thought me too delicate to suckle him and that confinement would not agree with me.' Thus a wet-nurse was obtained for Maurice. Although Mary parted with her child 'with a good deal of regret', she had to admit he was much improved upon his next visit to her. His nurse was the wife of O'Connell's foster brother, 'which reason I prefered [*sic*] her to any other Nurse though she does not speak a word of English which to me you know is unpleasant but as I have got her sisterinlaw [*sic*] Moll to attend also to him, I shant find it so disagreeable as I otherwise would.'[31] The only purpose the wet-nurse served was to breast-feed the child. A monthly nurse, in the above case Moll, was hired to attend to the mother and assist the *accoucheur*. This nurse was usually summoned only when labour began and stayed with the mother for one month from the date of her confinement.[32]

Upon Morgan's birth, the decision was made to send him to Valentia Island to wet-nurse. What part Mary played in this decision is difficult to determine from the letters. However, it would appear that she was loath to send her child so far away and attempted many times to arrange for herself and her two children to stay with O'Connell's parents at Carhen.[33] Mary's objection to her separation from Morgan seemed to be based solely upon her growing love and affection for the child rather than a fear over his well-being at the hands of a stranger. Never once did she consider nursing the child herself; she wanted the children and both their nurses to stay with her at Carhen and she expressed her regret to O'Connell:

> What I would give to have her [O'Connell's mother] keep my little darling at Carhen while I remained there but I fear I have no chance and, darling, what a pity it is (if we could help it) ever to send my sweet fellow to Valentia though I am convinced his nurse will take very good care of him for she absolutely adores him and she is one of the mildest creatures I ever knew and seems to be very well disposed.[34]

Mary realized, however, that the chances of having both children with her at Carhen were slim for, as she told O'Connell, 'old people have an objection to having young children squalling about them'.[35] Moreover, space at Carhen for two nurses, two infants and their mother was limited. Consequently, the choice to send a child out to nurse rather than bring in a nurse seemed to reflect the economic and practical concerns of the family situation rather than any desire on the part of the mother not to be bothered by a bawling child. Later, when Mary and Daniel had their own home in Dublin, the children were nursed there under the care and supervision of their mother. In the case of Morgan, despite Mary's wishes and regrets, the child was sent to Valentia. Mary had no choice but to accept the situation and to visit her son at regular intervals.[36]

Ellen, born in November 1805, was also sent out to nurse. Mary received reports from Ellen Connor in Tralee regarding the child's welfare.[37] No mention of Kate and nursing appears in the correspondence, but Edward (b. 1808) and his nurse lived with the O'Connells in Dublin. It would appear, then, that the hiring of a wet-nurse was a given in the O'Connell household. Yet, Betsey's birth in 1810 opened the issue to renewed debate. Betsey was born on 21 February but her nurse did not arrive until 16 March. During the interim Mary must have nursed the child herself, and little Betsey thrived. When Mary found herself dissatisfied with the new nurse, she wrote to O'Connell of her intent to dismiss the woman and, though the letter does not exist, she may have hinted at continuing to nurse the child herself. On 18 March O'Connell wrote to his wife in reply:

> Do, darling, what you please with nurses. Dispose of them precisely as you like … I cannot permit you (pardon the harsh expression) to nurse yourself. Darling, you are not stout enough to nurse, and I only blame myself every time you get the least cold. Think, my own Mary, of how your husband loves you and … do not harass yourself by nursing her. However, wife of my fondest heart, remember I only advise. Gratify yourself and you make me happy because to gratify you is my first pleasure, my only substantial delight. Indeed I should have preferred your curing the Iveragh nurse of her itch and keeping her but in this and everything else do … just as you please provided you leave yourself your strength and your health for the fondest of husbands and the sweetest of babes … and treasure if you can, keep the Iveragh nurse. Next to you and my babes I love Iveragh. But do *as you choose*.[38]

Because Mary was so soon pregnant again after Betsey's birth, it can be assumed that she did indeed follow her husband's wishes that she keep the nurse. John was also wet-nursed at the O'Connell home in Dublin. So close was he in age to his sister Betsey that the two children were nursed by the same woman. By this time, Mary was perfectly happy with the arrangement, for, 'such a pair of doats as she has nearly reared for me'.[39]

The criteria for choosing a wet-nurse varied. Though not entirely pleased with Betsey's nurse, Mary described the woman, who arrived up from the country, as 'a healthy looking young woman but as to *beauty* or *smartness* she has not much of either to boast of, but if my little *acquisition* thrives with her as well as she has with me I shall be satisfied as to her beauty'. Any hint of skin disease or illness made a candidate unsuitable.[40]

Often, the nurse was also suckling her own child. While this was acceptable, Mary was delighted at the improvement of Morgan, 'as his nurse has now no occasion to milk herself'.[41] As seen above in Betsey's case, finding a good nurse was not always easy. Edward's first nurse was dismissed because she became ill. The second nurse proved much better and, according to Mary, the child did not give the hired woman much rest. 'I never saw a child (God bless him) suck so much, and she has plenty of it for him as I take care to give her good nourishment.'[42]

Mary found that most of the wet-nurses 'agreed very well' with her children. Although it is difficult to determine with exactness, the length of time each child was nursed appears to have varied. Generally weaning occurred at or around eighteen months, although the child by this stage would already be receiving additional nutritional elements.[43] Maurice was nursed from his birth in June 1803 until August 1805. He handled the transition well, according to his mother, who reported, 'he is as quiet as possible and slept the Night as well as ever he did. He sometimes asks for her [the nurse], but then he does not cry or get cross at her not coming to him.'[44] Morgan's nurse brought him to his mother in Tralee in August 1806, two years after he was sent to Valentia Island.[45] Ellen, who was sent to Tralee to nurse in the late spring or summer of 1806, was back in Dublin by March 1807.[46] Little Ricarda O'Connell, born in May 1815, was still nursing in August 1816.[47] Daniel Jr's nurse, whose husband was in the military, continued to attend the child in March 1818, some eighteen months after his birth.[48]

The letters reveal that in the O'Connell family the practice of wet-nursing was considered normal and even beneficial to the children and their mother. In later years, Mary remarked to her son Daniel Jr that a family friend, Julia O'Brien, was breast-feeding her own infant. Mary wrote, 'she is suckling him herself of which she's very proud'.[49] Such a pointed reference suggests that nursing one's infant was still a rarity in Mary's circle of women friends. She seemed to harbour no anxiety for her children's safety or well-being at the hands of the nurse. On the contrary, Mary was very particular about the women she employed and quickly dismissed any with whom the child did not thrive. Her comments regarding her nurses were positive and even grateful. The descriptions given by both O'Connell parents of their offspring reveal happy, healthy, thriving children—a far cry from the traditional historians' view of the 'mercenary' wet-nursing phenomenon.

A discussion of nineteenth-century child-rearing practices would not be complete without examining the very real threat of infant mortality and childhood death. William Buchan's *Domestic Medicine*, published in 1784, claimed that one in two children would die before reaching the age of twelve.[50] Some historians argue that this high rate of infant mortality kept parents from forming emotional attachments to their children.[51] Recent studies, however, suggest that parents did indeed forge bonds of love and affection with their offspring from the time of birth.[52]

Despite the relatively high incidence of infant and child death, it is clear from the O'Connell correspondence that, for Mary and Daniel, infants were to be treasured dearly, even before birth. Morgan's early brush with measles, for instance, made his father's 'heart bleed'. He believed the death of their child would be 'a severe loss'. Yet he did attempt to offer his wife one small consolation. In the event of Morgan's death, she should 'remember that you have another boy—that you have the fondest most faithful husband'.[53] Little Betsey, who fell ill with whooping cough just two months after her birth, elicited the same lines of love from her father who believed 'it would turn my heart cold to lose the little love'.[54]

Although Mary did not seem to be plagued by miscarriages and still births as were other women in her family, the threat of a child dying was very real to the O'Connell family. In all, Mary safely delivered twelve children. It would appear that a thirteenth infant, unnamed, died during or very shortly after birth. Of the twelve children, seven survived to adulthood. Those who died in childhood were Edward, who lived seven months; Daniel Stephen, who survived fourteen months; Mary, who died shortly after birth; and Gloriana and Ricarda, who lived perhaps three years. It is clear from the correspondence that in the brief time that these children were alive, they were much loved and fussed over by their parents and siblings alike.[55]

The loss of one infant did not prevent the family from lavishing love upon the next child to come along. Nor does it appear that affection was reserved until a sufficiently 'safe' interval had passed that would ensure the child's survival. O'Connell wrote of Morgan just one week after his birth, 'This little rascal has certainly taken a lasting hold—but by no means to the exclusion of the other sweet fellow [Maurice].'[56] Of baby Ricarda, born in late May 1815 and nicknamed 'the little red duck' or 'Ducky', Mary frequently wrote to her husband, referring to her as 'a dear little infant' who was 'engaging as possible'. The child, she continued, 'is every day growing more and more on my affections'. She provided great amusement to the family. The boys continually doted upon her and, Mary reported, 'she is quite a little idol'. Every day that passed the child endeared herself more to her mother, who sent O'Connell affectionate accounts of the little redhead's teething, her walking and all her charming habits. With the birth of Daniel Jr, Ricarda became insecure about her place in her mother's affections. Mary informed O'Connell, 'I never saw a little creature become so attached to me as she is. She cant bear to see me take little Dan nor will she allow the girls or John to come near me. I fear I shall make her too bold or rather that between you and me she will be a spoiled child.' Unfortunately, Mary's fears were unfounded, for one month later, on 16 October 1816, Ricarda makes her last appearance in the O'Connell papers.[57] In April 1817 O'Connell wrote to Mary regarding the illness of Daniel Jr, who had been born the previous August. '[M]y heart is so sore for another infant', he told his wife, 'that I could not indeed I could not bear to be *taken in* about another darling.' Danny had contracted measles and whooping cough. It can only be assumed that Ricarda and Danny had fallen ill together. While Danny eventually recovered, the much loved Ducky did not.[58]

The O'Connells shared in the grief others suffered at the loss of an infant. '[P]oor Betsy O'Connell,' wrote Mary of her brother's wife who had just lost a child, 'it is only time that can reconcile it to her for indeed he was a stout Baby. She is with me every day.'[59] When his sister Ellen lost her child, O'Connell wrote to Mary, 'it is to her a grievous calamity. How deplorable in itself to have all her sufferings thus thrown away in giving life to a being that breathed but for an instant and then sunk in eternal rest.' He counselled Mary, who was staying with Ellen at Carhen at the time, 'Endeavour, my darling, to turn her thoughts from the sad subject. Perhaps you ought to avoid caressing your boy before her and if you think it useful to her to keep him from her sight you ought to be very careful in doing so.'[60]

Although Mary does not pointedly express her grief at her own losses in her letters to her husband, we cannot assume this to mean she felt very little. More than likely O'Connell was present when each child died and during the mourning period that followed, so Mary would never have had occasion to write to him on the subject. Within the extant correspondence there is not one occasion on which she reported the death of a child. Carroll

Smith-Rosenberg, in her study of female relationships, found that 'Virtually every collection of letters and diaries in my sample contained evidence of women turning to one another for comfort when facing the frequent and unavoidable deaths of the eighteenth and nineteenth centuries.'[61] Unfortunately, letters between Mary and her female friends and family no longer exist. It is probable, however, that her grief was expressed there.

The relationship between the O'Connells and their children was an informal and affectionate one. One example of this is the use of nicknames within the family circle. As a small child, Maurice, practically raised by his grandparents at Carhen, called his mother 'Mama Mary' and his father 'Dan'.[62] The use of nicknames by the O'Connells reflects a trend in the early nineteenth century. Informal modes of address revealed the growing prominence of the individual over the rank or position that given individual held in society. Moreover, these nicknames indicate the varying levels of intimacy amongst individuals and within family circles.[63] Several of the O'Connell children were given affectionate pet names by their parents. Kate was commonly referred to as 'Saucy Kate', and O'Connell often called Danny 'Miscreant', an appellation which Mary also picked up. Ricarda O'Connell, as we have seen, was known as 'Ducky'. Moreover, Mary insisted that Danny use her nickname of 'Mod' as the only acceptable form of address in the letters he sent her from boarding-school.[64]

As these pet names suggest, Mary and Daniel were careful to acknowledge all of their children as individuals. The personality of each child was taken into account when deciding on the best course for rearing them. Again, this emphasis on the individuality of each child reflects the many changes brought by domesticity. Unlike the philosophy of traditional patriarchy, in which children were valued for their potential to increase family wealth and advance the family name, domesticity placed a higher value on loving children in their own right. O'Connell's enthusiastic appreciation of girl children, for example, is indicative of the spread of domesticity in the nineteenth century.[65]

The O'Connell correspondence is peppered with descriptions of the children, their funny sayings and delightful mannerisms. Mary wrote to O'Connell about little Maurice, saying, 'He is quite familiar with me and when he wants to coax me he calls me pretty Mama May.' She described how the child 'regularly gets a pen to write to Dan [i.e. his father]'.[66] On another occasion the young child pointed to her bed and exclaimed that it was for 'Mama Maly to lolo'.[67] This was not merely the overzealous reporting of a first-time mother; three years later, Mary continued to recount the activities of the children to her husband away on circuit. While Morgan was 'as indifferent as you please, Ellen says you are in the study but our sweet little Kate, when she came into the room last night and was kissing me, she held out her little mouth toward the bed, and Johanna [the nurse] was obliged to take her to it. The little infant looked quite disappointed when she did not find you there.' Ten years after her first child was born, Mary reported on the ninth: 'Gloriana says you are gone to Mass when she is asked for you.'[68]

When Mary and Daniel married, his position as a fledgling attorney put them in a precarious financial situation, which was made worse by his disinheritance. Since O'Connell had no house of his own, Mary moved between her mother's home in Tralee and the O'Connell family home in Carhen. These circumstances, coupled with the decision to send their sons out to nurse, meant that Mary was separated from her first children at frequent intervals during their early years. She was, however, continually aware of their progress and kept fully updated as to their well-being.[69] O'Connell complied with her request for detailed accounts of the children, taking the time to note their physical appearance, their personality and their antics. The following excerpt regarding Maurice at ten months old, though rather long, is a lovely example:

> His little hair is grown. It is a shade lighter in colour than yours—his eyebrows are of the same shade but resemble mine in shape. He is grown taller though not much and has the appearance of being as fat as he was. His flesh is as solid as that of a grown person. His breathing is become much more clear and soft—so much so that I have no doubt but he will be as longwinded a fellow as any of his family. There cannot be a creature better attended to. Every being in the house doats of him. His grand mother perhaps most of all. He spends his mornings in bed with her—with both his arms round her neck cooing and shouting and whistling for her. And during the day he takes away her work or her book to make her play with him. The consequence is that she is grown extremely attached to him. He has a thousand tricks and I have been told a hundred stories of him that would be ridiculous to any other person but give fond delight to

the heart of a parent … My poor father idolizes him … He delights in his basket and walks in it about the house. He treads very firmly in it and walks about the beds by himself holding with one hand. There is a woman here making quilts in a frame and he is greatly pleased at walking about it without any person's help … It would make you laugh to see him screw up his little mouth to whistle. He is very fond of trying to do so and succeeds surprizingly [*sic*]. He has got but two underteeth. They are a good deal advanced and are of great use to him as he now eats some of every thing. He likes dry bread but infinitely prefers a potatoe [*sic*] and some milk … James is indeed attached to him … You desired me give you those details, and I well know how they will gratify you heart.[70]

Still, Mary's frequent absences in these early years were not without impact upon her young offspring. When she returned to Carhen in August 1805 after spending several months in Dublin setting up house, for instance, two-year-old Maurice did not even remember her. Mary, greatly upset at this, complained bitterly to O'Connell, who attempted to console her and warn her that she might be ill-treated by their youngest offspring as well.

How I could wish that Maurice had recollected you but should you be mortified by his very probably forgetfulness it be some comfort to you to know this is the last occasion on which he will refuse to acknowledge his little mother.—As for the other fellow I suppose he is able and willing to beat you. His nurse is making him as bold as a young Lion. I fear it is a bad experiment on his future temper—If you think so, speak to her about it.[71]

The situation did improve with time and Mary delighted in informing her husband just days later that 'he [Maurice] and I are the greatest friends'.[72] Though she still had her trials with the young child, she assured O'Connell, 'He is much attached to me though he sometimes calls me a bitch and desires me go to Tralee to Dada Dan.'[73]

O'Connell took an active part in the upbringing of his children as well. Education was very important to him. 'Nothing I do believe can give such delight to the heart of a parent as watching the first faint glimmering of rational ideas as they fall from the lips of [a] little *beginning babbler*,' he wrote to Mary upon hearing news of Maurice's new vocabulary, and he promised to teach the child his letters over the Christmas holiday.[74] When away, O'Connell always enjoyed news of his children. 'Write a volume about them,' he begged his wife. 'Dearest, let me get long letters from you—write to me much of yourself, much of our boy—they are the subjects that interest me.' As the children grew older, O'Connell praised and admonished them in letters from the circuit. Mary often remarked upon improved behaviour following receipt of these missives.[75]

For Mary, her children served a consolatory function in O'Connell's absences. 'I never can reconcile myself to your absence until I get your first letters, then the company of our babes and the happiness I look forward to when we shall again meet, in some measure consoles me for the lonesome feeling I have.'[76] The relationship between mother and child, however, was not seen in the child-rearing literature of the day to be a means of producing maternal satisfaction. Instead it was merely a 'vehicle for the child's growth'.[77]

Shortly after Maurice's birth, O'Connell outlined his ideas regarding the role of a parent: 'If we could shield him from every rude blast of adversity. If we can give him the big heart that swells with affection but that can grow cold when unfeeling oppression commands. May my boy have strong, distinct and marked traits in his character. The pitiful disposition that never soars beyond mediocrity shall never be praised before our son, darling.'[78] Of his daughters, O'Connell instructed Mary, 'I think, darling, you ought to control your girls a little more. They are to be sure very young but habits of selfwill and obstinacy are very apt to be acquired and are impossible to be eradicated. Ellen certainly has an adventurous spirit and Kate should not, I think, be allowed to be so *decided* in her opinion.'[79]

O'Connell, having escaped to the circuit, found it easy enough to give advice when far removed from the many complications involved in each disciplinary incident. For Mary, however, embroiled as she was in daily battles with several naughty children, his simple and practical advice may have proved difficult to follow. The letters suggest that Mary tended to be the more lenient of the two. Of Maurice she wrote, 'I think you will have something to do on your return *to keep him in order*. When I attempt to threaten him he only laughs up in my face and then I press the *bold fellow* to my heart and bestow on him twenty kisses.'[80] Yet Mary recognized the need for a balance between affection and authority, and worried lest she spoil her children.[81] Describing Ellen's behaviour on one occasion as extremely bold, she informed O'Connell, 'I am now going on a plan of keeping her out of my presence and confining her to the schoolroom until I see a thorough change for the better in her conduct and manner which I hope will have the desired effect as she seems to feel *it* very much.' The punishment obviously worked, for in her next letter to O'Connell, Mary reported that Ellen was back in favour.[82]

When not at home, O'Connell continually advised Mary in his letters regarding the discipline of their offspring. He had specific ideas about how each child should behave and how to treat them should they not. 'I am very anxious to know how Maurice has behaved himself since,' he wrote to Mary on one occasion. 'He ought to act as a man in my absence—but if he is one bit bold I entrust of you not to indulge him or let him dine in the parlour—Tell him besides that I shall be extremely angry with him unless he keeps his word with me about conducting himself properly.' Punishment, such as confinement to the nursery or exclusion from the dinner table, as well as the withholding of affection and praise, was used to deter the O'Connell children in their errant ways.[83] An 'early and gentle control' was O'Connell's maxim. 'Control them, heart, for me,' he told Mary. 'They will be happier for it.'[84]

Control consisted of setting a good example, administering firm discipline and lavishing the child with love. Obedience, then, came as a direct result of the child's desire for love and approval, rather than fear of severe punishment. Both parents gently encouraged their children to excel, as O'Connell wrote to John, 'surely you will endeavour to show yourself deserving of all our Love'.[85] The method seems to have been successful. Maurice O'Connell wrote to his mother on his fourteenth birthday:

> [I]t shall be my care, whilst I live, to endeavour to repay that love & tenderness with which you watched over my childhood & endeavoured to instil the seeds of virtue into my breast. Nor am I less grateful to my father, not only for his love, but for that brilliant example which his conduct has placed before my eyes. An example which it shall ever be my pride to imitate as I know that will [?see] me beloved & esteemed here and happy for eternity hereafter.[86]

Mary always held up the example of her husband to her children. She instructed Daniel Jr to 'gratify him by close attention to your studys [*sic*] and keeping your person clean'.[87] When Danny seemed to falter in his school work, Mary was quick to chastise him: 'Surely you will not commit so much sin as to neglect studying and doing all in your power to repay your good Father for the expense he is at for you.'[88] The O'Connells also granted rewards to well-behaved children. Money was often given in return for good marks at school. On another occasion, O'Connell requested that the children dine with him upon his return from the circuit. 'I think it would be a treat to the doats to dine at the table with their father,' he told Mary.[89]

On only one occasion is the use of physical punishment mentioned in the letters. In March 1811, Mary reported to her husband that she had had a huge scene with her eldest daughter Ellen, then five. Ellen was so resolved not to go to school one morning that Mary was 'obliged to beat her with a rod'. Apparently, Ellen's teacher had punished her for not having her hymn and doubled her work for the next day. Mary expressed her conviction that Ellen's teacher

> is severe and ill-tempered. She does not consider Ellen's youth and is forever complaining about her. She is, she says, an annoyance to the other children, that she is never at rest and as to her temper, it is very bad—my darling child that has the sweetest temper and disposition I ever saw ... I can't tell you how it hurts my feelings to have Mrs. Bishop forever saying she is ill-tempered.

Despite her dislike of the woman, Mary was well aware of her husband's desire that Ellen attend school there. Therefore, she insisted the child go, punishing her for her disobedience.[90] O'Connell's response sanctioned both Mary and the teacher's behaviour. 'I am greatly obliged to you for your firmness with my poor Nell,' he wrote. 'If you had given up the point she would have conquered you for life.' He further stated that Ellen was 'selfwilled and the tender indulgence she meets at home requires a greater degree of austerity abroad'.[91]

Despite the severe positions taken in the above incident, both parents were conscious of being too harsh. In 1820 O'Connell wrote to his wife regarding a chastising letter he had sent to his oldest son. He feared he had been too rough on the boy though he meant only to 'stimulate his industry'. He asked Mary to convey to Maurice that 'whether he wins or loses he will be equally dear to his father'.[92] For her part, Mary found O'Connell's letter highly effective. She further believed that her husband's example of early rising and his close attention to study had an even greater effect on her first-born. Of course she did allow that they must 'make allowances' for Maurice because he was so young.[93] In the case of Danny,

Mary was accused on more than one occasion of spoiling the child. In 1820 Ellen O'Connell reported to her father, 'Mama says she whipped him the other day but I don't think either you or I will attach much credit to that assertion.' She defended her mother, however, agreeing that Danny was such a 'bewitching little Darling and I don't wonder he should be a little spoiled'.[94] Ellen's assessment was probably correct. Danny was Mary's baby, her youngest child, born six years after his brother John. In between these two boys, Mary had delivered four other babies, all of whom died in childhood. It is no wonder she doted upon the child. The entire family teased Mary about her favouritism towards Danny. O'Connell commented at one stage that he was surprised she had let the nine-year-old child go to Glencullen to stay the night. He did not think she could bear the separation and would worry with him so long out of her sight. When she voiced concern over Danny's riding habits, O'Connell's teased, 'I quized [sic] you a little about Danny and you see I was right.' He admonished her to let the child jump his pony over ditches and even low walls, assuring her that Danny was an able rider.[95]

Mary was sensitive to criticism regarding the upbringing of her children. On one occasion rumours of such criticism reached her in Dublin. She quickly wrote to Danny at boarding-school, 'I am told Mr. Duncan [presumably Danny's schoolmaster] says to every person that you are a spoiled child by me. I don't really think I deserve he should speak of me in those terms and I should much regret you giving him cause to make this ill notioned remark upon your Mother. He should learn a *little discretion*. Tell him I *spoke* to you on the one disagreeable subject. I should wish him to know.'[96]

The relationship between mother and son was limited to some extent by the social constraints within which the masculine identity was formed. A female adult generally took precedence over a male child but only until the boy was about seven years old. At this stage, boys were sent off to school, separated from females. Here, male school masters, tutors and peers replaced his family as the centre of his life. This separation, which often allowed and even encouraged the denigration of women, was instrumental in shaping male identity and enforcing heterosexual behaviour. Mary found this to be true of her sons' experience at Clongowes. Each of the O'Connell boys entered the all-male boarding-school around the age of thirteen. 'What nice mannered boys Maurice and Morgan were when they went to Clongowes,' she observed in a letter to O'Connell. 'Indeed they may now well deny it. It is almost impossible to get them to divest themselves of the vulgarity they acquired at *that* college.'[97]

Usually, fathers became more involved in their sons' discipline, care and upbringing when the boy entered school. Both school and parental authority encouraged boys to strive to do their best, to win.[98] 'Mama desires me say ...' wrote Kate O'Connell to her brother Danny at Clongowes, 'that she thinks it a great shame for you not to be in the same class with Greg, you ought to work hard & get away from the little boys you are with. Consider it is no honor to be first amongst such little fellows. What is easy to you is difficult to them.'[99] John O'Connell further counselled his younger brother, 'Endeavour next term to get first in Examen. Nothing is of greater use to a person. It is in fact, the true way of getting first in compositions afterwards.'[100]

Corporal punishment was also a possible response to misconduct at boarding school. Upon hearing rumours that flogging was still carried out at Clongowes, she wrote to Danny: 'This practice has been long given up in every publick [sic] school and I can hardly think the Jesuits would be behind in the work of civilization,' she commented.

> Even from the army flogging is now quite abolished. I wish to have it in my power to contradict this report as I should regret any circumstance that would injure the establishment at Clongows [sic]. My feeling is that if a boy is base enough to deserve a flogging he should be expelled [from] the college. To you I trust there is no fear such a disgraceful punishment should be ever resorted to.[101]

Education for young girls differed drastically from that of boys. Formal education for girls was often rudimentary, especially amongst the lower classes. Even in the middle and upper classes the range of instruction was narrower for girls than for boys. The limited education available to girls reflected the attitude that women's proper place was in the domestic sphere; they did not need an extensive education in order to look after their homes and their children. In the middle and upper classes, however, women were encouraged to study languages, simple mathematics, history, poetry, art, music and even some philosophy, all with the aim of catching a husband and becoming a companionate wife.[102]

In the case of the O'Connell girls, Mary instructed them alongside the boys at home from a very young age, teaching them their letters and listening to them read. Ellen O'Connell claimed to have been able to read at the age of four. Shortly after she turned five, Ellen was sent to a school for girls in Hume Street, Dublin, run by Eliza Bishop. Maurice and Morgan O'Connell attended a boys' school kept by Elverina Wollstonecraft, an English widow, sister to Eliza Bishop. The girls were taught in the drawing room and the boys in the parlour. When Kate was old enough she joined her sister there.[103] Ellen was generally a good pupil, but at one stage she was bribed to give up her place at the head of the class in exchange for a paper flowerpot. Thrilled, she marched home with her trophy only to be 'well scolded and ordered next day to return the flower pot and inform the briber … that I could not hold to my bargain'. Ellen recollected that it was at this stage that O'Connell began to give her a tenpenny every Saturday if she held her place at the head of the class during the week. Impishly, Ellen began to lie about her place. O'Connell quickly caught on to her trick and alerted Mary to the girl's fibs, claiming, 'It could not happen but for the dislike you have conceived to the *mistresses* of her school, because their detection would be certain. I mean if you were occasionally to see them.'[104]

Although Mary continued in her dislike for Mrs Bishop and her school, Ellen and Kate remained there until, shortly thereafter, the O'Connell boys were moved to a different school and the girls were brought home, where their governess, Miss Lynch, took charge of their education.[105] As the children grew older, special instructors were engaged for Morgan, Ellen and Kate in French and Italian.[106] When the family removed to France, O'Connell decided that Ellen should also learn German and Spanish, while Kate was to be a student of French and Italian. Betsey's studies were as yet undecided.[107]

The O'Connell children, even the girls, received well-rounded and extensive educations. However, play was also important in the development of happy and healthy children. Horseback riding, skating, walking, carriage rides, gardening, hunting, dancing, fencing, music and reading were some of the many activities which the O'Connell children pursued in their leisure hours. The children also put on plays in their 'private' theatre and the girls worked in the gardens.[108] Gender did not seem to make much of a difference in the children's choice of activity. Both Danny and Ellen pursued musical interests, for example, and John dallied with poetry. Kate O'Connell was an accomplished horsewoman and often participated in hunts, although Betsey could never 'get over her objection to riding'.[109]

The lives of the O'Connell children seem to have been well balanced. Extensive education went hand in hand with sport and leisure. Physical punishment within the home appears to have been almost non-existent and outside the home it was strongly condemned. A good example of behaviour was set and expected to be followed. All the while, love and affection, sprinkled with firm guidance and persuasion, elicited the desire in each child to strive to do their best for the approval of both their parents.

A further duty of a parent was to see her offspring comfortably 'settled'. According to Randolph Trumbach, 'The settlement's most important business was ... to balance the claims of family continuity and greatness embodied in the position of the eldest son against a satisfactory provision for younger children and for wives; to mediate between the conflicting claims of kindred and patrilineage.'[110] It was a duty that Mary and Daniel took very seriously. The settling of children required 'a great deal of thought'. Consideration was given to the number and sex of children, even more so than rank, when determining their marriage portions. Obviously, the more children one had, the more difficulty one had in settling them all well. Sons were educated in the hopes of securing entry into the professions or the clergy while daughters were watched over and educated by their mothers, who carefully monitored their contacts in the hope of establishing a fitting match. A fitting match, of course, required a suitable dowry.[111] The difficulties the O'Connells faced in making good matches for their daughters demonstrate the intricacies of family aggrandizement and the important roles inheritance, dowries and good matches played in promoting the family's financial well-being, not to mention the happiness of the individuals involved.

Marriage in pre-Famine Ireland was a 'carefully negotiated bargain', whereby the bride provided a suitable dowry to her husband's family.[112] The Irish word *spré*, meaning dowry, was frequently used in pre-Famine poetry from every province. The word 'match', with all its economic connotations, was also well established by the early nineteenth century. Both words often appeared in connection with the theme that the poet would willingly marry the girl in question without benefit of a dowry. The universality of this theme demonstrates the extent to which the dowry system was in place in nineteenth-century Ireland.[113] In general, the size of the dowry varied depending on the status of the family. For example, small farmers in Co. Tipperary were thought to give around twenty or thirty pounds for their daughters' marriage portions, while middling farmers in Co. Kilkenny gave between fifty and one hundred pounds. Large farmers in Co. Cork were known to give anywhere between one and three hundred pounds.[114] In comparison to these figures, Ellen O'Connell's dowry of £5000 was astounding; however, it fell far short of the marriage portions allotted to members of the Irish aristocracy.[115]

Mary O'Connell was well aware of her financial shortcomings upon her marriage to O'Connell and was determined that her daughters not be stigmatized as she had been. Unfortunately, the economic difficulties plaguing the family from 1816 onwards made it difficult to settle the daughters well. Hunting Cap's death in 1825 came much later than O'Connell would have hoped or expected. Anticipating the windfall of his inheritance at any moment, he spent excessively, straining his resources. Following his uncle's demise, O'Connell was immediately able to dower Ellen at £5000, to be paid over four years. Ellen's marriage, to Christopher FitzSimon, could not have taken place without the death of Hunting Cap. Even with this inheritance, however, O'Connell still had trouble coming up with the necessary money. In 1826 he was forced to admit to FitzSimon, who had applied to him for an overdue payment, that the expense of recent renovations at Derrynane left him unable to comply.[116] With O'Connell's inheritance so quickly spent, Kate O'Connell was left to wait, 'banished' to Derrynane, until a change in fortune would give her the necessary dowry.

Mary played a substantial role in negotiating the marriage settlement between Ellen and FitzSimon. Her letters on the subject reveal the anxiety that plagued a young girl while these negotiations took place. Ellen liked FitzSimon; she had been corresponding with the land-owning barrister as early as 1822 while staying in France. However, she realized that should the matter not be settled in a way pleasing to her parents, she would have to obey their wishes and give up her attachment. Ellen's easy acquiescence to her parents' wishes was by no means unusual. Olwen Hufton explains:

> Every young girl was made aware that such were the rules of the game and that physical attraction, while not to be discounted, was of secondary importance. To love, care for, feel affection towards your partner, were obviously important considerations, but so was having something to your name. The

acquisition of means was therefore a goal towards which the young must work. For girls, this vision of the future, or life plan, was made apparent to them from childhood. It was an intrinsic part of social conditioning.[117]

Still, the task was not always easy. 'My poor Nell looks as sober as you please for which she is not a little quized by saucy Kate and Ricarda. You will of course have some communication with Colonel Fitzsimon [uncle to Christopher FitzSimon],' Mary wrote to her husband. She went on to instruct him carefully:

> You should ascertain exactly what he will do for his nephew and I must again impress on you, darling, that I will retract my consent if a jointure of £400 a year is not settled on Ellen and £500 in case she has no children. I also consider £5000 a very handsome fortune with such a girl as my Ellen, and no sacrifice should be made by her family inconsistent with their interest or her establishment in the world. In short, darling, should matters not appear to you as you expected or as you think I would approve of, be careful not to commit yourself beyond the power of redemption.[118]

O'Connell responded, assuring Mary that, 'I will take care of my Nell, my sweet Nell. Do leave that to me.'[119] Still, nothing was immediately done. Once serious negotiations began, Mary was excluded from the process, as women generally were.[120] She could only wait upon her intended to finalize the arrangement and its many economic details. On 7 March O'Connell told Mary, 'Depend on my making an arrangement complete with Col. Fitzsimon. Every day I like his nephew more and more.' Nearly two weeks later, an agreement was reached.[121]

Kate O'Connell did not fare so well. While O'Connell may have hoped to dower all his daughters equally, his constant battle with finances left little for the dowry of his second daughter. As Mary and O'Connell debated over Mary's return to Ireland in 1824, Mary's prime concern was the welfare of her daughters. Returning to Ireland and living somewhere other than Dublin was disagreeable to her and to the girls. Taking up residence in the country would only publicly advertise their financial difficulties and, consequently, damage her daughters' chances of attracting eligible suitors. Instead Mary argued that a year's delay in Windsor would allow them to save more money and 'then be able to show our girls off better', and O'Connell eventually agreed.[122] By the end of February 1824, however, plans changed again and O'Connell decided to bring them all home to Dublin, reasoning, 'We do not want to puff off our daughters by splendour and show, and if we keep for a year or so in the background, why they will only come forward with more effect and pleasure when the temporary privation is over—and in the interval I will be so very very fond of my girls that I will make up to them for any loss they may sustain.'[123]

The inheritance O'Connell received in 1825 allowed for Ellen's settlement but little was left over to ease the continuing family debts. Kate, then, would have to wait. The family removed to Derrynane, where it was thought more money could be saved. O'Connell reported his financial situation to his wife: 'I have paid so much money for interest that I am quite sick of being in debt and if I had but one or two years of strict economy I would be entirely out of debt and able to pay Kate's fortune on demand.'[124] The following month Mary confided in O'Connell her concern for Kate's future. Delighted that he was allowing them to return to Dublin, she wrote that it would have been 'unjust and cruel towards my Kate to take her to Dublin when all the gaiety was over. She is now at that age to enjoy life. You married Ellen at nineteen and why should you not marry Kate at least as early? I am [?sorry] you were not able to reserve her fortune for I feel quite sure it will be soon called upon.'[125]

Mary was wrong in her estimations. In 1830 she wrote to O'Connell as she prepared to join him in London, 'I am anxious to make a good appearance in London for the sake of our girls. It might be of great advantage to them.'[126] At twenty-three, Kate was still on the market. The following year, O'Connell, in an especially sensitive comment, told Mary, 'Tell my sweetest Kate I hope to live to see her love a husband more than she loves her father though she may rely on it that her father will never love her less than he does at present.'[127] In 1832 Kate married her cousin Charles O'Connell of Kerry, with whom she had eight children; no information regarding the dowry arrangements survives.

In March 1831 Mary O'Connell wrote to her son Danny, who was away at Clongowes Wood College. 'What would you think of the possibility of a *wedding* taking place at 30 Merrion Square South,' she asked teasingly. Although nothing firm had been set, Mary felt confident 'of Betseys having made a conquest of a Mr Ffrench, a Catholic young Gentleman of good fortune of Ffrench Lawn in the County Roscommon ... All I have to say farther that such a thing as a marriage may occur but when I cannot well tell you.'[128] The attachment between Betsey and Ffrench caused quite a stir in the O'Connell household. Mary's letters to Danny during the period were conspiratorial in tone; she admonished him to 'be very discreet' about the secret she was to tell him and to 'not mention it to any person until you get leave from me which shall be as soon as I think there may be a wedding. At present it is uncertain.' Still she could not help but speculate on the probability of the event. Nicholas Ffrench was introduced to the family by Maurice. Though not extremely handsome, he was, by Mary's account, 'a fine made large Man with a a [*sic*] very good countenance', and well liked by all—including Betsey. He had dined with the O'Connells the preceding December and, according to Mary, 'the first day he saw Betsy he was *capti*vated'.[129] So too was Mary. Ffrench was the sole heir to his father's estate and descended from one of the oldest Catholic families in Connaught. On 19 March Mary boasted, 'Betsy will probably change her name before next Month is at an end. This between you and me.'[130] Preparations for 'a certain event' were well under way by the twenty-third of March and within the month the couple were married.[131]

Settling the O'Connell sons into promising careers and fitting marriages proved no less daunting a task than settling the daughters. When Maurice O'Connell was but six years old, his father commented on the child's promising 'qualities of mind and of heart'. He went on to tell Mary, 'There is about him an ardour and a distinctness which please me much.' Mary agreed, responding, 'he really is a sweet, sensible fellow and, I trust in God, will yet answer your expectations and be a pride and comfort to both of us'.[132] In his early school years Maurice was a diligent student.[133] After a fine academic performance at Clongowes, however, Maurice, working with a private tutor, failed to win a scholarship to Trinity College. O'Connell was none too pleased with his son's growing inattention to his studies. In letters to his wife he continually asked for reports on Maurice's study habits. Comments such as 'Tell Maurice his fond father hopes that he *is* studying—*will* wont do,' and '*Stick* to Maurice and make him get though his examination,' began to appear more frequently in his letters, as did O'Connell's complete amazement that his first-born could be so very different from himself.[134]

In 1823 Maurice qualified as a barrister. This feat did not end the worries of his parents. Maurice suffered from a 'terrible increase of "fidgets,"' O'Connell complained to Mary in April of that year:

It is, my love, vain to conceal it from ourselves. It must be an organic defect or, if it be habit, it is increasing on him to a cruel degree. My heart is quite sore about him. I wish you would at once sit down and write to him on the subject ... He actually has got a trick of lolling out his tongue round his lips which is childish and absurd in its appearance. I would not write to you on this subject if it did not affect me deeply, deeply.[135]

Upon hearing her husband's description, Mary replied in a sensitive and sympathetic letter:

The description you give of my poor Maurice makes me truly unhappy, but if his restlessness is a disease, he is to be pitied and not condemned ... perhaps his constitution is more weakened by his growth. I will hope anything to be the cause of all this misery to you but an incurable disorder ... my earnest advice shall be that he should at once use the shower bath. When he is with me I shall take great pains with him, and if this fidgeting be merely a habit, I do not despair of his getting quite free from it.[136]

Still, O'Connell was not consoled, so certain was he that Maurice would 'never be cured of his shocking and foolish gesticulations ... What a cruelty it is of him to abandon himself to these miserable sillinesses ... I doubt whether you will not think it useless to go to the expense of giving him any profession.' Fortunately, by late June, Maurice's 'fidgety tricks' had improved.[137] His father, a member of the House of Commons since 1828, had him elected to Parliament for Clare in 1831. In 1832 Maurice was elected to represent Tralee, a position he held until his death in 1853.

There was a great deal of pressure placed upon the eldest son to marry in a way beneficial to his siblings' future and to the financial situation of the family in general. As a result, many attempts were made to settle Maurice with a suitably wealthy bride. In the autumn of 1827 Mary and Daniel conspired to see Maurice wed to a Miss O'Shea whose uncle was purportedly worth some £80,000. For unknown reasons, the match never occurred.[138] Then, in April 1829, Maurice had two new choices laid before him: a Miss Reddington and a Miss O'Brien. These matches also failed to materialize, as did a later one in 1831.[139] Maurice did eventually marry into a wealthy family. In 1832 he eloped in his yacht with Mary Frances Scott, much to the displeasure of his parents. Although the Scotts had money, they were Cromwellian Protestant landlords, and marriage to a Protestant was not considered a suitable match by Mary and Daniel. The couple had four children together before their marriage broke up.[140]

M.R. O'Connell describes Morgan O'Connell as 'a lively and cheerful young man'. In his youth, however, Morgan was a quiet and brooding child, and this greatly disturbed his parents. 'I know not why that child's heart is not as warm to either of us as that of our other children,' O'Connell complained to Mary. 'It sometimes afflicts me.'[141] Moreover, Morgan's efforts in school never met O'Connell's high standards. 'Morgan's great objection to apply himself will, I fear, be the means of rendering him unfit for any profession except the army which is the *last* I should wish for him. However if his inclination is in that way, there is little use in opposing him.'[142] Thus, at age fifteen, Morgan left Ireland as an officer in the Irish Legion. Assembled by John Devereux, the group set out to aid Bolivar in obtaining South America's freedom from Spanish rule.

He returned home in late 1821, placing Mary and Daniel at odds as to his future career path. O'Connell strongly objected to a military career for his son. He hoped Morgan might pursue law. Mary, however, disagreed.

> I totally and entirely disapprove of it. It [the military] is a Profession I never wished for any Son of mine but at present thinking of fixing Morgan to any trade … is quite idle. You dont know Morgan as [?I do] believe me he is too fond of liberty ever to submit to the control of any Person for a period of five years much less consent to be bound to a Desk … believe me it would be lost money to give him any other Profession but the Army. I repeat, I know Morgan better than you.[143]

Eventually, Mary's opinion prevailed and Morgan joined the Austrian army. By 1832, however, he was back in Ireland and his father supported him in his successful bid for a seat in the House of Commons representing Co. Meath. From 1846 to 1869 Morgan acted as Registrar of Deeds. According to M.R. O'Connell, 'He had little interest in politics, and just did as his father directed.'[144]

At one stage Morgan apparently made his desire to marry Anne Costigan known to his family. This match O'Connell regarded as 'folly'. He cared too much for Anne, daughter of their long-time family friends, to allow Morgan to 'trifle' with her, for the two 'would only produce a progeny of beggars'.[145] Writing to Mary he insisted that she 'Break the matter off … in the kindest way you possibly can.' Morgan acquiesced in this instance to his parents' wishes. In 1840 he married Kate Balfe, the daughter of a Catholic landlord in Co. Roscommon. The couple had no children.

Mary's third son, John, was the only O'Connell child to make a serious career out of politics. When John was six, O'Connell expressed his hopes that the boy might make 'a most excellent *priest*'. Eight years later, O'Connell reiterated this idea. 'How delighted I should be if it pleased God to give him a powerful vocation to His holy service.'[146] John had other plans. In 1826, aged sixteen, he wrote to his father from Clongowes:

> The subject of it [this letter] is the profession to which I have the most inclination. I do not say that I am to adopt because I know that that is entirely at your & at Mama's disposal. However there can be no harm in declaring that to which I have always felt and feel a strong natural bend. I mean the Navy. You or at least it was hinted to me [*sic*] that you intended me to be a lawyer if you will to be so, it must happen certainly ... Now tho I would not wish to displease you for any thing, I must declare that I have not any liking for the law that on the contrary I have a decided dislike to it.[147]

O'Connell's response is no longer extant but John's future actions indicate what his father must surely have said. John continued his studies at Trinity. In 1832 he joined his brothers in Parliament. He passed the bar and became a barrister in 1837 but his parliamentary career left him little chance to build up his law practice. Instead, he continued to sit for various boroughs for the remainder of his life and was a key player in the Repeal Association. He and his wife, Elizabeth Ryan, whom he married in 1838, had eight children.[148]

Daniel Jr was the last O'Connell child to be settled. The family pet, Danny, like his brothers before him, entered Clongowes in May 1830 at the age of fourteen. Extracts from a journal the boy kept reveal a somewhat monotonous existence at the school.

> May the 11th ... nothing of any consequence occurred for the rest of this day ... May the 13, 14, 15, 16, 17, 18, 19, 20, and all the days to the end passed over without any thing of serious consequence happening except that Gregory and I got the uniform. June the 1st ... we are beginning to dislike this place greatly.[149]

Study, exams and prayers made up the routine of most days alongside meals, bathing and sport. The event most looked forward to was vacation, granted each year from 1 August to 8 September. The days until its arrival were painstakingly counted. 'I was awoke this morning by the boys shouting for Vacation ... Vacation is at length arrived. Hurra, Hurra, Hurra. I am so very glad, hurra, Hurra Vacation for ever Hurra Hurra Hurra Hurra Hurra.'[150]

For his last son, O'Connell purchased a partnership in Madder's brewery—later renamed O'Connell's brewery—in 1831. Despite Mary's enthusiastic predictions of its success, and John O'Connell's compliments on the quality of the porter, the firm did not prosper and the O'Connells' connection with it ended in 1841, leaving O'Connell again in the predicament of seeking a profession suitable to his youngest son.[151] Not surprisingly, Danny also became an MP: for Dundalk 1846–7, Waterford City 1847–8 and Tralee 1854–63. In 1863 he moved to London to take up the post of Commissioner of Income Tax. He married Ellen Mary Foster in 1867. The couple had ten children.[152]

4

'regulating matters'

— DOMESTICITY —

As political theory regarding state power underwent significant
changes throughout the eighteenth century, the glaring contra-
diction between domestic patriarchy and the political idea of contractual obligation became increasingly obvious. Enlightenment thinkers
drastically revised prior notions of family and women; their secular, rational and contractual model of family relationships, based in natural law,
challenged the assumptions of a divinely ordained patriarchal family structure. Whereas previously, the patriarchal head of the household owned his
wife, children and servants, and viewed them as his own property, the
eighteenth century brought a more egalitarian view of marriage and
family. Companionate or romantic marriages, property rights for women,
divorce and improved child care characterized early modern domestic
lives.

As a result, women, and their role within the family, were seen in a new
light. Enlightenment thinkers reasoned that since women were naturally
more sympathetic, they were more moral and virtuous than men. Of
course, these moral qualities could be developed only within the proper
setting—the home. Consequently, Enlightenment thinkers justified the
conventions and customs of society which continued to bind women to the
home, by basing their theory on the 'natural instincts' which governed the
relationships of women and men. An improvement of women's position,

however, came through 'the new evaluation of their domestic role, through which they would contribute to the moral regeneration of society'.[1]

As men's work moved out of the home and into the professional arena, women found themselves increasingly isolated from the public sphere occupied by their husbands and sons. As the home ceased to be a place of productivity, it became 'the setting for the internal life of the family, its physical qualities—cleanliness, order, comfort—reflecting the achievement of the woman at its heart'.[2] Beginning with the middle classes in the late eighteenth century, domesticity—'the family's awareness of itself as a precious emotional unit that must be protected with privacy and isolation from outside intrusion'—combined with romantic love and improvements in mothering to usher in a revolution of sentiment which effectively sealed the family off from its traditional economic interaction with the outside world.[3] The increased emphasis on domesticity throughout the nineteenth century saw the middle-class conjugal family become an object of veneration. The culture of 'true domestic womanhood'—characterized by piety, purity, submissiveness and domesticity—furthered the idea of the home as a haven from the harsh world.[4]

For many women, the domestic sphere was the only place in which they could gain the satisfaction and even power unavailable to them in the public work place. Indeed, L.A. Clarkson, in his study of late-eighteenth-century Carrick-on-Suir, found that 'masculine authority generally prevailed in matters of business, property and marriage, but that in household management female power was paramount'.[5] For the wives of professional men, 'the business of complementarity, or smoothing the path by promoting the right public image of private solidarity, careful management or moral strength' became the hallmarks of a woman's role. A smoothly run household brought standing to a family within the community. To this end Mary O'Connell strove throughout her life to create a nurturing environment for her children and a safe haven for her travelling husband, while maintaining the standards necessary to remain within the accepted boundaries of society.

In general, Mary took great delight in her housekeeping duties, especially when she thought her actions would please her husband. As she cleaned and prepared O'Connell's study for his arrival, she confessed, 'It is a great amusement and pleasure to me darling.'[6] Mary was directly involved in the purchasing of provisions for the family. She was fully aware of current prices and of fluctuations in the economy. She was also a shrewd dealer and would not allow herself to be cheated. She expected value for the money she paid. When she purchased six bottles of port which she found to be of inferior quality, she immediately sent them back. When a hogshead of claret arrived as a gift from O'Connell's uncle, Count O'Connell, she sold it to aid in the purchase of a piano.[7]

Overseeing the bottling of wine, port and claret was another task for the woman of the house. 'It was a troublesome dirty job,' Mary reported to O'Connell in 1807—a job made more troublesome by unreliable servants and tradesmen. Of the wine cooper, Mary hoped that he wouldn't 'turn out as great a rogue as the other. They are all I believe alike.'[8] The chore proved little better the following year as Mary complained, 'the cyder is not yet jarred nor can I get Brady to do it. He is puting [sic] me off from day to day saying it is not fit. In my opinion he is no judge. At all event he is a great torment.'[9]

Mary became exasperated when O'Connell interfered in the running of the household. '*Pray* what was the necessity to order six dozen of bottled cider and six of bottled ale, love, just at this time?' she demanded of her husband in 1825. 'I perceive I must exert *my authority* and *try* to keep you in *proper order*.'[10] Still, Mary often used O'Connell to perform tasks for her while he was away on the circuit. While O'Connell was in Cork in 1809 she asked him to 'Reserve some of the poundage pigs to be converted into bacon for your use.' From Kerry she demanded a hundred common salt salmon and a crock of corned butter. From Ennis she requested lobsters.[11]

O'Connell frequently relied on Mary to act as an agent for his business transactions. He would often send her money with instructions on which bill to pay and how much. 'It is a great ease to my mind' to be able to do so, he told her.[12] Paying bills was not, however, a task Mary enjoyed. Though she fulfilled all his commissions, she longed for him to come home, 'so soon you can settle those matters yourself'.[13] Her letters reveal a persistent insecurity over her ability to act as an agent, brought on not only by a lack of self-confidence but also by the difficulty of the task itself. Settling bills and directing money over long distances were not simple matters. Moreover, O'Connell's directives were often complicated. For example:

> Pray beg of Rick to take that bill for £400 which I left with Bernard to Mr. Cooper of Merrion Square. He lives within two doors of Judge Day's, and beg of him to give up for it a bill of mine for £361 due to Mr. Cooper of

Cashel and to get *the difference*. If Cooper of Merrion Square refuses he must not get the £400 bill … If you get *the difference*, lodge that also with R Hickson, College Green, for me.[14]

Other times, problems arose over poor penmanship and miscommunication. In attempting to send Mary money to purchase a jaunting car, O'Connell wrote that he was 'unable to make out your figures. How much money do you say you have.'[15] Such confusion reveals the difficulties of conducting a marriage and managing a household via the post. 'I fear I have made a blunder in depositing Mr. Connors [*sic*] bill in the bank when it was not payable here but Love I merely followed your directions without looking to see where it was payable,' she wrote. 'I hope, heart, it will not be any inconvenience to you.'[16] This mistake made her much more leery when, a few days later, she received a sum of money with a letter stating the enclosed amount to be five pounds more than what she actually got. 'This, love,' she told O'Connell, 'is neither a mistake or a blunder of mine. I got his letter in my room and not a creature in the room when I opened the letter and when I counted the money, which I did over and over again lest I may mistake in the reckoning of it.' She concluded that the amount was five pounds short and she wrote to the man responsible.[17]

Despite her own feelings of inadequacy, Mary would not be patronized. 'I must scold you', she informed O'Connell, 'for telling me in a postscript not to lodge the bills until they were accepted. Now, heart, what do you deserve for this *insult*. Surely I must be a great *fool* to go lodge bills before they were accepted.'[18] As time wore on, she grew even more confident in handling her husband's affairs. When O'Connell eventually hired James Sugrue to look after these matters she was affronted, especially considering O'Connell did not inform her of his actions. She wrote to her husband slightly annoyed, 'as I consider myself perfectly *competent* to pay your bills and acceptances'. Nevertheless, she did concede that 'it was to save me trouble that you employed him … My *figures* are indeed very bad. I am not surprised, my heart, that you should not be able to make them out.'[19]

Any type of refurbishment or redecorating within the home generally fell under the supervision of women. In 1811 the O'Connells began renovating the house on Merrion Square. A study, a gallery and a parlour were to be added and O'Connell instructed his wife to get a contract made up with the builders—'It is impossible to be sufficiently guarded with those kind of people.' Mary did as he directed, arranged for estimates and signed the contract for work herself.[20]

In October 1813 they undertook refurbishment of the 'back premises'. Although O'Connell thought it late in the season to start, he instructed Mary to do as she pleased. His next letter, however, outlined his own plan to turn the building into a pantry and bedroom for the servant James below and a study above. 'It should be so contrived as to enable me to set up my present bookcases … I would require also a dressing closet back of the study, and perhaps some other *conveniences* could be arranged for myself personally,' he directed. It is unclear if these plans were carried out. During the summer of 1814 Mary and the children removed to Mallow while remodelling was taking place. These were probably the adjustments talked of in late 1813. By March 1815 plans were again under way—this time to repair the roof and to put double doors in each room.[21]

In September 1819 news reached Mary that O'Connell intended to start building onto the house at Derrynane. She strongly disapproved of this and wrote to him on the subject. 'I really think it would be throwing your money away, at least for some years. Only think of the short time you have to spend out of Dublin and would it be worth your while to build? Consider it well before you involve yourself.'[22] It is unclear whether Mary's opinion put a halt to O'Connell's plans, but more than likely the lack of funds made building impossible at this time.

Later, when the family were settled at Derrynane, Mary functioned as a land agent for O'Connell. He charged her with the overseeing of the renovations to the house, the selling of oxen, the harvesting of rabbits, the slaughtering of pigs and the curing of bacon. Mary's difficulty in selling the bullocks, however, and O'Connell's consequent anger at the low price she finally got for them, led her to declare, 'I will bid adieu to the subject of bullocks, cows and pigs for the future in my letters. Let these matters be between you and your agent.' The low price she made from the oxen was his own fault, since he refused to respond to her inquiries as to how low she should go in price. 'I never will again pay your commands such *implicit obedience*,' she vowed. Still, she would not resist advising him on the renovations to the house, arguing that a third storey was unnecessary, and she contradicted his orders regarding the layout of the wine cellar.[23] The constant money troubles placed Mary in perhaps a more powerful, or certainly more central, position regarding the management of household funds. Moreover, lack of capital meant that Mary's duties were expanded at times to include areas normally attended to by hired help.

O'Connell frequently used Mary as a buffer against debt collectors and borrowing kinsmen. When a cousin applied to O'Connell for a loan, O'Connell had Mary respond to the letter, informing the relative that her husband had 'completely drained me of money', and that 'nothing but a circumstance of that nature could oblige me to decline any wish'.[24] Mary also used her husband whenever she was unable or unwilling to make a payment. For example, when the wine cooper demanded three or four shillings, she refused, 'telling him that as soon as you [O'Connell] returned you would settle every thing and pay him for his trouble'.[25]

Although O'Connell allowed Mary a free hand in spending the money he sent her as she saw fit, Mary did not follow his loosely defined accounting system. Instead she insisted on keeping detailed accounts of all her expenditures, in order to document that 'not a penny was laid out that could in any way be avoided'.[26] Not until 1827, after several years of economizing, when the family was living at Derrynane in an attempt to save even more money, did O'Connell finally insist that Mary enter into a book the sums spent for household necessities. 'We will then easily calculate what saving is made by your staying at Derrynane,' he concluded.[27]

Mary also assisted O'Connell with his legal practice by forwarding him newspapers and briefs or sending him copies of dockets. She accepted retainer fees on his behalf, keeping the money and accompanying documents for his perusal. On occasion she acted as his secretary, writing letters and arranging engagements for her absent husband.[28]

Mary's tasks became more onerous still when she was forced to move with the children to France in an attempt to live more frugally. With O'Connell gone on the circuit, Mary was left to arrange the move. In addition to packing up house and family, Mary arranged their passage on the ship that would carry them to Bordeaux. Preparations for the journey included readying provisions for the long voyage, for passengers brought their own wine, spirits, soda water, milk and other supplies. Mary also was in charge of trying to let the house on Merrion Square for the time they would be away, as well as selling the carriage and horses and dismissing or relocating the servants.[29] These responsibilities all weighed heavily upon her and she was hesitant to close any deal without consulting O'Connell. With regard to the house, O'Connell counselled:

Why do you delay to close any bargain you think prudent? Do not, my first and only love, pay me so bad a compliment as not to be convinced that whatever you do I shall approve of. Indeed I should feel extremely happy to get £400 a year for the house and any thing like £100 for the horses ... You would delight me even if you made a bad bargain because I would then show you how sweet it was to me to have something to forgive you ... In future only let me know what you have done. Do not delay to consult me as to what you are to do ... If you set the house let the agreement be in writing. The lease should be if possible—half a year rent in advance but do not stick much at that—or mention it until after you are agreed in everything else. The rent should be payable quarterly. The rent should be over and above taxes ... See my love that all this is expressed in the agreement—but I am very much afraid that you never will get such a rent or such a price for the horses as you expect.[30]

Unfortunately, Mary's efforts failed and she was not able to secure the potential lessee. O'Connell instructed her not to give in to their requests but at the same time he gave her 'the most ample discretion to do so if you think fit'.[31] In the end, the house was never let, nor were the horse and carriage sold. The servants, except for the housekeeper, did go, and O'Connell was left alone in the house with only his son Maurice for company.[32]

Once in France, O'Connell had planned for Mary to take lodgings in Pau. Initially it was thought that William Finn, husband of O'Connell's sister Alicia, would be there to make the arrangements for them.[33] Finn, however, was delayed leaving Ireland and so the task fell to Mary, Alicia, and Ellen, who spoke French. It was a daunting task to find suitable accommodation for such a large party. Place after place was rejected on the grounds that it was too small, underfurnished, too far out of town or in poor repair. Finally, concessions had to be made and lodgings were settled upon although, according to Ellen, 'Mama told [us] it is a very disagreeable situation and that no carriage can drive to the door.'[34]

Situated under the rock on which Henry IV's castle stood, the exterior of the house was 'mean looking'. Inside, however, things improved, as Ellen O'Connell recorded in her journal:

On entering the hall, the dining room is to the left hand—it has two windows looking out on the Esclair. From this you go into the drawing room which is a large room hung with red braided damask silk curtains & furniture of the same—a handsome time piece ... The windows open out over a narrow [? illegible] of running water which turns the Castle … there is a third window at the side to which four steps lead up and which opens into a wooden gallery, one side of which looks onto the courtyard of the house and the other commands a magnificent view of the mountains. Inside the drawing room & on a line with it is Mama's bed room in which there are two beds—I am to sleep in one of them.[35]

Kate and Betsey would share another room while Morgan, John and Danny would divide the two bedrooms upstairs between them. The house also contained three servant rooms for Pierre, the servant man, Catherine, the cook, and an unnamed housemaid. Ally and William Finn took their lodgings elsewhere.[36]

As in every other domestic situation in which Mary found herself, she had difficulty with her servants. During their stay in Pau they changed menservants three times; the first, presumably Pierre, was 'too stupid' and the second, who spoke no French, made too many blunders as a result. Moreover, Mary was tormented daily by the lady of the house, 'a large scolding talkative woman of forty'.[37]

Despite these pitfalls, Mary attempted to create an atmosphere for her children similar to that of Dublin. In the first place, she engaged instructors for her children. The drawing-master came every day save Monday; the dancing-master came Monday and Thursday. The children also took music and riding lessons. Morgan and John attended college every day, Morgan learning French and John studying French and Latin. At home, Ellen tutored her younger sisters in French and Italian. In the evenings they attended soirées and balls or dined at the homes of other expatriates.[38]

Upon their return from France and England in 1824, the arrangement of the household staff at Merrion Square changed drastically. In an effort to save money, Mary did not reinstate the housekeeper. By this time she found their servant woman, Hannah, had enough experience. Two menservants—a footman and James—and two women servants were all she thought necessary. Horses, and the necessary servants required to keep them, were out of the question. Many preparations, however, would still have to be made to have the house ready for their arrival that spring. The house was to be painted, the walls of the lower part whitewashed and the bedrooms papered. Moreover, the garden needed to be cleaned, 'the middle laid out for a grass plot, the beds round the well of the garden laid out for planting and sowing seeds'.[39]

Displays of hospitality often proved tiresome for Mary, draining her phys-ically and emotionally as well as financially. Visitors were common at the O'Connell home in Dublin, and often Mary had little notice of their arrival. Lack of space was a constant problem, and one which O'Connell seemed continually to overlook. As a result, Mary was left with either squeezing people in—by purchasing a standing bed, for example—or attempting to find a polite way to retract an invitation. In 1813 Mary told O'Connell, 'it is unpleasant that we shall not be able to accommodate him [John, O'Connell's brother] with a Room. I fear I must disinvite Mary Hussey. James [another brother of O'Connell] will be here the latter end of this week consequently will occupy the back Room and it is quite impossible for me to spare another.'[40]

A larger dilemma arose in 1815 when Mary, nearly seven months preg-nant, found her house in danger of being overrun with visitors. She wrote in a panic to her husband in Cork, 'tell me, love, how I am to accommo-date every person'. The doctor had forbidden the children to sleep in the new addition to the house until May and, 'Should your uncle [Count O'Connell] come I must put your mother off until October.' She contin-ued that James was leaving and although she would like him to stay she could not manage.

> In short, I am most unpleasantly situated … Should he [Count O'Connell] come I will write to your mother and tell her exactly how I am situated, and as she is a woman of sense and reason I am convinced she will give me every credit for the wish I feel in not having her come to us until I can settle her and her servant comfortably, which would be in October. She could then stay until the next summer and probably have Ally's [i.e. Alicia Finn's] society during the Winter and Spring.[41]

On another occasion, without informing his wife O'Connell offered to his cousin the use of his horse while in Dublin, much to the inconvenience of Mary and her servants. Upon receiving a further directive from O'Connell, she sternly replied that she would attend to his request

> the moment John can spare time from his attendance on Mr. O'Connell who I am told has your directions to get the Pony as often as he wishes which surprises me not a little. Now that James [the footman] is away the entire business devolves on John and surely it is unreasonable to expect he

can attend inside and outside and go of [sic] messages. William will not nor cannot attend to the mare and if every Person who wishes for it is to get it, you must hire a groom to convenience them … if you wish Mr. O'Connell should get her his servant must make her up for John cannot attend me if he is to attend [him].[42]

In the early years of her marriage, Mary was shy about entertaining when O'Connell was not present. Having word that a relative of her husband's was coming to Dublin, she wrote, 'I almost *dread* his arrival. He will so teize me for your not being here all for his own sake. I wish heart you could come home sooner.'[43] Although twenty-eight years old and a mother of three, Mary had been mistress of her own home for less than a year. She soon grew out of her unease, however, and began hosting parties, often in her husband's absence. She wrote to O'Connell in 1819 regarding one such occasion:

> I hope to prevail on that family [the O'Maras of Glencullen] to dine with me on Sunday next to meet Mrs. Mahon [probably wife or mother of Nicholas Mahon] and the [Purcell] O'Gormans. I thought you would wish me to pay a compliment to Mrs. Mahon and I therefore asked her. I shall ask [John] Finlay and his wife to dine with me. I will depute Mr. O'Mara to act for you. He is such a pleasant man. I think he is the very best substitute I could give my friends for the loss of your society. You will say it is a bold thing for me to ask company in your absence. I assure you I would cheerfully give up the pleasure except for the above mentioned motive. I get hares and grouse constantly from Mrs. O'Mara.'[44]

Dining was not the only means of socializing and Mary did not limit herself to her own home. As mentioned above, the family often attended the races in Mallow. These brought crowds of people to town and led to a proliferation of dinner parties and soirées.[45]

While in France, Mary often attended the theatre.[46] Accompanied by her oldest children, she also went to balls.[47] In Dublin, Mary and the girls attended a ball at Dublin Castle in 1826. By 1830, however, Mary decided against going to the St Patrick's Ball at the Castle. Although the girls, Morgan, and the FitzSimons attended, Mary found that 'Going out by day and going out by night are very different to those who are apt to take cold as I am.'[48] In London she enjoyed the opera.[49] Walking or taking a turn in the carriage was another form of socializing and one in which Mary and her children participated regularly, weather permitting, no matter the location in which they found themselves.[50] Of course, even walking was governed by certain rules and conventions. Mary reported to O'Connell from England:

> the Girls are this moment returned from a lovely walk with Danny as their Beau. It is quite usual for Ladys here to walk together without Gentlemen or Masters. This however I should not allow my Daughters to do if they had any Male Acquaintances here but they have none except dancing acquaintances to whom they merely give a passing salute. They go out as little as possible without me and never out to the Country.[51]

If she did not go out of an evening, she passed the time by reading and playing cards. Mary read newspapers primarily, although she would occasionally read a novel or listen as one of her daughters read aloud. Sometimes guests would be invited for dinner, or the family would dine at the home of a friend.[52]

O'Connell often counselled Mary on the types of people with whom she should or should not associate. Even before their marriage, he wrote to her on this subject, asking her

> not to go to any other great or small party to the Lady's you mentioned in your last. Indeed my soul, she is not fit company for you. She is not either a suitable companion for my Wife ... in future my wife will frame some excuse to avoid any intercourse with beings whose purity does not equal her own. I know, my love, that you will not be displeased at my premature assumption of authority.[53]

Even after marriage O'Connell commented on her choice of friends. 'I am glad you have seen Mrs. O'Mara. Her husband is a very sincere friend of mine. I should be glad if you had occasion to cultivate her acquaintance.'[54]

Mary was especially sensitive to any snubbing she perceived by her 'peers'. 'Miss O'Neill [Eliza, an actress] has left town without returning my visit. Strange conduct. She returned every other visit.' O'Connell assured Mary she was over-reacting. 'The neglect of Miss O'Neill is impertinent but of course only to be laughed at ... It is not worth a single thought.'[55] Even amongst family Mary often felt insulted. 'Mrs. Bess [wife of O'Connell's brother John] never called upon me since I came here though she was several times in town and yesterday she was a quarter of an hour outside Mrs. Rice's door in her carriage and never even sent her servant to inquire for me,' she told her husband on one occasion. 'This is not the way you and I would act if they were in the neighbourhood of Merrion Square but indeed darling, very few of your family ever act by you as you do by them.'[56]

In England she felt herself to bear even more the brunt of bad manners and snobbery. 'This is a most horrid stupid place for young people. The stiff starched proud English will not visit without letters of introduction,' Mary complained from Southampton in 1823.[57] Introductions were just another means by which society attempted to create barriers limiting access to their level to those below, for an 'inferior' was always introduced to a 'superior'. After an introduction, the 'superior' had the choice of following up the introduction.[58] 'The Mr. Hill here is married and has a family,' she reported to her husband. 'They live at the Polygon but I fear he is a bad Catholic and his wife and children are Protestants. This introduction took place ten days since and strange to tell neither Mr. Frederick Hill nor his wife have visited me … So much for English manners. They are to be sure the coldest people in the world.'[59]

Her complaints resumed a few days later. 'Not all of *those* introduced to us by Mrs. Conway have as yet paid us a visit. We are Irish Catholics. This is against us.' She continued more angrily over a week later, 'there is neither private nor public amusement going forward in this stupid, prejudiced place. Neither your schoolfellow nor his family, the Hills, have condescended to pay us a visit.'[60] O'Connell's reply attempted to soothe his wife's hurt feelings. 'Darling,' he wrote, 'your disappointment at not having your visit returned shows how idle it would be to attach any importance to courtly smiles. I am quite sure you do not; but it is the more unaccountable because Serjeant Goold assured me that the Lord-Lieutenant declared he would invite us both to one of his state dinners.'[61]

Gradually, Mary herself was able, through etiquette, to snub her husband's political enemies. When the Lord Mayor of Dublin, Robert Way Harty, attacked O'Connell in a speech given in late 1830, Mary remarked, 'How glad I am I did not visit the Lady Mayoress … His head has been turned by the compliments there paid to him and he forgets that he was once one of the people and glad to have their support.'[62] Later, as Mary grew more comfortable in her station, she too exercised judgement on the women around her. Ellen O'Connell reported an incident at the races in Mallow in which a carriage drew near theirs in which sat two lovely girls, 'though my mother said they were painted'.[63]

A lack of money, as we have seen above, could greatly increase the duties required of a wife. Similarly, social standing required socializing, which also added to a woman's tasks. Luckily, when money was plentiful, so was help. Mary, as an upwardly mobile middle-class housewife, was eventually able to employ servants to aid her in her domestic duties. Having such a large family created immense amounts of work aside from the attention required by each child. Furthermore, rising standards of cleanliness demanded enormous amounts of washing both of children and of clothes.

A large noble household might employ between six and thirty servants; a gentry home might employ between six and twelve. More modest, middle-class homes would have three or four servants on hand.[64] Domestic service was the largest area of female employment in nineteenth-century Ireland. Most servant women came from the country, as city-dwellers believed them to be more dutiful and loyal. The O'Connells often chose girls from Kerry, relying on the good name of the servant's family to ensure honesty and productivity. For many country girls, domestic service provided the only means by which they might leave their homes for the towns and cities.[65]

Many qualities were desirable in a servant. Since much of the work was physically taxing, strength and stamina were an obvious requirement. Carrying water and wood, cooking and laundry were all labour-intensive. 'Quiet and unobtrusive … steady, advanced in life, and … religious,' were ideal characteristics listed by O'Connell.[66] Most servants, however, fell far short of this desired profile. Servants' laziness, stealing, rudeness, drunkenness and otherwise improper conduct were common complaints of mistress and master and grounds for dismissal, though flaws were often overlooked because finding help was so difficult. The perceived problem reached such proportions that in 1825 the Dublin Society for the Improvement and Encouragement of Servants was established. Formed due to the 'difficulty of procuring well conducted Servants, who will continue for a considerable time in one service', the society took the names of members 'who wanted good and faithful servants, and also, the names of such well recommended servants as were seeking employment'. Through the society 334 members applied for servants and, of the 635 servants enrolled, 155 gained employment.[67]

The O'Connells do not appear on the list of subscribers, but perhaps they should have, for Mary described in her letters several troubling episodes with servants. One such instance occurred at her mother's home in Tralee. Mary's brother John and the servant girl had embarked upon a less than prudent relationship, which Mary sought not only to end, but to keep from her mother. Mary let the girl go, telling her mother the servant's impertinence was the cause. '[M]y mother', she told O'Connell, '... has every suspicion of her not being honest but not the slightest of her being improper in conduct.' It is probable that the girl was pregnant, for young John was sent for and instructed to come home as soon as he possibly could.[68]

With O'Connell away, it became Mary's job to deal with the servants, including hiring, paying, promoting and firing them.[69] In 1814 she wrote of promoting Frank, who 'surprises me he gets through the business so well—unfortunate Thomas I was obliged to discharge—almost constantly intoxicated since you went away. If Frank continues as he has began [*sic*], I will be satisfied with him as a Footman.'[70] The following year brought problems with a young servant boy named Peter. 'I cannot be tormented with him,' Mary wrote to O'Connell, 'he will not act as he ought to do and the Brat is such an excellent servant but his principles are so bad.' She decided to send him back to Kerry where she hoped O'Connell's brother James could make some use of him, for, in her opinion, 'he would make a most excellent Butler's Servant particularly with a Master that would keep him in order'. Following this experience Mary resolved she would never again 'be troubled with a little Boy'.[71]

Recent research indicates that many nineteenth-century women found it particularly difficult to deal with male servants. Lacking the aura of an aristocratic lady, the middle-class woman was subject to attacks on what male servants considered her female inferiority. In addition, a male servant spent the majority of his time in tasks and duties outside the house and away from the direct supervision of the mistress, thus lessening her control and influence.[72] Mary O'Connell certainly clashed with her male servants on more than one occasion, as the letters attest.

In 1819 Mary, 'provoked by receiving the greatest impertinence', was again forced to dismiss a footman. Apparently the servant—whose tasks included waiting tables, delivering messages, accompanying guests home and assisting his master or mistress when travelling—had hired a helper without Mary's permission and then expected her to pay the man's wages. She described the ensuing incident to O'Connell:

In truth, William thought he could do anything he pleased, that he would not be parted with, and since his last engagement his stubbornness knew no bounds. The conclusion of his address to me was to the following effect: 'The devil mend me for coming back to you, and when my two years are up I will leave you there.' This happened in the hall of our house in town in presence of my children and other servants. Immediately on my coming home here I sent Morgan to tell him to give up his things, that he should never drive my carriage again, that I was ready to pay his wages when I got the clothes from him. He sent me word he would not leave me nor give up his things until he was paid up to the 20th February next, the end of his two years. This I of course refused to pay, and Morgan told him I would pay him four guineas which was coming to him, that the law was open to him, that if he was entitled to be paid the two years in full he knew his remedy. He still persevered in refusing to give up the things and insisting on the two years' wages.

Finally, the servant gave up his things and left without his money. 'I cannot tell you the state of agitation his conduct threw me into,' Mary concluded. 'The ingratitude of the fellow I felt more than anything else. I am truly sorry I ever took him back and I hope, heart, that nothing will induce you to ask me to take him again.' Ironically, the helper, whose employment started the entire row, stayed on to take care of the horses and even drove Mary to mass that day.[73]

Long-standing servants could hold significant influence within the family they served. O'Connell's footman James, for example, was active in promoting the dismissal of a new servant maid whom he did not like. After failing in his efforts to sway O'Connell, the servant asked Maurice to intervene on his behalf. Although O'Connell refused to part with the girl, the fact that James felt it within his rights to demand her dismissal is telling as to the elevated status of particular staff members within the O'Connell home.[74]

Another servant of long standing was Hannah, who first came to Dublin from Tralee in late 1810. O'Connell hesitated to send her despite Mary's specific request, for his sister-in-law had warned that the girl was 'idle and impudent'.[75] O'Connell's doubts were obviously misplaced. Although Hannah was apparently somewhat dull-witted, she was asked to accompany the family to Clifton in 1817. There Mary found her 'most attentive. I am really quite surprised she gets on so well, her memory so different from what it was at home.' Mary attributed the improvement to the servant's busy days and increased duties.[76] Hannah also travelled with the family to France. By this time she was a valued family servant, and her ignorance was looked on with affection. O'Connell inquired after her in his letters, wondering how she got on with the French servants: 'I think poor Hannah must often be at a loss how to get on at all. I should be glad to see her attempting to make herself understood by a person who knew nothing of English.'[77]

References to Hannah and to another servant, Julia, are frequent in the letters and reveal that their status was somewhat ambiguous. O'Connell often asked after them, inquiring as to how the weather agreed with them, worrying if he thought they were not well.[78] When Hannah married James, O'Connell's footman, the couple were separated every time O'Connell left Mary. Thus Mary and her husband during this time would often send the regards of one servant to the other via their own correspondence.[79]

Mary and O'Connell were consulted when their servant Julia hoped to wed. It would appear that the family's spiritual advisor was also in on the negotiations, for O'Connell wrote to his wife in 1827, 'The secret Mr. L'Estrange hinted at is what you conjectured—Julia's proposal of a marriage—but of course you alone are to decide.'[80] Mary must have approved of the match because, later, she and her son Danny acted as godparents to Julia's first child. References to this woman in Mary's letters to her son reveal that in some cases servants were regarded as close friends and were looked after as such.[81]

Another servant of ambiguous standing was the governess. The lack of professions for middle-class women who had some education but whose families were unable to provide for them meant that many of these women went into domestic service as housekeepers, lady's companions or governesses.[82] As a result, the line dividing the social status of the lady of the house from that of some of her servants could be very thin. Such was the case with Mary's relationship with her children's governesses. The family's first governess, Miss Lynch, was engaged as a nursery governess for Ellen and Kate in 1808. Whereas Ellen later described the woman as 'well connected and competent to teach English', O'Connell believed 'her manner injures the children. She obtains no respect.' Although he felt it would be cruel to inform her of this or to dismiss her, he still thought the children would be better off without her. In the end, the woman was sacked for stealing in 1812.[83]

She was replaced by Mary McCarthy of Cork, who stayed with the family only a short while, from March to September 1814. Under this woman's tutelage, Ellen undertook to learn Latin in order to 'stir him [her brother Maurice] to emulation'. She and Kate were fondly attached to Miss McCarthy and often took turns sleeping with her at night. O'Connell too found her to be 'a most amiable and interesting young woman'. She did not stay with the family long, however, and her departure to aid a distant cousin came quite suddenly, much to Mary's consternation.[84]

Theresa Conry became the new governess in the autumn of 1814. A convert to Catholicism, the woman had 'a plain but sensible face, and a very good figure but a bad taste in dress. She was very clever and good, but rather hasty in her temper.' Despite Ellen's praise, O'Connell preferred Mary McCarthy, who apparently became available again. He wished they could take the woman back, but they had no valid reason for letting Miss Conry go. Still, he proposed to Mary to approach Miss McCarthy and to 'Put it [the position] distinctly *in her way* at any rate.'[85] As it turned out, Miss Conry stayed with the family until the spring of 1815, at which time another governess had to be found. O'Connell left all these details up to his wife, instructing her to 'Do what you please.'[86]

The new governess, Mary Jane Gaghran, took command that summer and O'Connell directed Mary to watch the woman carefully. 'If she does not take a decisive tone of command with them [the children] at once, if she does not preserve their respect without relaxation, it will be in vain to attempt to regain it. Darling, it will require your interference to impress this on her mind.'[87] Contrary to O'Connell's misgivings, Mary had nothing but praise for Miss Gaghran, whom Ellen later described as a 'tall graceful young woman of 28 years or thereabouts—with a very expressive if not handsome face. She was a good musician & well skilled in English & French.'[88] Miss Gaghran settled down directly to business and, before her first month was out, provided a report to O'Connell via Mary of her thoughts on the children. Regarding Ellen, the eldest daughter, the governess 'promised to exert herself to get rid of all her bad habits and ... begged I would say to you that she expected you would see an improvement in Ellen as she had made up her mind to act with determined manner by her.' Mary reported further that the governess found Betsey and Kate very docile and thought that 'before many days elapse John will consent to spend an hour or two in the School Room every day—Miss G. is trying to conciliate him and already she has made some progress'.[89]

Diligently applying herself to her duties, the new governess instructed the girls in English, writing and French. She took the children on walks about the Square and to events such as band concerts or military exhibitions.[90] When the family removed to Clifton in 1817, Miss Gaghran accompanied them.

It would seem that the young woman was off to a good start. Yet, while the girls, especially Ellen, were extremely fond of Miss Gaghran, Mary's relationship with the governess, though initially quite good, gradually deteriorated. Although Mary 'pass[ed] over many little unpleasant traits in her manners' for the sake of the children, she did believe that Miss Gaghran was exceedingly competent. She continued in her assessment of the woman:

> I also am sensible how necessary it is for parents to overlook many little things in a governess when not injurious to the morals of their children. None of us [is] without our faults and therefore I make every allowance for the frailty of human nature but I must say this, that never was a governess so well treated by any person than Miss G. is by me. She is naturally haughty and, having authority at the early age of sixteen to this day, is the only way I can account for the very great opinion she has of herself. She has it to fault.[91]

Later, when Mary removed to France, the governess was left behind, much to the sorrow of the young O'Connell girls. The woman's presence in Dublin resulted in a row between Mary and her husband, when O'Connell visited the former governess at her home (see chapter 2). This argument between Mary and Daniel did not affect the relationship between the governess and the O'Connell girls. Ellen O'Connell began writing a journal to the woman, as was common amongst female friends of the era. As she departed Ireland, she thought with sadness 'of my best friend and the length of time that would intervene until I should see her again'. The two corresponded frequently during her absence, the arrival of the former governess's letters moving Ellen to tears. She remained close friends with the woman even after marrying.[92]

One of the dominant requirements of women's work was unselfishness. Only by giving up self-interest did a woman achieve 'the purity of motive' which in turn allowed her to make her home a moral sanctuary.[93] When members of the family fell ill or were confined, for example, the added burden of serving as nursemaid fell upon the woman of the house. In 1801, living in her mother's crowded house in Tralee, Mary wrote to her then fiancé O'Connell of her sister-in-law's confinement and delivery of a healthy baby boy. 'How I wish to God she was able to come downstairs,' Mary lamented, 'for I have hardly a moment to myself with housekeeping and attending her and my mother who is still confined with her arm.'[94]

In April 1808 the O'Connells' housekeeper, Mrs Ryan, fell drastically ill. 'She was attacked yesterday with a violent stitch in her side,' Mary reported, 'and though blistered and blooded, she still continues very bad.' Mary initially attributed her reluctance to go see the woman to her own pregnancy. She was convinced that 'it would not be proper for me to run any risks at present'. She did, however, send Mrs Ryan wine, and inquired as to her improvement every hour. A few days later, still refusing to visit the woman (who was probably being treated in a fever hospital), Mary told O'Connell that she would go 'but really I don't like to be seen going [? to the] place she is in. If I could be of any use ... most cheerfully would I go to her.'[95] On 19 April Mary informed O'Connell of the housekeeper's death. O'Connell was left executor of the will but the burden of arrangements fell to Mary. She gave money to defray the funeral expenses and she organized the sale of the woman's furniture. 'This is a most unpleasant business to me,' she told her husband, 'however there is no other Person interested about the poor woman to have what is proper done for her but me. Her sister has not gone near her.'[96]

The O'Connells did not hesitate to consult their family doctor in relation to servants who had taken ill. In 1809 a serving girl, Jenny, was sent home to Tralee where a Dr Kearney hoped the country air would restore her.[97] Other sick servants, as in the case of the housekeeper, were sent off to the fever hospital. A good-natured mistress would then send extra comforts to the ailing servant. Mary records one such instance in her letters of a servant girl placed under the care of a Dr O'Riordon, who was known for his work at the Cork Street Fever Hospital.[98] Despite the fact that the girl was recovering, Mary had already hired a replacement and would not take her back. She felt the girl 'was not equal to the station she undertook'. Mary was not completely cold-blooded, however, as she realized the girl would be amply provided for by her mother, the last cook employed by the O'Connell family.[99] While the life of a domestic servant was by no means easy, many were better off than the majority of the working classes. In general, domestic servants were better fed, had better living conditions and suffered from a lower mortality rate than others of their class, due in part to the actions of their employers.[100]

Mary O'Connell's domestic duties were many and diverse. The extent of her tasks and of her influence demonstrates the increased effects of domesticity in binding the woman to the home, while at the same time giving her increased power within that sphere. Mary's experience is also extremely revealing in that it gives the modern historian an insight into the very precarious position which middle-class women held in society during the early nineteenth century. Lacking the aura of the born and bred gentry, these women continually struggled to control servants and define their status within their new class by adherence to strict rules of propriety.

While an increasingly affluent society allowed many middle-class women to surrender the physical and administrative tasks of household management to others and to lead 'a life of elegant but idle gentility',[101] such was not the case with Mary O'Connell, as we have seen. Although balls, soirées and dinners made up part of her social life, O'Connell's financial imprudence required Mary to retain an active part in many household tasks and even to expand her role to include the duties of agent, accountant, and real estate speculator.

5

'all our friends'
— CORRESPONDENCE AND KIN —

During the nineteenth century the work of maintaining kinship bonds generally fell to women. 'Kin work' or 'kinkeeping', which involved cultivating contacts amongst families and relatives, tied households together and was an integral part of any woman's idea of a fulfilling family life. Economic modernization, which took men away from family firms and farms and placed them in jobs with non-kin, further increased the work involved in maintaining kin ties.[1] Prolific letter writing, gossip, mutual aid and extended visiting, a hint of which we find in Mary's correspondence, characterized family life and allowed extended familial relations to flourish.

When families and kin became geographically mobile, letters, predominantly written by women, sustained connections between relations. Personal letters relating 'trivial' matters became as common, if not more common, than post relating to business. Despite complaints about the continued inefficiency of the mails in Ireland, letters could be sent and received with increasing speed and ease. Thus, it is no coincidence that the most common and acceptable letter-writing style was natural and unaffected, as if author and recipient were merely having a chat.[2]

Mary's letters were spontaneous, unpretentious and witty. As she was often separated from her family and friends, letters connected her with the things that made her life full and worthy: her children, her husband and her extended family. The importance of letters can be seen in her many references to and complaints about their delay or absence. Indeed, a good portion of nearly every missive dealt with the actual mechanics of how one intended to send the letter, and the status of any letters received, unanswered or in transit. Mary was particularly exact in these details. For example, she wrote to O'Connell, 'Your letter my Darling of Wednesday I received this morning and though you allow me no *merit* for writing to you on Monday I *hope* you will for *writing* to *you* yesterday when I got no letter from you nor no *apoly* [apology] this day for omitting to write on Sunday.'[3]

Moreover, in her letters Mary makes reference to the many other people with whom she corresponded and the information they imparted. The frequent appearance of second- and even third-hand information in the letters reveals the intricate network of family and friends whose amassed knowledge Mary redirected from her writing desk to suit her own ends. From her pen flowed information, gossip, love and anger, by which she strove to bind her family together.

Generally, the events of Mary's married life happened on paper, as during her courtship and early years of marriage she was forced to live apart from her husband. Sessions of the circuit took O'Connell away from home for at least three months every year. Mary was in England and France for a total of two years due to financial troubles and health problems. And later, O'Connell's growing political success meant meetings, elections and parliamentary sessions that required still further separations. Constant letter writing was the only means to hold their marriage together through so many separations.[4]

In Mary's eyes, O'Connell was never as faithful a correspondent as she was. O'Connell was aware of her displeasure and his letters are filled with apologies and excuses for their delay. The press of business was usually the cause of his inattention.[5] Mary, however, was rarely forgiving. 'I cant tell you how much it surprises me that you should let two posts pass without writing me a single line. There is some excuse for your not doing so any of the week days but surely my heart you could find time to write on Sunday,' she chastised. On another occasion, after eight days with no word, she burst forth angrily, 'Good God, heart, why don't you write to me if you are well?'[6] Her entreaties often took up most of the letter:

> It is so very unusual with you to be so long a time without writing to me that I am realy [*sic*] quite uneasy. Only recollect it is eight days this day

since you last wrote. I teize myself with a thousand conjectures which end in the firm belief that only business alone would prevent you from writing. I do not allow myself to think it is illness because I am sure if it was some Person would have the humanity to let me know it … I know it is unreasonable of me to expect you can write to me often when you are engaged in business, but all I would ask is to hear from you at least twice within the week … [7]

O'Connell could hardly disagree with her. Despite his lapses, he too was 'dying with anxiety' should any time pass without word from her.[8] Although the two bandied about the expression 'No news is good news,'[9] usually no news meant illness, accident, death or disaffection, and so they begged one another for long, news-filled letters to assure themselves of the other's good health and fond regards. 'Dearest, let me get long letters from you—write to me much of yourself, much of our boy—they are the subjects that interest me,' O'Connell implored Mary during one of their many separations.[10]

Both Mary and O'Connell were aware, however, of the shortcomings of letter writing as the sole means of developing their relationship and communicating their feelings. O'Connell found writing 'tedious and clumsy' when trying to convey his true feelings to his wife. 'Language is quite inadequate to express the intensity of my love,' he complained. Still, he owned, he could not exist but for her letters.[11] Mary too found his notes to be her 'greatest comfort' when he was away. '[H]ow I delight in your letters. You write in such good spirits and exactly as if you were talking to me. I never can reconcile myself to your absence until I get your first letter,' she wrote to her husband.[12]

Since letters were the primary means of communication between separated parties, people went to great lengths to discover the exact times mail went out and came in, the quickest routes by which to send their missive and the exact time it would take to arrive or to be received. For example, 'A letter put into the Dublin office on Saturday morning will reach me on Tuesday morning' in London, O'Connell informed his wife.[13] Of course, miscalculations could be made. Mary's firm belief that there was a Wednesday post from Tralee led to a 'wrangle' between her and her husband, who neglected to write by it, when in fact no such post existed. The incident became a joke to them when O'Connell again found himself in Tralee. 'Notwithstanding all my promises, the *post of Wednesday* has passed without my writing,' he teased.[14] In 1820 Dublin mail reached Carhen in forty-eight hours. Still the postal service was inefficient, a fact which greatly plagued O'Connell. Of Tralee, where mail was carried on foot only twice a week, he often complained, 'No Dublin post from Monday until Thursday. It is really vexatious that somebody does not *vindicate* the town. There is a daily Dublin post to Listowel because the Knight of Kerry exerts himself. I am you see in a passion on this subject.' One year later, in 1821, the situation was rectified. The post from Dublin went every weekday to Tralee.[15] To avoid delays, one option was to send notes with any friends who happened to be travelling, allowing the message to arrive more quickly than the post would carry it. Sometimes, however, friends failed to follow through with their commissions.[16]

On occasion, then, mail was slow and even unreliable. Poor weather accounted for some of the delay. Letters could be misdirected. Robberies sometimes occurred in which mail was stolen. In some cases a postal employee would lose letters or, even worse, read them.[17] At one stage O'Connell professed his hatred of the city of Cork merely because of its undependable mail service.[18] Even when the post was regular, other difficulties arose. 'The post is quite regular here,' O'Connell told Mary from Derrynane, 'but I am obliged to write on post days before I get your letters. This gives our correspondence the appearance of tediousness.'[19] Sometimes letters never reached their destination, much to the dismay of both author and recipient. On one occasion, three of Mary's letters to Ennis never arrived. 'You have no Idea darling heart of my Vexation on receiving your letter on Monday Night. I was unhappy and mortified at the uneasiness which I am well aware you suffered at not hearing either from me or Kitty and well may you impute it to illness for believe me nothing else would deprive me of the delights of writing to you,' Mary assured her husband when another lost letter caused him distress.[20]

One can imagine the frustration and the wild assumptions drawn when waiting for an expected letter. Problems took on even greater proportions when distance and miscommunication hampered a correspondent's message. Many of the disagreements that appear in the letters were the result of miscommunications, generally due to the lack, whether intentional or not, of letters. Not hearing from O'Connell made Mary 'cross as a cat' and 'completely sours my temper', she told him in 1824. Jealous of the attention he gave to his political business, she felt 'inclined to *wish* the Catholic Association at the bottom of the sea'.[21] O'Connell was no less annoyed when expected post failed to arrive. 'Good God, what can be the cause of your silence?' O'Connell wrote to his wife in a burst of temper. 'I could not write to you on Tuesday, and yesterday I allowed myself to be too angry at not getting a letter from you to write. I am unable to write connectedly from anxiety. You or some of my darling girls must be ill, or my boys. There must be some reason for this silence. If there were none it would be very, very cruel.'[22] Another occasion of delayed mail sparked an argument in the autumn of 1810. Mary wrote angrily to O'Connell:

> From the style of your letter written from Carhen last Sunday you must have been seriously displeased with me but let me ask you, how was I to act? For nearly a week I got no letter from you, not knowing the cause of your delay and expecting you to leave the country every day. I thought the surest way was to direct my letters to Tralee thinking if you were not there the letter would be forwarded to Iveragh ... however before this reaches Kerry you will be convinced how much you have wronged me indeed Dan I am a little piqued with you for thinking me capable of giving you intentionally the slightest uneasiness. Were you delayed in the Country by amusement I should not vent my disappointment or punish you in the manner you give me credit for [i.e. by not writing] ... This nasty letter from Carhen has dispirited me. It is the first serious letter I ever got from you and I exactly feel like a spoiled child.[23]

When Mary and the children moved to France, letters became the sole means of communication with her husband. Neither O'Connell in Ireland, nor his family in Tours, could rely upon hearing about one another through friends, newspapers or gossip. Complete dependence upon letters to impart news and maintain family unity during this separation resulted in the development of several rules to follow when putting pen to paper. O'Connell was very particular in how he planned to write his letters and he insisted his family adhere to his guidelines. His long letters from Dublin took on a journal format in which he wrote a bit each day, usually sending several days' entries at one time. He implored the family to write in a natural style, 'to chat as it were ... by letter'.[24] Unfortunately, the letters from his family did not always live up to his standards. The children, he complained, 'did not write with that *flow* which I could wish for'.[25] Nearly a year after their separation O'Connell again remarked to his wife, 'You see how particular I am ... I wish heart you would follow the example and seperate [*sic*] your letters in distinct paragraphs by the dates and I am sure you will merely because I ask you.'[26]

112

Long letters, of course, were imperative. A common practice of the day was to write a full page and then turn the page sideways, writing across the margin. O'Connell detested this practice and gave stern orders against it. 'I would rather pay three times the postage than get such letters,' he instructed his wife.[27] Mary and the children enjoyed teasing him over his fastidiousness, punning that it would make him *cross* to have anyone *cross* a letter to him.[28] Despite this particular aversion, O'Connell had difficulty tolerating wasted space. 'Only think of Nell beginning her letter half the page down as if she was writing a compliment card,' O'Connell chastised. 'I forgive her for that and making three lines of being my dutiful etc., because she wrote me a great deal about you all … I pay double postage for a letter and a cover … so that I ought to get two full sheets in every letter just as I write to you all.'[29]

Letter writing was a necessary skill and as such was included in a child's education. While O'Connell was generally delighted with the letters he received from his children—he especially remarked upon the natural style of his daughters' missives—he nevertheless found it imperative to employ a writing instructor for his sons. Mary also encouraged the children to write and continually directed her sons to correspond with their family members, particularly their father. When Maurice and Morgan were enrolled at Clongowes, for example, Mary instructed them to write weekly to O'Connell.[30] For the O'Connell children, writing to and receiving letters from their father was a great delight, and they jealously competed with one another for the honour of sending him a line. To her father, Ellen O'Connell wrote of her sister, 'Kate is not a little vain of the letter she received from you. I am quite tired of looking at her kissing and hugging it. She even carries it with her to bed every night.'[31]

Without the constant flow of messages between O'Connell and Mary during their many separations, their marriage might not have survived. Moreover, letter writing was the means by which Mary remained connected to her extended family, whether she was situated in Dublin or far removed in southern France. So far away from her Kerry kin, Mary felt very keenly any neglect from her correspondents there. '[T]hey have quite forgotten that such People as Kitty [her niece] and I all exist,' she complained to O'Connell, 'not a single line have we had from any one of them … tell Betsey [her sister] I am quite jealous with her and my Mother. Neither of them wrote me a single line … though they ought to know their letter would be a great pleasure to me … in short tell them all we are much obliged by their kind remembrance of us. It cant be their *devotion* that prevents them from sparing time to write to their friends here.'[32]

Extended and separated families, such as Mary's, relied on letter writing to maintain kinship ties. News often reached family members second- and even third-hand. Mary described one example in a letter to her husband:

> your Father ... I heard (from James Connor) was ill but I got no letters from any person which makes me hope no news is good news. The letter I got from Connor written on Sunday mentioned that on his arrival in Tralee on Saturday the report was that your Father [at Carhen] was ill but that if there was a confirmation he would instantly send an express for you to Ennis. I heard nothing since so that I trust in God the report was without foundation. I know you will be glad to hear I had a letter from my Mother yesterday saying Edward was better ... I write this by Hussey who goes in the mail this Night knowing you will get it sooner than through the Post office and should you be gone from Kerry he will have the kindness to forward it to you.[33]

Three days later Mary reported to her husband that she had received a letter from Ellen Connor, who had heard by the Iveragh post that O'Connell's father was much improved. Thus O'Connell became the fourth-hand recipient of the news. In this instance no fewer than six people were involved in spreading the word regarding the illnesses of O'Connell's father and Mary's brother Edward.[34]

Of course, receipt of a letter was not the only means of hearing all the news. Mary could always find someone to tell her of her husband's whereabouts or well-being. For example, the driver who took her husband to Cork gave her a good account of O'Connell's safe arrival in that town.[35] The author of any letter was well aware that the message might be read not only by the recipient but shared with others. Therefore, missives containing any private or revealing information were accompanied by directives either to burn the letter or, at the very least, not to show it to anyone.[36] Lost or misplaced letters often landed in the wrong hands, resulting in serious consequences. '*The Quarrell* between Kitty and Bess [O'Connell's sisters] originated in some expression of my poor Kate's in a letter to Ally which Ally *lost* at Grenagh,' O'Connell wrote, explaining one such incident to his wife.[37]

To ensure that nothing like this might take place, Mary often begged

O'Connell to destroy any of her letters he received while at Derrynane. O'Connell, however, refused. 'I will *not* burn your letters,' he told her. 'I could not do it even now, but the moment I get to Derrynane I make them up in sealed parcels and lock them up so that no person can possibly get at them. Be assured that I keep them with the utmost safety.'[38]

As O'Connell's fame grew, the need for discretion became even more apparent. He always sent Mary detailed accounts of political business in London, saying, 'Let me know if there be anything which I ought to write about and which I do not. I wish I could be more detailed. I will endeavour in future to send you a regular journal.' However, he gave Mary instructions regarding names which should not appear in print, specifically, 'the names of the person [*sic*] who may give me information because the newspapers are so ready to catch up any and everything that it is not safe to mention names to anybody'. On other occasions he instructed, 'Do not let any thing I write appear in any papers,' or 'This is entirely between you and me.'[39] Once, when writing from court in Waterford, O'Connell was obliged 'to cover every line which I write to prevent *accidental* over reading.'[40]

Mary often relied upon newspaper accounts of her husband's comings and goings when letters failed to arrive. She found 'the greatest delight' in reading of his speeches at political meetings or his arguments in court.[41] While this generally provided an accurate account of O'Connell, sometimes such widespread coverage proved bothersome. For example, seeing a report in the local paper of his own illness, O'Connell was forced to write quickly to his wife to calm her fears.[42]

Newspaper accounts of O'Connell's speeches also kept Mary informed as to what O'Connell was doing. Aware that she followed his speeches closely, O'Connell was able to comment on them in his letters and she, in turn, was able to reply. O'Connell went to great lengths to see that Mary was supplied with the many papers in which his speeches were printed.[43] Because O'Connell's political business was carried out almost wholly in the public forum, Mary was much more a part of the public sphere of her husband's life than the wives of bankers or businessmen. As her sons entered politics, published accounts of their actions allowed her to follow their public lives as well. The public nature of her menfolk's business allowed her to step outside her private role as wife and mother in order to make her own political judgments:

> I admire your letter on the subject of the dinner to Lord Clanricarde very much, and I perceive by a paragraph in the Herald that you purpose to bring forward at the Catholic Association the resolution formed by you and Mr. Butler respecting the Catholic cause. I shall be very curious to read the debate on this question. I expect a great deal of opposition though I hope I may be disappointed … I hope you continue to wear your warm night-shirts.[44]

Between letters, newspaper accounts and word of mouth, the dissemination of information, by modern standards, was surprisingly quick in nineteenth-century society. Not all news that spread was favourable, accurate or meant to be known. Gossip frequently found its way into the O'Connell correspondence. Generally, the O'Connells were the gossips but on more than one occasion they themselves were the subject of rumour and hearsay. Interesting in their own right, these often judgmental and even hurtful accounts also reveal the many functions of gossip and scandal within the social circle of the O'Connell family.

Gossip can be defined simply as talking about a person or persons who are not present, for the purpose of either amusement or entertainment. For example, O'Connell wrote to Mary in January 1810: 'Robin Hickson of the Square has become a Roman Catholic publickly—this has given some amusement to the talkative inhabitants of Tralee.'[45] In addition, gossip can be linked to social control and to the maintenance of a group.[46] The case of the love-sick Charles Phillips, author of Curran and his Contemporaries, was an instance in which gossip was used to express and maintain the values of the group and sanction those who failed to ascribe to these standards. Moreover, the scandal was entertaining. O'Connell told the tale to Mary:

> I never knew a man so altered and, indeed, so insane with love. It seems that the lady promised to write to him on Thursday; she forgot the promise, and he was very uneasy that day. Friday came and no letter; Saturday, no letter; Sunday also without a letter! And off he set on Monday morning in the day coach. I never saw anybody so dull and stupid, nor have I seen so much agony as he exhibited as he was daily disappointed of a letter. He has suffered a great deal, and has, as you may imagine, not a little disappointed public expectation here.[47]

In the above example, gossip acted as a channel through which people reaffirmed their shared values and ideas regarding appropriate and inappropriate behaviour. In a further example, Mary found herself the subject of gossip when news of her marriage to O'Connell was finally revealed several months after the event had taken place. Rumours flew around Tralee once word got out.

> One is that your mother is so exasperated that she never got out of bed since John went home. I listen to all those stories and am quite indifferent about what they say or can say as I know it all proceeds from envy. What astonishes them most, they exclaim, is my seeming indifference at your being disinherited by your uncle for so they will have it, because they would wish it.[48]

Gossips compete with each other for status within a group by imparting information regarding their competitors. Mary fell victim to such a situation when two of her letters to O'Connell were purportedly taken from his coat pocket by his sister, Ellen O'Connell, when he was visiting Derrynane. Ellen apparently made the contents of the letters known to 'every individual who came across her'. Mary reported the incident to her husband:

> Had she even adhered to truth in her statement it would have lessened the baseness of the act. One of those letters was relative to your mother's coming to Dublin, written indeed very differently from what was represented to your mother by Mrs. O'Connell [Ellen] and which representation was the cause why your mother did not come up last October ... To the best of my recollection I never wrote to you on the subject in any way that I would wish to conceal from her ... In this [second] letter, which Mrs. O'C stole, I strongly objected to Peggy Morgans being an intimate of my family ... but in short the whole of the letter has been grossly misrepresented, and your mother has given credit to it which surprises me not a little as she ought to be quite aware of the facility with which Mrs. O'Connell always told lies. God forgive her ... burn every letter that you get from me. It is the only way to secure them.[49]

Gossip could also be used as 'a hallmark of membership' in a particular group.[50] Social sanction against individual actions was particularly useful in maintaining standards of behaviour, especially with regard to marriage practices. By the early nineteenth century, strict parental control over the choice of a marriage partner was in definite decline; but gossip, a more subtle tool, still worked to limit free choice.

117

Potential marriages were always a hot topic for speculation. News of impending nuptials was usually accompanied by a judgment as to the suitability of the match. Moreover, the 'leakage' of information allowed women a formative role in the early stages of establishing relationships. Women exchanged news regarding the appropriateness of partners and worked together to arrange events at which well-matched partners might meet. The dowry sizes and social connections of the potential partners were discussed. While women had very little say in the actual negotiation of the marriage contract, their role in a couple's courtship up to that point was pivotal.[51]

When Maurice O'Connell expressed an interest in a young Miss O'Shea, his father was delighted. Writing to Mary, O'Connell speculated on the rumour regarding the woman's uncle and his supposed fortune. Should the man 'be really worth £80,000 and has the interest of his niece at heart, he ought to make an adequate settlement on Maurice', O'Connell surmised. 'In short I am in greater spirits on this subject than I was but we must be cautious.'[52] Another example involved the relationship between O'Connell's sister Ellen and Daniel 'Splinter' O'Connell. O'Connell's mother told the story of 'a report that was spread all over the country that they were married or so far engaged'. What made the rumour worse was that 'Dan O'Connell of Portmagee would have proposed for Ellen but for the report' of her intended marriage to Splinter.[53]

People gossip in order that their own definition of events or situations prevails, and to maintain a flow of gossip back to themselves.[54] O'Connell used gossip as a smokescreen to deflect attention from himself and his illicit courtship of Mary O'Connell, while at the same time generating conversation about her to satisfy his own desire to talk about her with others. In April 1801 Mary first informed her fiancé of the rumour that she was engaged to Peter Hussey, a young barrister from Tralee. To her surprise, O'Connell responded, 'You are probably indebted to me for all the jokes you suffer about Peter Hussey. My quizzing him on the subject might have given rise to the report. I declare to you most solemnly that I found pleasure in talking on the subject as it afforded me an opportunity of speaking about you without exciting suspicions of that which for the present I wish to conceal.'[55]

A further example in the letters between Mary and O'Connell reveals how gossip was used between family members to encourage intimacy. By sharing private information, family members were able to establish a sense

118

of solidarity. O'Connell was not above imparting gossipy bits of information gleaned from his business dealings. Although professional discretion would not allow him to discuss the personal details of cases with his colleagues, in 1814 he told Mary about the scandal of his cousin Con O'Leary:

> Last week he was to have been married to Miss Cronin of Rossview and at present he has everything arranged to marry a Miss Purcell who is near forty. The match with Miss Cronin was broken because her father desired that O'Leary should promise not to admit his son by Miss Allen to sit at the table whenever he came to visit his father. O'Leary flew off in a rage.[56]

O'Connell was privy to this bit of tattle because he drew up the marriage article. By sharing the tale with Mary, by effectively allowing her a view into his public life, he contributed to the intimacy between them.

Talk, or gossip, between family members reminded correspondents of their common interests and values and their exclusivity as a kin unit.[57] In 1823 Ellen O'Connell apparently wrote a letter to her father in which she mentioned a young Protestant gentleman by the name of Mr Jackson who had taken an interest in Kate. O'Connell, in his next letter to his wife, instructed her to be cautious in this matter and not allow it to be said that his daughter had formed an attachment to the man. His gave three reasons for his objections:

> [F]irst darling I would insist that all her children should be brought up Catholics. I would not consent to any exception—secondly we know nothing of the family or means of the young gentleman. Thirdly, he was said to have been of a sarcastic and indeed something of a slanderous temper. He may to be sure be falsely accused and for my own part I can not recollect I ever saw the slightest reason to think that he was guilty of any such disposition. I only repeat the rumour to put you on you [*sic*] guard.

By 11 December O'Connell wrote of his relief upon hearing that Mr Jackson had departed and Kate was, for the time being, saved.[58]

We have seen how correspondence and gossip worked to link families and maintain social and cultural values. Even with the rise of domesticity, there is no evidence from the O'Connell papers that kith and kin became any less important to the individual or nuclear family, and indeed a concerted effort was made to retain these links. Lawrence Stone argues that by 1750 two key factors defining the modern family were well established: 'the intensified affective bonding of the nuclear core at the expense of neigh- bours and kin', and 'a strong sense of individual autonomy and the right to personal freedom in the pursuit of happiness'.[59] We have already seen in chapter 2 that O'Connell's choice of marriage partner, while a mark of personal freedom, did not preclude a strong sense of family identity and responsibility. Furthermore, the O'Connell correspondence does not sup- port Stone's theory that relationships within the nuclear family intensified at the expense of extended kinship ties; quite the contrary. Rather than separate the family from its large network of kin, the domestic ideal of the nineteenth century intensified relations between the nuclear family and its in-laws.[60]

Patriarchy, with its patrilineal and primogenital ideology, had deemed matrilineal ties less important; when a woman was incorporated into her husband's patrilineage, she was disengaged from her own.[61] Domesticity, on the other hand, tended to reinforce ties with the wife's family.[62] In the case of Mary and Daniel O'Connell, it would appear from the correspon- dence that Mary's family held an important place in the nuclear family's affections. Mary maintained close ties with her mother, brother and sisters, and saw to it that her husband and children did as well. In fact, in the case of Mary's sister's family, O'Connell went to extreme lengths to guarantee their very survival.

Upon the death of her father in the summer of 1819, Ellen Connor wrote to Daniel O'Connell, her uncle, 'May God forever bless and protect you. What would become of us but for you?'[63] The situation of the Connor children was bleak. Betsey Connor, Ellen's mother and Mary O'Connell's sister, had died in 1815 from complications arising from the birth of her eighth child. The death of her husband James four years later left the chil- dren, ranging in age from four to twenty-three, in dire financial straits. Left 'unsettled' by the premature death of both parents, the children could rely only on the generosity of kin. Mary and Daniel O'Connell took it upon themselves to provide for and settle each of the Connor children in a good marriage, or in a respectable profession, or both. It was a daunting task. 'The affairs of that family are in a sad way from the dreadful fall in the times,' O'Connell confided in Mary. 'I am afflicted to think of the dismal prospect they have before them.'[64] Whenever he was in Tralee,

O'Connell took time to visit with the Connor children. He would dine with them during his stay there, much to the delight of his nieces and nephews. 'I really think *they* feel the same affection for you that they did for their poor father,' Mary commented.[65]

The only way to see the Connor girls, Ricarda and Ellen, securely settled was to marry them off. Thus, when William Neligan, an attorney in Tralee, took an interest in one of the Connor daughters, Mary and Daniel hopefully looked on, for he was 'a most excellent and respectable young Man'.[66] O'Connell dallied in Tralee after the assizes ended and reported back to Mary: 'I would of course be more explicit with you if the case was *ripe*—but it is only breaking to myself. It is Ellen I believe and not Rickarda that Neligan thinks of and as far as I can judge from observation she too is quite satisfied under present circumstances or indeed under any circumstances it is most desirable.' Mary concurred and hoped Ellen had 'too much good sense to refuse him'.[67] The wedding, set to take place after Easter in 1821, never occurred. On 26 May James O'Connell wrote to O'Connell that he had three letters regarding the match (one being from Ellen) and all parties involved were under the impression that O'Connell had promised £1000 for Ellen's dowry. James knew nothing of it and was at a loss as to how to proceed. Most likely this misunderstanding and the young woman's lack of fortune ended the relationship between the couple. Ellen Connor never did marry.[68] Ricarda Connor eventually married John Primrose Jr in 1830. Primrose acted as O'Connell's agent from 1822, and thus Ricarda's connection to the family remained very close.[69]

O'Connell's financial contributions to the Connor family cut into his own purse, much to the dismay of his ever-vigilant brother. As his wife and children prepared to depart for France to 'economise', O'Connell received a harsh warning from James: 'If you continue to manage the affairs of James Connor's family, which contrary to my earnest request you undertook, you will be involving yourself much more every day.'[70] Even Mary worried over O'Connell's assistance. While she implored O'Connell to look after the affairs of her sister's children, she was somewhat taken aback at O'Connell's decision to enrol Maurice Connor at Clongowes. 'I thought there was money necessary to be given on the entry of any Boy to that school,' she puzzled.[71] Whether O'Connell paid for the boy's entrance or not is unclear, although it seems likely that he did. Maurice was later joined by his brother Dan. In 1822, however, O'Connell had to take them out of Clongowes as they could no longer afford the fees. Dan Connor was sent to a mercantile house to work as a clerk. At the age of eighteen, he joined the Austrian service. His brother Maurice returned to the family home in Tralee.[72] Maurice later went on to study medicine in Edinburgh and became the resident medical officer in Westcove, Co. Kerry.[73]

Through the years, each of the Connor children benefited from the guidance of Mary and Daniel. Charles Connor, after much trial, error and gentle persuasion from his aunt and uncle, found his niche in the priesthood.[74] Under O'Connell's tutelage, Edward Connor studied for the bar and, in 1823, O'Connell reported to Mary, 'We made a clumsy effort to have him sworn an attorney a year too soon but failed.' The young man did eventually pass, however, and was able to support himself in his profession.[75] And finally, in 1827, O'Connell arranged for William Neligan, Ellen Connor's ex-fiancé, to take her brother James, the youngest of the siblings, as an apprentice. James later set up his law practice in Tralee.[76]

The spread of domesticity which allowed such strong matrilineal ties to be maintained in the above episode also promoted a growing social network amongst women. A stronger emphasis was placed upon the divisions between public and private spheres. The gender-role divisions that characterized nineteenth-century society and its cult of domesticity resulted in the emotional, as well as physical, segregation of men and women. As restrictions were placed upon male–female relations, women could spend days, even weeks, solely in the company of other women or children, dividing their time between home, church and visiting.[77]

At the centre of this female world was the relationship between mothers and their daughters. While boys went away to school as early as age seven, girls spent their entire single lives at home, where they established and maintained a closer relationship with their mother and sisters. Daughters, patterning themselves after their mothers' example, were expected to remain more family-centred and more interested in the goings-on of family members, whereas their brothers were preoccupied with school and careers.[78]

The demographics of nineteenth-century Irish life also contributed to the establishment of a distinctly female realm. There was often no clear distinction between nuclear family and extended kin. The range in age of siblings varied dramatically, allowing a daughter to function as both sibling and mother figure to her sisters and brothers, depending on their ages. The few surviving letters from Kate O'Connell to her younger brother Danny, then aged fifteen and away at boarding-school, provide an example: 'I hope you wash yr. hands at least every morning. If you don't give yourself this habit now you won't be able to be clean when you are at home,' the twenty-four-year-old instructed him.[79] Women frequently took charge of their own siblings, or those of their husbands, after marriage. O'Connell's sister Alicia lived with them in Dublin, for example. Cousins moved between relatives' homes for short and extended visits. Along with grand-mothers and aunts, a large group of maternal figures were readily available to every young woman.[80]

The links among kinswomen continued with marriage. It was common practice for women to write to the fiancée or new bride of their menfolk to welcome her into the family. O'Connell made this request of Mary when his brother James took a new bride. 'Write to her, love,' he asked his wife, 'to press her in the strongest terms to come to your house. Call her Jane and sister … Do this for me, darling, in your best style, and seriously I know no woman, nor indeed any man either, who can write better than you.'[81]

With each rite of passage, a woman found support in her network of female friends. Mary delivered her first child in the home of her own mother. For the birth of Morgan, she left Carhen and again returned to her mother in Tralee. Later, in Dublin, her spinster Aunt Nagle attended Mary during the births of several of her children. In many cases, an unmarried older woman provided the service of companion and nurse-maid in return for her keep. In an era when marriage was the ultimate social achievement, spinsters gained a place in society through such forms of assistance.[82] Mary, likewise, remained for months on end at Derrynane to assist in the delivery of her daughter-in-law's first child, much to the annoyance of O'Connell.[83] Upon the birth of a new child, women acted as godparents to their friends' infants. Moreover, female children were often named after their mother's close friends and relatives.[84]

Times of sickness and death also called for the support of women friends. For example, while Mary took the waters in Mallow in 1814, her sister-in-law, Betsey O'Connell, looked after the youngest O'Connell chil-dren in Tralee. Betsey again took charge of an O'Connell infant in 1817 when Mary and her older children removed to the spa town of

Southampton.[85] In 1844 Mary's daughter Betsey O'Connell travelled to her sister's home to help with a sick child. Little could be done for Ellen's child, who was not expected to live through the night, but Betsey remained to comfort her sister during the horrible hours of waiting. Her tasks also included writing to her father of the tragedy.[86]

Visiting, another form of kin work, further contributed to a female culture. Unfortunately, letters between Mary and her female friends and relatives are no longer extant and thus we are unable to examine fully the extent and depth of her relationships with other women. However, passing references within the letters between Mary and Daniel reveal that Mary nearly always had a female member of the extended family as a guest in her house.[87] Women frequently moved between homes of family members, acting as companions to one another and assisting in times of illness or at the birth of a child. Often the house was overrun with visitors. In August 1815 Mary wrote to O'Connell in Tralee, 'With the three Connors and my own half dozen, I assure you I have a noisy house.'[88] Likewise, Mary's sister frequently looked after Mary's children in addition to her own brood of eight.[89]

When husbands were away, visitors were especially welcome. O'Connell himself realized the benefits of securing ample companionship for his wife during his absences. When Mary was feeling particularly low in spirits during a stay in Mallow, O'Connell insisted that her mother, her sister Betsey or her niece Ellen Connor come to stay with her. 'Their society will keep up your Spirits,' he wrote.[90]

Visits produced reciprocal benefits. Mary's mother, for example, often came to Dublin for long visits, usually during the winter months, to alleviate the boredom of her life in Tralee. In later years, however, Mary's mother looked after the children when Mary and Daniel were away.[91] For a young girl, an extended visit to Dublin provided the exposure necessary to secure a suitable husband as well as providing companionship to a daughter near the same age. 'If you were here you would pity poor Mary McCarthy,' O'Connell wrote to Mary of his cousin in Kerry. 'I have a great mind to ask her to sleep with Ally for the winter. If you give me leave, I will do it.' Alicia, O'Connell's sister, was staying in Dublin with Mary, and Mary McCarthy did join her there.[92]

For an older woman, a young visitor provided companionship, someone with whom one could talk, sew, play cards, read or go calling. 'I wish you would hurry Betsy O'Connell to me, her society would be a great comfort to me,' Mary wrote to O'Connell. When Betsey finally arrived in April with her son, Mary told her husband, 'I can't tell you how glad I was to see her.'[93] On another occasion, Mary lamented the departure of her sister and niece from Dublin, telling O'Connell, 'You may judge how lonely I feel when I tell you my Dear Betsey and Ellen left me this morning ... I would have urged her more than I did to remain sometime longer with me ... My dear Ellen how much I miss her society.'[94]

Continually living in an environment surrounded by other women of all ages was particularly beneficial to young adolescent women. Having a close companion or a role model in the form of a governess, aunt or cousin, worked to relieve tension that is today so common in the relationship between mothers and daughters. Likewise, sisters shared a particularly close bond. While marriage inevitably and permanently parted sisters, many remained emotionally close. Even after Ellen O'Connell married Christopher FitzSimon, she kept close ties with her sisters. She corresponded with Kate regularly, writing by nearly every post. Later, Betsey joined her sister Ellen at Glencullen. Similarly, Kate O'Connell joined her sister Betsey after the latter's marriage and move to Ffrench Lawn.[95] Mary was also extremely close to her sister Betsey Connor. The two frequently corresponded, and her sister's death in 1815 came as a 'severe loss' to Mary.[96]

Kinship ties influenced the domestic, economic and political make-up of the family unit.[97] These ties took various forms. Economic ties, for example, bound the Connor family more firmly to the O'Connells than to, say, the family of Mary's brother Rickard. Physical proximity was another factor in establishing close kinship ties. O'Connell's sister Alicia, although some years younger than both Mary and Daniel, was especially close to the family, and in particular Mary, because she lived in the O'Connell home in Dublin and travelled with Mary to France during her two-year separation from O'Connell. Likewise, political and work-related interests kept O'Connell closer to some relatives than to others.

Of course, none of these kin ties could be satisfactorily maintained without the kin work of women. Letter writing and visiting, though tasks not strictly limited to women, were just some of the means women employed to remain connected to their extended female family members and friends. Women's discussions and gossip, whether by letter or in person, connected extended family members and maintained community and kinship systems. For women, this work was essential to their emotional stability and central to their way of life. The kin work of women, then, was central to all kin affairs.[98]

6

'a most treacherous complaint'
— SICKNESS AND HEALTH —

One of the most prominent characteristics of the correspondence between Mary and O'Connell is the space devoted to commenting on the health of the writer, recipient, children, relatives, friends and anyone else who had fallen ill. These statements of good health and tales of sickness reveal an obsession with well-being; and rightly so. Illness was rampant in nineteenth-century Ireland. Even a mere toothache could result in infection and, possibly, death. Some treatments did more harm than good. The absence of antibiotic drugs meant that an illness was generally left to run its course, often with disastrous results.[1] Epidemics were common and often deadly, sometimes wiping out entire families. The letters between Mary and Daniel relating to sickness and health served many functions: assuring well-being, advising means of preventing future illness, consoling in times of sickness and evoking sympathy, attention and help when needed.

A primary function of letter-writing was to ascertain or confirm the good health of the parties involved. In some cases, no news was hailed as good news, but in general, the omission of a statement of well-being on the part of the author, or, even worse, the absence of a letter altogether, signified illness. As Mary told O'Connell, 'nothing but illness could make me *silent*'.[2] Likewise, Mary became alarmed when letters from O'Connell failed to arrive. 'What has prevented you from giving me even a line to say you are well?' she scolded. 'Business is no *excuse* because, love, in your greatest hurry you would find time to say (Mary I am well).'[3] O'Connell was not always obliging. Mary wrote to him the following year, 'Good God, heart, why don't you write to me if you are well ... I watch every person's countenance and think when I see two people whisper [to] each other that it is something that is the matter with you.'[4] Mary herself was found guilty of the same omissions on occasion.[5]

Often the mere appearance of a letter written in 'a neat hand' was enough to signify the good health of the author, yet this too could prove deceptive. Detailed and truthful accounts of well-being were always preferred.[6] Mary was known for keeping her illnesses from Daniel. Not wanting him to worry over her, she frequently understated the seriousness of her condition or neglected mentioning having been sick at all. O'Connell was well aware of Mary's propensity to conceal information and even called her 'a fibber' on the subject of her health. He often begged Mary to be 'quite candid ... it now, I may say, corrodes my soul to think that you may still imagine you were doing me a kindness by concealing from me the exact state of your health'.[7] A large portion of each letter was reserved for accounts of health and sickness of not only the author and recipient but all family, friends and mutual acquaintances. O'Connell, for example, wrote to Mary in November 1834:

> Poor Jane has been very unwell with a sore jaw—an ulcer from a toothache. She was not to [see] me until after the Doctor should arrive. I saw her looking as well and as handsome as ever. The attack is nearly over. I also saw my poor Biddy who looks exceedingly ill. I fear she is not long for this world ... I have great pleasure in telling you I just saw your dear mother looking extremely well but she did not appear to be in spirits. Her health is mercifully good the dear darling woman. Aunt Chute is in present possession of her reason, Ellen Connor is fat and well. You see darling I have given you a full detail of all our friends. I myself am blessed be God perfectly well.[8]

In addition to recounting the state of one's health, another favourite pastime in regard to illness was offering advice. Prevention was the key to well-being; even when the author of a letter assured the recipient he was fine, the recipient would frequently return a list of practical precautions to follow in order to avoid becoming ill in the future. 'Let me entreat of you to take care of yourself and to wear the flannel waistcoat that has the sleeves,' Mary wrote to her husband one bitter December. 'Cheer up your spirits, my love. Take care of all things cold or damp,' O'Connell counselled.[9] Caution and prevention were crucial to maintaining health and Mary practised both. In one instance she would only dine out 'if I find my cold better. It is very slight but at this time of the year it is better [to] be too cautious than run any risks of cold.'[10] Should a person fail to take the necessary precautions against ill health, little sympathy was lost upon them. 'It is your own fault that you have a cold in your head,' O'Connell scolded Mary in 1825. 'Nobody need have a cold at Derrynane unless *they* earn it for themselves.' He would further become angry at her for 'allowing your spirits to desert you as they do'.[11] Staying healthy was a matter of individual responsibility.

Each aspect of life was approached with health in mind. Choice of clothing, for example, required careful monitoring. 'My throat would have suffered, I believe, had I not taken the precaution of putting flannel about it this morning that I had no fear of feeling the soreness—and now I have hardly a vestige of the hoarseness,' O'Connell wrote.[12] Furthermore, only one month after their initial correspondence, he took the liberty of telling Mary that he believed 'the present fashion of the female dress is most unsuited to this weather. Women do not wear half as much clothes as they used to do. But for my sake, my darling, you will avoid this preposterous fashion. I like fashionable dress when it suits the health and convenience but the present is a most dangerous one.'[13] O'Connell was correct in his appraisal of the current ladies' styles. As politics turned to the ideal of democracy, so too did fashion. Following the styles of France's first republic, gowns became high-waisted and classical, made of cheap white muslin. The low cost of the fabric allowed those of lesser wealth to dress fashionably as well. Good weather in Ireland in April 1801 further promoted the sheer, loose style which grew so popular it became the eventual uniform of femininity. When it was replaced in the 1820s, health-conscious women found no respite in the new fashion standards. As women's bodies were moulded to fit current designs, constricting stays, ladies' vests and tight corsets accordingly came back into vogue.[14]

A more obvious example of personal responsibility for illness is apparent in the use of inoculations. Inoculation for smallpox was introduced in England as early as 1718, though it met with great opposition and was not without its dangers. Benjamin Jesty, a Dorsetshire farmer, was the first to successfully perform the cowpox vaccination not only on his cow, but on his wife and sons, in 1774. In 1796 the English physician Edward Jenner discovered that immunity from smallpox could be produced by the mild condition of cowpox. This discovery led him to develop a smallpox vaccine from the cowpox virus.[15] This much safer vaccine for smallpox, involving a less intricate procedure, was made public in 1798 and quickly became an accepted remedy. Those who chose not to protect themselves and their children were immediately blamed once they fell ill. Most probably all the O'Connell children were vaccinated for smallpox. Mary makes reference to having John inoculated for 'cow pock' just three months after his birth in 1810. Ricarda, born in 1815, was nearly one year old when she received the vaccine. The child 'did not make the battle I suspected she would with Mr. Kearny. She is such a fine tempered little Babe it is easy to manage her,' Mary reported to O'Connell.[16] In general, Mary and Daniel took full responsibility for maintaining the health of their family and adopted any preventive measures at their disposal.

As letters sought to assure and advise, they also worked to console. Awaiting the birth of their first child, O'Connell encouraged Mary in her times of sickness, 'you will not suffer your spirits to be depressed. Think, my angel, what tortures your illness must give to the heart that adores you, and do therefore endeavour to preserve your health.'[17] He further assured her upon the baby's birth, 'Do not make yourself uneasy about any of the little illnesses which are incident to his time of life.' O'Connell expressed his conviction that the child's strong constitution would serve him well.[18] At the illness of her brother Edward, Mary placed her trust in God that 'his youth, will, and the great attention he is paid will yet restore the dear Fellow to us all'. At the same time she consoled O'Connell, whose father was quite sick: 'I will allow you must naturally feel a great deal at the loss of so kind and affectionate a parent but, Darling, I know you won't be unreasonable, should it please God to take him to himself.' When Morgan O'Connell's health improved Mary assured her husband, 'you see my darling you have nothing serious to apprehend for him this turn'.[19]

By discussing one's illness, listing symptoms and advising courses of action, the writer and recipient normalized illness, making it less mysterious. 'I felt myself excessively unwell,' O'Connell informed Mary. 'I had in fact strong feverish symptoms upon me. I had a chill, a headache and pain in my bones. I however took a warm bath, ate no dinner, drank three bottles of soda-water which served me as if I had taken a dose of salts, and slept off my illness.'[20] O'Connell frequently barraged Mary with questions regarding her health. 'Do you cough or is your chest sore?' he would ask, 'Have you consulted any physician? Tell me the exact truth.'[21]

A further consolatory function of the letters arose from accounts of other people's sickness. This allowed the correspondent quietly to underline the fact that she and her family had been spared. In 1807 Mary's sister Betsey Connor suffered from 'a *bile* [? boil] that is formed in her breast and must be lanced'. Although Betsy recovered quickly, O'Connell found it to be 'so troublesome a complaint' that he wrote to Mary, 'How fortunate I am darling that you were never attacked in that way.'[22] In some cases, finding blame for another's illness, be it in the afflicted's living habits or moral depravity, provided assurance that the condition in question would not invade the life of the writer. Of his law partner James Connor, O'Connell confided to Mary that his propensity to catch colds was perhaps the man's own fault, for 'going out at night always exposes him to violent colds and colds were never more prevalent'. O'Connell, on the other hand, was in good health and assured his then fiancée that he was taking excellent care of himself.[23]

Likewise, the prolonged illness of Mary's niece, Ricarda Connor, evoked the same lack of empathy from O'Connell, who argued that Ricarda's good spirits were the cause of her continued poor health. Because she was sitting up, laughing and chatting, she 'accordingly increased her feverish propensity and her pulse is again high this day. She can not be got to take care of herself.' Four days later he recounted to his wife, 'She is in as good spirits as ever she was—and indeed her good spirits contribute to keep her ill because they make her careless and inattentive.'[24]

Finally, illness, as presented by the author of a letter, could sometimes be used as a method of persuasion, of gaining sympathy and of eliciting assistance from the recipient.[25] In November 1804, for example, Mary found herself in Tralee, surrounded by people with measles and afraid that her new-born child, Morgan, would catch it. She first apprised O'Connell, in Dublin, of the situation on 14 November. Two days later she wrote again, informing him that she was 'uneasy about the measles as well as the intense cold of this horrid house'. She planned to leave within a fortnight. By 18 November she was nearly frantic, for there was 'not a quarter of the Town that the measles are not in and to crown all, Tom Connor [Mary's nephew] has got them'. The boy's case was 'favourable' and 'at his age there is not the smallest danger to be apprehended with care and caution but to an Infant it is a most treacherous complaint. They seldom or ever get over it.'[26]

O'Connell agreed with his wife's assessment.'Poor babe how my heart bleeds at losing him so early in his days for much indeed do I fear that he will not escape contagion.'[27] He advised that if Morgan was still safe, he ought to be sent off with a nurse at once. Mary, however, was not to travel until she was fully recovered and had the doctor's permission. By 21 November Mary had gained that permission. She was desperate to leave; all of her sister's children had taken ill. Yet within two days, the doctor had rescinded his orders, saying that exposing the child to the cold and haz- ards of a journey at this time of year was more dangerous than exposing him to measles which, he believed, was of a favourable kind in this instance. Mary resolved, therefore, to stay and wait out the illness. She wrote to O'Connell again on 25 November, in much brighter tones, having every hope Morgan would escape contagion. The Connor children were improving and had very mild cases. Still, she would consult the doctor about moving the child when he turned one month old on 30 November.[28]

It is unclear what occurred over the next few days, but it appears that, despite Mary's upbeat letter of the 25th, the doctor's assurances did noth- ing to relieve her fear. Perhaps the epidemic grew worse, or perhaps she just had too much time on her hands with which to imagine the worst. In order to escape contagion she essentially quarantined herself and the baby. She would not go to her sister Betsey's house, nor would she allow any of the Connors to come to her lodgings.

To make matters worse, she had asked O'Connell on more than one occasion to write to his parents and request that she and Morgan be allowed to come to Carhen to stay until after Christmas. She wished that Morgan be kept there instead of being sent to wet-nurse on Valentia Island as was the current plan. O'Connell, however, was hesitant or neglectful in making that request. Mary implored him once more to ask their permis- sion 'on receipt of this without mentioning that I had wrote or spoke to you on the subject, and do not omit mentioning if your mother has no objection to it. Perhaps it would be better for you [to] write to herself about [it]. In my opinion it would.'[29] The matter seemed to call for delicacy. Mary wanted no mention of her name in the request, for reasons she would not reveal to O'Connell until they met. She was fearful O'Connell's parents would decline an invitation, for 'I know that all old people have an objection to having young children squalling about them.'[30] If that were the case, Mary would be forced to remain in cold, damp lodgings, separated from not only her husband, but her other son Maurice as well. In the end it was Kitty, O'Connell's sister, who wrote to her mother, not to ask if Mary and Morgan could come to Carhen, but to tell her they were coming as soon as the weather improved. Still, Mary thought it best if O'Connell wrote as well, to smooth things for her arrival.[31]

Alone and insecure, worried for her child's safety, isolated from her husband, her first child and her friends, with no home of her own, Mary felt an increasing sense of desperation. Perhaps she was looking for much-needed attention and guidance; more likely, she adopted a distressed tone to propel O'Connell into action. In any event, despite the doctor's assurances and her calm acceptance of her situation as depicted in her letter of 25 November, she wrote frantically to O'Connell for advice on 28 November. Her instinct was to take the baby and leave for Derrynane as soon as possible, yet she wavered in her action. 'I am still undetermined as to remaining here,' she wrote. 'Our Babe will be a month old on Saturday and I have a great notion of setting out for home should the Weather continue as it has done these four days back—in fact my heart I am at a loss how to act. Some advise me to take the child home, for fear of the measles, and others desire me act as the Doctor tells me so that between advice from them and from the Doctor, I scarcely know what to do.' She desperately wanted just fifteen minutes to speak with him and decide what should be done. 'Doctor Connell will be the only Person to blame if my Infant takes the measles,' she warned dramatically. Mary concluded that O'Connell's reply would direct her actions.[32]

There is no direct reply by O'Connell in the surviving correspondence. His letter of 4 December declared his hope of being with her in a fortnight. By 8 December the danger of measles had passed and O'Connell expressed his joy that Morgan had escaped. Although Kitty had been called home to Carhen in late November, Mary and Morgan remained in Tralee until O'Connell joined them there on 23 December. Together they travelled to Carhen, where they spent the Christmas holidays with O'Connell's family.[33] In this instance, Mary's dramatic account of her situation did little to win sympathy from O'Connell or to propel him into arranging her removal to the more comfortable Carhen.

Ideas on maintaining optimal health varied. Exercise, for example, was considered necessary and good, but strenuous exertions were viewed as dangerous. Mary credited her continued good health in Clifton in 1817 to 'the exertion I am obliged to make here … The quiet still life I lead at home cannot be conducive to my health.' She went on to report that 'Having something to think of and a good deal to do is equally as good … for my health.'[34] O'Connell too promoted moderation, once telling Mary that the fasts of Lent agreed with him for 'Almost all the diseases of persons in the upper classes do at middle life arise from repletion or overmuch food in the stomach.'[35]

It was also widely held that any form of mental anguish or stress could bring on physical illness. Likewise, physical illness would in turn disturb the mental state or 'spirits' of the afflicted. Thus it was always necessary to keep up one's spirits. O'Connell frequently admonished Mary to do so 'least [sic] your mind should injure your state of health'.[36] Despite O'Connell's constant reminders to 'endeavour to preserve your health which can only be done by letting your mind be at ease', Mary seemed to fall ill regularly due to low spirits. For example in 1803, upon telling Hunting Cap of his secret marriage, O'Connell awaited word from his uncle regarding the tenuous state of his inheritance. Mary, some four months pregnant in Tralee, fell ill. She attributed the bout of illness to 'uneasiness and grief … at parting with you [O'Connell] and lest your uncle's displeasure should affect you too much'. Moreover, the illness of her brother Edward in 1808 kept her confined for two days due to 'the excess of … grief and affliction'.[37] Often a physical illness was exacerbated by poor spirits. O'Connell observed to Mary that Betsey Connor, who fell ill in 1810, would improve if she did not torture herself with 'useless apprehensions'.[38]

Accidents frequently occurred and could prove just as dangerous and certainly as inconvenient as illness. O'Connell often wrote of falls and injuries sustained from them. A slip in Limerick in 1809 landed him hard on his right hand, tearing the middle finger and part of the thumb rather severely and preventing him from writing to Mary.[39] Tumbles from his horse were common, especially on his frequent, and sometimes hazardous, journeys around the Munster circuit. When O'Connell's colleague Denys Scully took a fall from his horse in May 1823, he suffered a concussion. O'Connell dismissed the incident, claiming, 'the quantity of blood he lost from his head only served to do him good'. He perhaps became more sympathetic to his friend three days later when he too took a tumble from his own horse, injuring his elbow and leg.[40]

The common cold was perhaps the most frequently invoked illness in the letters. The general belief was that a cold was the result of becoming chilled or of exposure to a damp environment. Other temperature changes could also bring about a cold, such as drinking a cold beverage after being warmed by some strenuous activity or a breeze blowing through a window on a warm day. Dressing lighter in hot weather was viewed as a sure way to catch a cold. Colds were believed to cause pores to close and thus prevent perspiration. Without perspiration, the body could not effectively rid itself of waste products. Treatments for colds therefore revolved around inducing sweats, and included hot drinks, applied heat and 'diaphoretic' or 'sudorific' medicines.[41]

No symptoms were taken lightly in the O'Connell family, especially in light of past experience with sickness. This explains O'Connell's insistence that Mary have a bothersome tooth drawn, as 'The continuance of the pain necessarily affects your whole system ... and only weakens your constitution.'[42] When Mary was ill with a cold, she became alarmed at the onset of a sore throat, for she recalled 'how fatal sore throats were this summer in Dublin. But I confined myself one day to my Bed and the next to my room by which means I got perfectly rid of it.'[43] Confinement was the simplest means of treating a minor ailment. A few days in bed and another few near the warm fire of a sitting room often proved fully restorative.[44] Yet sometimes more drastic measures were needed.

With regard to treatment, emphasis was placed on functions which were monitored in terms of ease and 'dis-ease.' Since the systems of the body were regarded as integral, pain or disease in one area or organ could easily affect the entire person. 'Local' dysfunctions were viewed in terms of general 'constitutional' health and, consequently, were treated indirectly by bleeding, purging or blistering.[45] Ricarda Connor was 'blooded twice in a few days and confined to her Bed' for an illness affecting her lungs, and Dr LeBatt recommended applying a blister to one-month-old Betsey O'Connell for the whooping cough.[46]

Treatments such as these were intended to expel poisonous toxins from the system or to lure the ailment to a safer place within the body. The common belief was that 'distempers' could move from one area or organ to another, determining the intensity of the illness. Based on the theory that good health was the result of a proper balance of the four bodily fluids or humours—blood, phlegm, choler (yellow bile) and melancholy (black bile)—most remedies were designed to force a disease out of the body by ridding the body of bad humours through purges and diuretics, as well as inducing fevers, sweats and boils.[47]

The pains of treatment were frequently as bad as, if not worse than, the illness itself. While some wondered if the treatment was worth it, others felt that a remedy only really worked if it was painful or unpleasant. Aside from purges and emetics, festering was another unpleasant method of expelling bad humours. Festering involved allowing a created or existing wound to fester so that it would gather or generate pus. Blistering referred to the process whereby a vesictory was used, be it an irritating ointment or plaster, to form a blister. Both methods attempted to create a watery discharge 'which may in some measure supply the want of critical evacuations'.[48]

Bloodletting was an even more dramatic method of expelling bad humours.[49] Bleeding, according to a domestic medical treatise of 1784, was considered necessary

> at the beginning of all inflammatory fevers, as pleurisies, perpneumonies, &c. It is likewise proper in all topical inflammations, as those of the intestines, womb, bladder, stomach, throat, eyes, &c as also in the asthma, sciatic pains, coughs, head-aches, rheumatisms, the apoplexy, epilepsy, and bloody flux. After falls, blows, bruises, or any violent hurt received either externally or internally, bleeding is necessary.[50]

By this description, it would appear that bleeding was recommended for nearly every ache or pain. Certainly its mention in the O'Connell correspondence was frequent and offhand, suggesting the practice was quite commonplace. Still, O'Connell had reservations regarding bloodletting. At Mary's suggestions that Maurice be bled in 1816 for recurring headaches, he replied, 'I was myself very subject to those headaches, and bleeding was never resorted to—besides bleeding always leaves a permanent injury though it may give a temporary relief.'[51]

Ideally, bleeding was performed as near to the affected part as possible and a lancet was the tool of choice. However, when a vein could not be found it was necessary to resort to leeches or cupping. A bandage was placed tightly between the area intended to be bled, approximately one inch from it, and the heart. The bandage was kept tight to reveal the vein, but once the blood began to flow it was loosened. The amount of blood drawn varied, depending on the size, age and constitution of the patient.[52]

Pills, draughts, ointments and powders were also used in treating illness. Most were based upon folk remedies with basic ingredients such as rhubarb or aloe. Others, such as mercury or quicksilver treatments, were less common and extremely dangerous. Classified as a 'sialagogue', medicine promoting the flow of saliva into the mouth, mercury induced vomiting, purged the intestines, increased the flow of urine and generated perspiration.[53]

Several references to mercury treatments appear in the O'Connell papers. Ellen O'Connell, Mary's sister-in-law, underwent mercury treatments under the care of Dr Moriarty for 'a type of rheumatism' which made her legs swell and caused terrible pain. Mary's niece Ricarda also underwent a mercury treatment under the care of Dr Leyne in Tralee for an unnamed ailment.[54] Mary's daughter Ellen was treated with mercury for what appears to have been jaundice. O'Connell wrote to Mary in November 1834, 'Ellen enjoys pretty good health although in the morning she looks yellowish. It wears off during the day.' The following day he reported, 'Ellen looks much better this day. She is taking blue-pill and cannot stir out but she is now in excellent spirits and her appetite is improving.'[55] The 'blue-pill' was *hydrargyrus muriatus corrosivus*, or mercuric chloride. Introduced for the treatment of syphilis in 1750, it was usually applied topically to any inflammations or ingested, after being diluted, to induce vomiting and excretions. Mercury was believed to be useful to any type of skin inflammation, not just those brought on by venereal disease, and particularly those outbreaks caused by insects or parasites. It was also used to clear the gastro-intestinal tract.[56]

Members of the extended O'Connell family occasionally underwent operations or surgical procedures. As early as 1809, O'Connell writes that his mother underwent a 'painful operation' for an unnamed malady. O'Connell's uncle Hunting Cap went under the knife on at least two occasions. In 1816 he travelled to Cork for a procedure and in 1824, after surgery for some type of gravel or stone, he was rewarded with 'immediate relief'.[57]

The treatments discussed above, especially bleeding, doses of mercury and surgical procedures, all required the care and guidance of a surgeon. Simpler treatments, however, could be performed without professional assistance. Mary often administered her own remedies to her sick charges. She treated eight-year-old Kate for worms after O'Connell noticed the child's foul-smelling breath. The common treatment was a mix of rhubarb, jalap and calomel disguised in honey or syrup.[58] On another occasion she sent her husband cajeput oil for a bothersome tooth. This oil came from the West Indies and was used externally as a 'warm stimulant, antispasmodic, and a diaphoretic', not only for toothaches but for painful joints as well.[59] These examples of home care notwithstanding, the correspondence reveals that the O'Connell family frequently and unhesitatingly called upon the services of physicians for even the most trivial of illnesses, and relied heavily on their advice. Several doctors are mentioned throughout the letters. It would appear that the family had a medical consultant in nearly every place they frequented, including England. These men were called to treat parents, children and servants for anything from a cough or torn ligament to kidney stones and brain fevers.

Physicians were called or consulted at even the slightest sign of illness in the O'Connell children. Writing about four-year-old Morgan, O'Connell told Mary that 'when I went to kiss him he started and seemed very feverish and uneasy. Do not my dearest hesitate to send for Physicians for him should my babe prove at all seriously attacked.' Mary appeared to follow her husband's advice. Doctors were regularly brought in to attend to her children in both minor and extreme cases.[60]

The case of the severe illness of Ellen O'Connell in November 1814 demonstrates the uncompromising attitude of Mary and Daniel with regard to the health of their children. Ellen's experience, as recorded in her memoirs, documents the progressive stages of sickness and treatments, graduating from home remedies to a doctor visit to a second opinion to surgery. Ellen fell ill on her ninth birthday, probably the direct result of a vicious toothache that began in Mallow that summer. Though the tooth was drawn in Cork, most likely infection had already set in. Once it became clear that Ellen had fever, her hair was cut to allow ice caps to be placed on her head. To comfort her daughter for the loss of her hair, Mary promised she would buy the girl 'sprigged muslin caps lined with pink'. Ellen herself recalled years later that when the ice caps were placed on her head they gave a 'delicious feeling of coolness'. Yet they did not reduce the fever, and delirium set in.

Up to this point it is probable that no doctor had been called and Mary relied on common knowledge and age-old remedies to treat her daughter. Those failing, however, Dr O'Riordon was called to see the girl along with a Dr Tuomy.[61] Their opinions of Ellen's condition differed, Tuomy calling it water on the brain while O'Riordon diagnosed a brain fever. O'Connell did not hesitate further but called in a Dr Mackey. Multiple consultations were common; it was accepted that eminent physicians or specialists would be called in if a case was serious and, as this case demonstrates, practitioners did not seem to resent it.[62] Mackey agreed that a brain fever—probably meningitis—was the cause of Ellen's distress. Her head was thus blistered and she was bled in both arms by leeches. It is difficult to tell from Ellen's account of her illness how much time passed between the ice caps, the blistering and the leeches. Most likely, however, a few days were allowed to pass, perhaps even a week, in order to ascertain the effectiveness of each remedy before the next, more drastic measure was undertaken.

The fact that Ellen was bled in the arms by leeches is worthy of note. Generally, bleeding was limited to the area of the body most affected by the illness, in this case Ellen's head. Only in instances where a vein could not be found was bleeding by leeches advocated. Many physicians opted to bleed children by leeches as well, for no other apparent reason than that they were uncomfortable taking the lancet to a small child. This method, however, was not condoned in some medical circles as it was difficult to discern how much blood had been drawn by the leeches, which were often difficult to stop, and the wounds incurred by this method were slow to heal.[63]

In Ellen's case, Dr Mackey eventually found the leeches to be ineffective and, 'in one critical moment', decided to lance the child's temporal artery. Ellen recalls him approaching her bedside with his hand full of cotton wool, in which his lancet was concealed. He told her he was going to put a leech on her head, at which point he lanced the artery and she cried out in pain, 'Oh! that leech has a sharp tooth!' Fortunately, Ellen recovered, but her illness lasted some two months and was serious enough to warrant calling in a priest for last rites. In later years she suffered weakness and headaches for which family doctors prescribed country air and bathing.[64]

The treatment of Ellen's illness demonstrates Mary and Daniel's concern over the health of their young children. The worried parents anxiously availed of all the medical options available to restore the young girl's health. Nine-year-old Ellen was no exception. It would not appear from the letters that age, sex or personal preference affected the zeal with which Mary and O'Connell attended to the health of their children.

In 1834 O'Connell wrote to Mary regarding their son Danny's illness. The young man, then eighteen, had taken ill in late November or early December of that year while in London. Concern for him was so great as to elicit a letter to O'Connell in Dublin from John Richard Elmore, who was sending the boy home.[65] O'Connell immediately determined that the boy should be sent to Kerry, where Mary was currently residing and where Dr Maurice O'Connor, a family friend and physician, could attend him. At first O'Connell concealed the illness from Mary, perhaps fearing he was overreacting. Yet when Danny arrived in Dublin on 7 December, O'Connell was shocked at his appearance. Though in good spirits and claiming to be improved, the boy was emaciated and his voice weak. According to plan, O'Connell sent his son off to Kerry where his mother could nurse him back to health. O'Connell described Danny's symptoms to Mary as 'consumptive … which I so much dread though his lungs were not affected. It certainly is not pulmonary consumption—but—in short darling let us not deceive ourselves whether favourably or unfavourably— Make Maurice O'Connor be quite candid with you.' In the end, Danny's complaint was diagnosed as a stomach disorder and he soon recovered his health. Yet the furious flow of concerned letters between Kerry and Dublin attests to the zealous concern over the welfare of the youngest O'Connell child.[66]

Although the O'Connell family placed great faith in their doctors, they did not value the opinion of each physician equally. Dr Moriarty, for example, was considered by O'Connell to be 'a sorry Quack. Leyne is the only scientific Physician in Kerry.'[67] The shift in favour of more scientific medicine brought with it changes in medical terminology and a more technical common language of sickness.

Much of the terminology of nineteenth-century medicine revolved around 'nerves'. As humoral theories faded out, the vocabulary of nerves was used to describe the connection between the mind and the body.[68] The ancient Greek physician, philosopher and medical writer Galen was one of the first to realize that 'some exciting stimulus passed from the brain down the spinal cord through the intercostal nerves to the muscles to cause their contraction'. The brain, according to Galen, produced an 'animal spirit' and sent it to the organs of sense and motion through the nerves.[69]

The modern understanding of nervousness began with Dr George Cheyne (1671–1743), author of *The English Malady*, in which he described as nervous patients those who formerly would have been diagnosed with hypochondria. Cheyne's understanding of the body combined humoral theory and his own new nervous concept of disease. Borrowing from Galen, Cheyne believed that 'All nervous distempers whatsoever from Yawning to Stretching, up to a mortal fit of Apoplexy seem to be but one continued Disorder, or the several steps and degrees of it.' The symptoms of nervousness arose, he contended, from 'a Relaxation or Weakness, and the Want of a sufficient force in Elasticity in the Solids in general and the Nerves in particular'. The body, according to Cheyne, was a mass of solids and non-solids. The non-solids, or humours, moved throughout the body, mixing with the solids. If the humours were too corrosive or biting they could literally shred or eat away at the solids—the muscles, the sinews and the nerves.[70]

Contemporary to Cheyne were two University of Edinburgh scholars who also supported the idea of nervous disorders. William Cullen (1710–90) coined the term 'neurosis', which he broadly defined as 'sense and motion injured' without fever or any local disease. For Cullen, neurosis was caused by a literal tightening or loosening of the nerves themselves. This broad definition encompassed a plethora of medical illnesses such as fainting, coma, apoplexy, cholera, asthma, diarrhoea and melancholy. Cullen's ideas greatly influenced nineteenth-century views of illness.[71]

The second influential Edinburgh medical scholar of the period, Robert Whytt (1714–66), published his observations on nerves in 1764. According to Whytt, a nervous sensation in one part of the body was carried by the nerves to the spinal column, up to the brain and back out along another nerve to another body part, thus causing the manifestation of a symptom. As a result, many related symptoms could be present at the same time, for each body part was sensitive to the other via the nerves. Nervousness, according to Whytt, could be either a natural defect in the constitution or could be produced by a long illness or an 'irregularity in living' which weakened the entire system.[72] Higher classes were thought to have more delicate nerves. Moreover, the wealthy could afford spicy food, meat and strong spirits which could turn the non-solid juices of the

141

body bitter and corrode the nerves.[73]

Problems arising from nerves were often considered to be more common in women and children. To classify an illness as 'nervous' was to suggest it was not serious. Mary frequently appeased O'Connell by informing him that a fever which confined her for weeks was of a 'nervous' nature, or that her cough 'realy [sic] is nervous'.[74] 'Nervous fever' was treated in medical books as different from regular fevers. According to one medical text, nervous fevers increased greatly in the late eighteenth century, due mainly to a 'different manner of living and the increase of sedentary employments; as they commonly attack persons of a weak and relaxed habit'—in short, women. Accompanied by low spirits, loss of appetite, weariness, 'deep sighing and dejection of the mind', these fevers were to be treated by keeping the patient cool and quiet while supporting their strength and spirits with a nourishing diet and 'generous cordials'. In some cases vomiting was to be induced or blistering attempted, but in no instance was the patient to be bled.[75]

Young pubescent and adolescent girls were thought to be especially at risk from nervous disorders. These adolescent neuroses usually took the form of illnesses such as the 'green sickness' or chlorosis. Defined as an 'obstruction from the womb-vessels of females, when their courses begin to flow', its symptoms included a 'sallow, pale, or greenish colour of the face, a difficulty of breathing, [and] a sickness of the stomach at sight of food'.[76] To guard against this condition, girls were advised to take fresh air, to exercise and, if all else failed, to cure the dreaded 'wasting' by marrying. It is difficult to tell if 'wasting' was anything more than a label pinned upon awkward, shy or difficult children. It does not appear that the mothers of these girls felt any alarm at the physical or mental state of their pubescent daughters. It can be assumed that the mothers believed their daughters would grow out of this phase; if not, marriage and child-bearing would solve the problem.[77]

Men too could fall victim to neuroses. Both James O'Connell, Mary's brother-in-law, and her son, Maurice, suffered in their early adulthood from cases of what O'Connell defined as 'fidgets'. James fell ill in England, the victim of 'those restless and fidgety manners which ... you know were not at all natural to him.' He could no longer stay in England and returned to Ireland where 'Whatever restraint may be necessary (if any shall) may as well be imposed here ... Indeed if he be not recovered by now there is no use in medical treatment for his complaint.'[78] Happily, these 'fidgets' improved and no more mention of them is made in reference to Maurice or James O'Connell.

Geographical and environmental conditions were also viewed as capable of causing illness or aiding well-being. According to medical historians Roy Porter and Dorothy Porter, 'Altitude, the lie of the land, exposure to winds, the composition and porosity of the soil, landscape features such as rivers, forests, lakes, and mountains, proximity to the sea—all these were believed to impinge on health, and thus critical when choosing a residence or travelling.'[79] Climate was equally important. Excessive humidity, rainfall, moisture or damp was regarded as dangerous. This preoccupation goes a long way in explaining the Georgians' propensity to 'travel in search of health'. Trips to the south of England, to the sea, to the spa and to the baths were commonplace.[80] Mary O'Connell's peregrinations are a prime example of this phenomenon, as she moved between town and country, Ireland, England and France, all in search of good health.

Mary O'Connell especially believed in the benefits of 'different air'. Writing to her husband, she mused, 'it is realy [*sic*] singular the effect that change of air has on me'.[81] O'Connell agreed with her, claiming, 'I think change of air has always done you good and that you would feel the benefit of Dublin the more if you were out of it a few months.'[82] Country air was generally considered a remedy for any ailment, either physical or mental. Dr Barry recommended country air for Ellen O'Connell, who suffered from headaches, a result, the doctor claimed, of her severe illness in 1814.[83]

While country air was restorative for some, others found well-being in the city. Mary, on her 1814 trip to the spa at Mallow, found no relief in the change. Upon her removal to Cork, O'Connell wrote, 'You will get, I trust, well from the Cork air; but at all event Dublin is a certain restorative.' Mary concurred that Dublin somehow agreed with her, saying, 'were I to remain in Dublin for ever I should not feel the slightest affection [*sic*] which is a most fortunate circumstance'.[84] Country air, especially Kerry air did little for Mary. To O'Connell's unending disappointment, Derrynane never agreed with her as much as Dublin and even London. Perhaps it was not so much the 'air' of the place that affected her as an atmosphere of loneliness, boredom and seclusion. When Mary was feeling particularly depressed and sickly in Mallow in 1814, O'Connell insisted that her mother, Betsey or Ellen O'Connor come to stay with her for 'Their society will keep up your Spirits.'[85]

A further popular belief held that only the air of one's birthplace or home was the remedy. Despite Mary's insistence that her sister remain with her, Betsey Connor, afflicted with a cough, 'seemed impressed with an idea she would never get well while she remained in Dublin'. Though distressed to see her companion leave, Mary held every hope that the native air of Kerry and Dr Leyne's care would cure her sister's illness.[86] Likewise she objected to O'Connell's brother James coming up to Dublin, despite the doctor's opinion, telling her husband, 'Country airs particularly his native airs would be very conducive to the establishment of his health.'[87]

'Air' cannot be confused, however, with 'weather', as Mary pointed out to O'Connell in 1825 while wintering in Kerry. 'Rest assured,' she wrote, 'the air of Derrynane was not the cause of my illness. The [?attack] on my chest did not last above an hour … I was but three days confined to my room but *that* was caused by the badness of the weather. If the air of this place disagreed with me my chest would never be free.'[88] Bitter weather was indeed a threat to good health. Mary and the children were frequently confined to the house and even to certain rooms in order to avoid the cold and damp weather so persistent during Irish winters.

Bathing was the most common reason for travel in the Georgian era. Visits to baths and spas for the purpose of taking in the waters, which were believed to have 'healing properties', were highly recommended by the medical profession. Cold baths were considered particularly conducive to good health, especially for 'inhabitants of populous cities, who indulge in idleness, debauchery, or sedentary or studious lives'.[89] Thought to 'invigorate both the body and the mind', cold-water bathing was advocated for 'all rheumatic pains, paralytic weakness and stiffness', as well as improving circulation, clearing obstructions and promoting secretions by giving 'permanent vigour to the solids'. Moreover, in the case of children, immersions in cold water cleared pimples and other skin eruptions, produced sweat and dissipated 'the acrid serum which corrodes and inflames the skin'. Cold water bathing also cured thirst, caused sleep, produced urine, prevented fever and rendered the bather 'insensible to cold air', and thus helped prevent colds. For those of a nervous disposition, the 'bracing qualities of cold water' were thought to be especially beneficial for they increased the quantity of blood in the brain and thus raised dull spirits.[90]

Like many of her contemporaries, Mary and her children frequently travelled for the purpose of bathing. In summer months, they were often found in Clontarf, outside Dublin, and in Mallow. Since sea-bathing was the most highly recommended form of cold-water bathing, O'Connell, himself 'a great advocate for plunging infant[s] into cold salt water', entreated Mary to bring the children to Derrynane in the autumn of 1811 where they might bathe.[91] It is unclear if Mary did go. It is thought that she never visited Derrynane while Hunting Cap was still alive. However, her intention to go to Derrynane and the absence of correspondence between Mary and Daniel from 22 August on suggests that perhaps she joined him there.

Kate was bathed particularly for some ailment of the heart which presented itself around the time she turned three.[92] A doctor recommended that John be bathed as it would strengthen him after a long illness. Apparently, the child protested violently at this sort of treatment and O'Connell abandoned his previous advocacy of the practice, claiming, 'A violent dislike to bathing is a kind of warning nature gives against the use of the bath.' Moreover, John 'has a very large head and the cold bath is dangerous for persons of that configuration'. With his opinion clearly stated, O'Connell left the decision up to Mary. Left to struggle with the adamant child, Mary was at a loss. Ellen refused to go as well and John put up a fight on every occasion, yet the doctor continued to recommend bathing as the best means of strengthening the child's constitution. The issue was resolved for her when the weather turned foul and they were unable to take the waters for several weeks. The baulking John was then given a slight reprieve. In the end Mary agreed with her husband, informing him, 'anxious as I feel about the use of the cold bath for him I will not press it further. Probably there is some reason in what you argue against it. At all event he shall not bathe.'[93]

In the spring of 1817 Mary travelled to England, where she settled herself and her children in Clifton, near the spa town of Bristol. Bristol was a great summer resort town, bustling not only with 'invalids', who came for the therapeutic benefits of the waters, but those accompanying them as well. In addition to several wells of various temperatures, amusements could be found in the ballroom, coffee house or one of the town's many taverns. Accommodation was available in a great number of lodging houses, and above the town sat the village of Clifton, 'where there are Downs extending several miles, where the company ride out for exercise'. The air of these downs was thought to be 'pure and beneficial'.[94] The waters of the Hot-Wells, one of the most famous baths, were said to be especially helpful in cases of diabetes or any kind of physical or inflammatory disorder. At a temperature of 76 degrees, this well was considerably hotter than others, such as the Rock-House, which only reached 50 degrees. Those frequenting the Hot-Wells were advised to

> go to the pump-room in a morning, and drink half a pint of it, then walk about for half an hour and take a glass of the water, and about five o'clock in the evening another half pint should be drank, and exercise taken as before, after being thus accustomed to three doses daily for awhile, the quantity may be encreased to three half pints in the morning, at intervals of half an hour between each, and the like in the afternoon. These six half pints are the usual quantity each person drinks daily during his stay at the Hot-Wells, which is generally from May to September, and which is called the Season.[95]

People travelled not only to find healthy climes, but also to escape unhealthy ones. Epidemic diseases were often blamed on environment. Those who could afford the means of escape did so. Cholera, for example, was greatly feared. Arriving in Britain in 1831–32 from Asia, cholera caused more widespread panic and had greater repercussions than epidemic diseases such as fever, smallpox and tuberculosis.[96] It made its first appearance in Ireland in Belfast in March 1832 and appeared in Dublin one week later. By mid-April the disease was reported in Cork, and by May it had appeared in at least fourteen of the thirty-two counties.[97] Those of means, such as the O'Connells, hoped to escape the plague by moving to safer environs, which generally meant the countryside. 'Should the cholera come to Ireland,' Mary wrote to her son Daniel in 1831, 'we shall certainly go to the Abbey [Derrynane].'[98]

Long confinements, painful treatments, doctor visits and travel all added to the general inconvenience of poor health. One sick individual in the household could greatly hamper life's daily interactions and activities. Illness and incapacity resulted in a shift in one's relations with others, be they family, friends, servants or doctors. Masters nursed servants, children worried over parents, burdensome relatives became indispensable and doctors became all powerful.[99] A sickly servant caused an upheaval in the household hierarchy as well as a disruption to the master's routine. The prolonged illness of the O'Connells' housekeeper, Mrs Ryan (see chapter

4), put Mary in a state of anxious turmoil for several weeks. When O'Connell's footman fell ill while he and O'Connell were away on the circuit, O'Connell informed his wife that he was like a fish out of water without the servant, who was forced to take to his bed for three days.[100]

The complexities of illness during the nineteenth century, therefore, were many and varied. The letters of Mary O'Connell allow a glimpse at many aspects of health and well-being in pre-Famine Irish society. What is most apparent from the O'Connell correspondence is the modern view the family, specifically Mary, took toward illness. Folk medicine and superstition found no place in Mary's life when it came to the health and well-being of her family members. Embracing Enlightenment philosophy, she adopted all the current and progressive methods of preventing ill health—however backward some of these methods might seem today—and unhesitatingly relied on scientific doctors to cure her loved ones in times of sickness.

7

'a pattern of piety'
— RELIGION —

The nineteenth century was a period of reform within the Catholic Church in Ireland. Changes included measures intended to reach the masses through the work of the priesthood, primarily within the context of the parish church. In some parts of Ireland, however, parishes with inadequate churches or no church at all were commonplace. As a result, the Irish home was often the centre of religious practice: prayer, religious education and the sacraments all took place there. It naturally follows that women, specifically wives, as caretakers of the home, were likely to influence the development and practice of religious rituals.[1] Catholic reform, in effect, transformed women into agents of the Church. Within their families, they taught their faith's rituals and beliefs. Furthermore, the Church's teachings of renewal and rebirth, its emphasis on the family 'and the entire business of solace and succour for suffering', appealed particularly to women.[2]

The correspondence between Mary and O'Connell reveals many of the common, everyday religious practices of the O'Connell family. Religion held a very important place in Mary O'Connell's life and, as such, was a major factor in the life of her family. Mary's influence is particularly noticeable in her husband's return to practising Catholicism in 1816. Moreover, she oversaw the rites of passage, frequently commented upon in the correspondence, which further mark the family's strong religious beliefs. Mary led the family in carrying out their faith through prayer and ritual and even in encouraging others to join their strong and close-knit religious community.

Mary took great pride in her family's attention to their Catholic duties, for she felt that she was responsible for their faith. She encouraged her husband and offspring in their efforts while regularly attempting to carry out her own religious obligations. When she married O'Connell, he was a confirmed deist. His return to the Catholic faith can in no small way be attributed to her constant and firm persuasion.[3] She frequently wrote to him, encouraging him to observe the Lenten fasts, to refrain from taking meat and to attend to his Easter prayers. 'You see, heart, how good I want you to be,' she told O'Connell, 'I do, darling, because I doat of you. I would wish you to be attentive to your religion and thankful to God for all his blessings and favours to both of us ... In gratitude to the Almighty ... we should at least attend to the duties of our religion.'[4]

O'Connell's religious life is an area about which historians still know very little. His education, steeped as it was in 'the traditions of seminarian gallantry' and 'simple, severe spirituality', seemed to have had no impact upon his faith.[5] It appears that from late 1794 he drifted steadily toward scepticism, influenced by his reading of Thomas Paine's *The Age of Reason*. This anti-Christian, pro-deist work gave O'Connell the tools with which to view religion in an entirely new light. Still, O'Connell clung to some nagging doubts regarding his 'unconversion', writing in his journal, 'The prejudices of childhood and youth at times frighten and shake the firmness of my soul.'[6] He consoled himself, however, with the thought that should his scepticism be an error and Catholicism the truth, a good and forgiving God would 'not punish for the unbiased conviction of the soul'.[7] Oliver MacDonagh, in his biography of the Liberator, concludes:

> We can never speak with certainty, or perhaps even confidence, of another's spiritual condition. But the evidence to hand does seem to indicate that O'Connell 'lost his faith' during 1794–5, and committed himself deliberately to another, Paineite deism, early in 1796. In doing so he did not, however, rid himself of doubts. Rather he exchanged doubts that Christianity might not be true for doubts (or at least extra-rational fears) that it might be, after all.[8]

O'Connell gradually returned to the practice of Catholicism, and signs of this 'conversion' came as early as 1809 when Mary wrote to her husband at the Tralee assizes, 'I can't tell you what real happiness it gives me to have you this sometime back say your prayers and attend Mass so regularly, not to say anything of your observance of the days of abstinence.'[9] Mary marked O'Connell's full return to the faith as occurring in the spring of 1816. Delighted, she related the family's joy to her husband, telling him that Maurice had 'thanked God with his hands clasped for your *conversion*'.[10] During Lent that year she wrote to her husband, praising him for his 'attention at present to your religious duties, and it is a delightful reflection to me that amidst all your bustle and business you continue a pattern of piety to all of us'. She also 'had the happiness of being at Communion as my *health* will now permit to be more regular than I have been this time back, I shall with the assistance of God try to follow your example. God be thanked, darling, the times are changed. You are now a better *Christian*.'[11] O'Connell too seemed content with his decision and expressed this pleasure to his wife, writing, 'I promise you, love, I feel myself beyond any comparison happier in *this* change which, with the grace of God, I hope will prove complete.'[12]

Mary, moved and strengthened by her husband's return to faith, still continued to encourage O'Connell. The following year she reiterated her concern over his religious devotion. Encouraging him to attend to his Easter duty, she admitted, 'I know, darling, you don't like to be spoken to on this subject but you will excuse your wife who idolises you and who feels equally as anxious for the salvation of your soul as she does for her own and for her children's.'[13] By 1820, however, O'Connell was boasting of his own dedication as he informed Mary, 'I must run off to get *my fish* for this week; I am a great papist.'[14]

Religion, then, held an increasingly important place in O'Connell's life. Without it, he believed, happiness in the afterlife would be elusive. O'Connell urged his son John to 'remember always that we are in this world only on *trial* and that there is not happiness hereafter without genuine religion or indeed, my child, any true happiness here without it'.[15] He reiterated the point in a letter to Mary, saying, 'As to religion darling surely it has not made any of us gloomy. Mr. Colemans maxim is—beaucoup de piete, beaucoup de gaiete … For my part I would not think any religion sincere that did not make the person more affectionate and considerate.'[16]

With O'Connell's 1816 'conversion', religion took an even larger role in the daily mechanics of family living. Mary seemed especially affected, and her religious practice intensified. She met more frequently with Rev. L'Estrange and she often attended prayers.[17] This intensification was perhaps also a result of personal grief and anxiety, for between the years of 1812 and 1815 the couple lost three infants, Daniel Stephen, Gloriana and Mary, to illness. In January 1815 Mary's sister Betsey Connor died from complications due to childbirth. In addition, Mary's brother Maurice suffered from a severe illness, leaving Mary with the impression upon his visit that spring that 'he is coming to die with me'.[18] The year 1815 also saw Mary carrying her eleventh child. Added to these worries, her husband's wounded honour and financial imprudence kept her from a happy and uneventful pregnancy. O'Connell's February duel with John D'Esterre and the latter's resultant death had forced O'Connell into hiding, while a chaotic mass of callers, with whom Mary was left to deal, descended upon the house in Merrion Square. Barely had the dust settled from the D'Esterre affair before another crisis took its place. In March 1815 James O'Leary, a Killarney merchant, went bankrupt and O'Connell, who had acted as security for the man, was liable for £8000.[19] This placed the family in dire financial straits and caused a bitter argument between the couple. After several frantic letters, angry, apologetic and forgiving, peace between them was eventually restored. Thus amidst family and financial turmoil, the Veto question and Napoleon's return from Elba, Mary successfully delivered a healthy baby girl in May 1815.[20] By December, despite O'Connell's traipsing around the countryside in an attempt to duel with Peel, she was pregnant again.

Though less eventful than her last, this pregnancy was not without its worries. Morgan was rather ill for several weeks in March and her niece Ricarda suffered from an extended bout of poor health; Mary hosted a wedding that summer as well as having one of the boys' school chums spend his vacation with them; and frequent trouble with a servant continued to vex her until she was forced to dismiss him. In July O'Connell wrote to his wife regarding her loss of spirits.[21] Anxiety continued to plague her in August. She struggled to keep up her spirits, writing to O'Connell, 'I trust in the Almighty. I have no reason for any apprehensions in my approaching confinement … .[the doctor] paid me a complimentary visit to day and promised he would not in any account be out of the way. He is indeed to do him justice always most attentive to me.'[22]

To compound matters, O'Connell would not be present for the delivery as his law practice would keep him busy on the circuit.[23] With all these extra concerns weighing on her mind, it is little wonder Mary attended three masses the day before giving birth to her last child, Daniel Jr. As well as increased mass attendance, during this time Mary regularly welcomed Rev. L'Estrange to the house for counselling. However, Mary's control of her temper finally snapped when she learned O'Connell was considering not returning to Dublin before heading off to Kerry to see his sick mother and to attend to some business there. She wrote to her husband that if he did not come home before going to Kerry, 'I should be most highly *offended* with you. Your Mother is not in that dangerous state that you should hurry off to her, and James Butler [the gentleman with whom O'Connell had business] having lived so long a Bachelor, the delay of a Week cannot add much to his *age*.'[24] Although he had promised his mother that he would come to her directly from the circuit, O'Connell, probably well aware that Mary had just cause to be wrathful, secretly hurried home to Merrion Square, hoping to appease his wife and his mother at the same time.[25]

Thus, for a period of nearly four years, Mary faced unusual hardship and worries at the hands of providence, which took her sister and three children while seeing fit to give her two more, and of her husband, whose financial and political antics kept them both living on the edge. The tragedies confronting the O'Connells seemed only to strengthen and renew their religious belief. As the couple overcame each new obstacle before them, their love and trust in one another grew stronger, providing more reason than ever to give thanks and praise to the God who watched over them.

The strong religious conviction of Mary, and later Daniel, was apparent in the upbringing of their children and in their home life. The rites of passage within the Catholic Church were significant events in the lives of most Irish Catholics. These rites were generally marked by the celebration of a sacrament. Some sacraments were considered more important than others. For example, the rules governing communion, confession and marriage were not so stringent; baptism and extreme unction, on the other hand, involved rigid regulations.[26]

The sacrament of baptism was one of the most important rites of passage for the people of pre-Famine Ireland. Like their contemporaries, the O'Connells took special care to see that their children were baptized shortly after birth in order that their eternal salvation be secured in the event of an untimely death. O'Connell's attendance at his daughter's baptism in 1815, the year before his 'conversion', prevented him from visiting his sons in boarding school. His willingness to remain for the ritual, despite his less than fervent religious belief, signifies the importance of the event. Years later, referring to one granddaughter, O'Connell wrote to Mary insisting the child be christened post-haste. 'Let her not be subject one day to the awful effects of any accident whilst unbaptised,' he instructed. 'Why should any risk be run,' he demanded the following week, 'in so vitally important an affair!'[27]

Baptism was celebrated with a gathering of family and friends. The event usually took place in the family home and would be followed by some form of refreshment. The O'Connells, especially Mary, were frequently invited to christenings and seemed to enjoy attending them.[28] Mary reported one such occasion to her son Danny, then in school at Clongowes. The child being baptized was the son of long-time family servant, Julia O'Brien. Danny was to be the godfather of the child but could not be present at the baptism. His brother John stood in for him, and a woman who lodged with the child's family was the godmother. According to Mary, 'she is protestant but that is of no matter when there is to be a Catholic to hold and answer for the child'.[29]

Like the first sacrament of baptism, the sacrament of extreme unction, a final rite of passage, was also highly significant for it ensured forgiveness and eternal salvation. Most Irish Catholics, including the O'Connells, considered this rite to be sacred. The importance Mary and O'Connell attached to the sacrament can be seen in their attempts to convince Betsey O'Connell, Mary's sister-in-law, to take the last rites, as Mary's daughter Ellen had when she fell ill at the age of nine. Seriously ill in Tralee, Betsey continually refused the sacrament out of either fear of its weighty meaning or a sense of her own unworthiness. In any event, Mary and her husband worried over her precarious situation and on more than one occasion encouraged her to submit. In March 1826 O'Connell wrote to Mary, 'I spoke a *little* this day to Betsey about religion but got no great encouragement. I did not select the proper mode.'[30] By October 1827 Betsey, still ill, had yet to see a clergyman, and O'Connell, finding the woman in a 'very precarious way', spoke to her husband, Mary's brother, on the subject. Rick, the product of a 'mixed' marriage, had been raised a Protestant after his father, but promised to speak to his sickly wife. Betsey died in December. The letters make no further mention of the issue, presumably indicating that the woman finally accepted the sacrament before death claimed her.[31]

After baptism, a child faced a second rite of passage with the sacrament of first communion. Little is said in the correspondence regarding the first communions of the O'Connell children. The first three O'Connell boys all made their first communion on 21 June, the feast of St Aloysius, the patron saint of their school, Clongowes Wood College. Mary encouraged Danny to follow this tradition as well. She took an active interest in his religious education, demanding to know the name of his director, his number at school and 'every particular'. The feast of St Aloysius passed, however, without Danny attending communion. Instead the fourteen-year-old first received the sacrament on 31 July, the feast day of Ignatius of Loyola, the patron saint of the Jesuits. The reasons for the delay are unclear. Mary herself never knew why the child waited. She hoped, however, that it was not due to 'neglect or foolish scruples'.[32]

Attending mass and receiving communion was a meaningful part of the O'Connell family's religious life. To partake of communion, it was necessary to be free of sin, a goal achieved by attending confession regularly. Alluding to communion, Mary wrote to O'Connell in 1825, 'Kate and I have been doing good this morning as *well* as you. Betsey was too *scrupulous* to go without being three or four times at confession. She will I trust go on Christmas day at the latest.'[33] Although Mary went to mass regularly, it was only after 1809 that O'Connell began to attend mass nearly every Sunday, scheduling his travel and business around the service. 'I really would not lose Mass for any consideration,' he wrote to his wife. 'No man has so much right to be grateful to Providence as I have.'[34] Should Sunday mass be missed, attendance on another day seemed to be acceptable.[35]

The mass as Irish Catholics know it today took form in the years following the Famine. Attending church in pre-Famine Ireland was very different. Due to restrictive penal laws, most chapels in pre-Famine Ireland were unadorned. Lavish displays, flowers, singing and music were a rarity. The buildings used for mass often served as market places or meeting houses as well. These simple chapels, with poor roofs and mud-packed floors, were merely mass-houses, not churches—places where mass was said on Sundays and holy days but that had little spiritual meaning within the community otherwise.[36]

As the nineteenth century progressed, however, the chapel became the 'heart and hub' of the Church in Ireland. Built in areas of high accessibility, the local chapel was the central point of any community.[37] Mary frequently attended mass at Townsend Street or at the Church Street Chapel in Dublin. The presence of a chapel within a community was a determining factor for Mary in choosing a place to live when journeying abroad. For example, when house-hunting in England, Mary suggested Ryde in the Isle of Wight, because it was cheap and the society good. The final selection of the place, however, rested on the question of whether 'there is a Catholic chapel in the town or neighbourhood'. Only if this condition were met would she consider it their 'best plan to spend the summer months there'.[38]

In November 1834 O'Connell attended mass for the first time in the newly erected St Andrew's in Westland Row, the parish church for Merrion Square and one of the first Emancipation Churches.[39] 'It is large and airy but not at all cold, not a single blast of cold air can get in whilst its size will keep it cool in summer. It is quite a blessing to have such a church near us, darling.'[40] The arrival of 'big chapels' or churches such as these marked a turning point in the history of the Catholic Church in Ireland. As the nineteenth century continued, religious practice in Ireland moved away from traditional folk religion to a more modern, orthodox Roman Catholicism.[41]

Occasionally mass was celebrated in the O'Connell household. When Rev. L'Estrange visited Merrion Square, the family heard mass frequently, sometimes as often as three times in a week. During a stay in Mallow in 1814, Mary 'gladly accepted' the offer of a Mr Burke from Cashel to say mass at their house. At Derrynane, a Mr Teahan and Mr O'Flaherty sometimes offered their services.[42] By 1827 O'Connell was determined to obtain the services of a priest at Derrynane. 'The house cannot remain without one,' he told Mary.[43] In the end, Mary had little need for a priest at Derrynane for she departed Kerry in January 1828 and was rarely there again until 1830. By this time, her nephew Charles Connor had been ordained a priest and served Derrynane as chaplain for the summer of 1830. No more mention is made in the correspondence of a resident priest at Derrynane; the *Catholic Directory* of 1836 lists Patrick O'Connell as the parish priest there.[44]

Like first communion and first confession, the sacrament of confirmation was another rite of passage in the life of an Irish Catholic and most

were confirmed at some time in their lives.[45] For girls it was especially relevant. From early childhood, young girls were groomed for their future role
in society as wives and mothers. Whereas the childhood and adolescence
of boys included marks of growth and progression towards manhood, for
a girl this preparatory period between the ages of five and seventeen was a
time in which she had no real place or role in society. Religious confirmation, and the general commotion surrounding it, may have acted as a filler
during this interval before a girl's coming out.[46] Much fuss was made over
the confirmation of a child, which generally occurred around the age of
ten or eleven. Upon Ellen O'Connell's confirmation, Mary gave her
daughter permission to write to her father. The girl delighted in informing him, 'I have been longing to write to you ever since I got my new name
that I might have the pleasure of signing it.' She signed herself 'Ellen
Bridget O'Connell'.[47] Betsey and John, being so close in age, were confirmed at the same time in March 1821. The absence of O'Connell at all
three of these occasions suggests that the event was perhaps more exciting
and special to the child than to the parent. On both occasions, O'Connell
was informed only after the event had taken place.[48]

Society viewed marriage as another significant rite of passage. The
church attempted to regulate both the choice of marriage partner and the
procedures by which a couple was joined. Marriage was forbidden in cases
where one partner had been previously married or was currently promised
to another, the couple was too closely related (i.e. consanguinity as far as
third cousins) or the parents of the couple refused permission. The last
could be overlooked if consent was unreasonably withheld. Furthermore,
the Church discouraged marriage with a Protestant or between those who
could not financially support a family. The marriage must be performed
by the couple's parish priest, by a clergyman authorized by him, or by the
bishop of the diocese. Marriage in another parish required a certificate
from the couple's parish priest. Priests were strictly forbidden to marry
anyone outside of their own parish unless given the proper authorization.[49]

Many couples, Mary and O'Connell included, sought a means of
evading such restrictions. They chose the method most often used by
those attempting to avoid Church rules—a clandestine marriage.
Generally performed by a 'couple-beggar' or suspended clergyman, the
clandestine marriage, though condemned, was not invalid, for the civil
law made no distinction between a parish priest and an 'irregular clergyman'. Clandestine marriages, however, were looked upon with disapproval

due to the lack of publicity surrounding the ceremony. A commitment made in secret was a fragile one, allowing a husband more freedom to desert his new bride, leaving any children from the union dependants of the state.[50] Still, such marriages were fairly frequent. The registers of eleven couple-beggars who conducted weddings in Dublin between 1799 and 1844 record an estimated 30,000 such unions.[51]

The six sacraments discussed above affected the lives of most Catholics in Ireland. The seventh sacrament was that of Holy Orders for men entering the priesthood. The O'Connell letters allow an interesting look at the journey towards this unique rite of passage as they detail the story of Mary's nephew, Charles Connor, in his struggle to find his niche.

Charles's mother was Betsey Connor, Mary's sister, who married O'Connell's law partner, James Connor. Betsey died in January 1815 from complications relating to the birth of her last child. She left seven children, ranging in age from six to nineteen years old, along with the newborn infant. In or around June 1819 her husband died as well, placing the Connor children in a difficult financial situation. The burden of the Connors' predicament fell squarely on O'Connell's shoulders and he set about arranging their financial matters. For many years thereafter, O'Connell saw to the boys' education, attempted to arrange the girls' marriages and struggled to find each Connor son a lucrative profession. As the case of the second son, Charles Connor, demonstrates, settling the children was not always a simple matter.

In November 1823, at the age of twenty-two, Charles left Ireland for London where, with a strong recommendation from O'Connell in hand, he hoped to find employment. By Christmas, Mary reported to her husband that Charles had joined her in Southampton. 'As the poor fellow had no situation as yet in London, I asked him to spend the Christmas holidays with us.' She further informed O'Connell that Charles was 'an excellent creature and most religious'.[52] With his cousin Maurice O'Connell Charles returned to London, where, Mary believed, 'it would be of the greatest service to him to move in the Society which I hear from every Person is of the very best kind in this Town and neighbourhood'.[53] Despite Mary's firm belief that Charles would 'get a situation' in which he would 'give his employer every satisfaction', the young man wrote to her in late January that no position could be found. Mary transcribed her nephew's words in a letter to O'Connell:

> I bear this disappointment with resignation. The fact is I do not regret it as I have entertained very seriously the notion which you intimated to me my uncle formed of my entering the Church. Believe me I am in perfect earnest. If I have your opinion that it would be wise I shall forthwith set off for Dublin, thence with my uncle's recommendation to Maynooth as soon as he pleases.[54]

Obviously, Mary and O'Connell had discussed this possibility of a religious vocation for Charles before, and Mary had apparently intimated as much to her young charge over the Christmas holiday. She was delighted at the direction in which Charles's thoughts had turned and she resolved immediately to write to him her most zealous encouragement as well as direct him to return to Southampton; the sooner he left the temptations of London the better. To O'Connell she wrote, 'I am fully convinced he possesses everything necessary for embracing a clerical life. He is truly religious and extremely well disposed, and I have not a doubt should it be the will of God to call him to his ministry, he will be an ornament and acquisition to the Church.'[55]

O'Connell was thrilled with Mary's news—and probably relieved that yet another Connor had finally been settled—replying, 'May the great God guide him for his holy service ... Tell him from me to consult his conscience and his God and if he feels strength to dedicate himself entirely to the sweet yoke of religion let him do so.' Furthermore, O'Connell offered 'cheerfully' to pay the boy's expenses to Dublin and to write to Maynooth about getting him 'on the establishment'.[56]

By the first of March Charles was in Dublin. On the twelfth of that month, as his uncle had arranged, he was received by Dr Murray, the archbishop of Dublin from 1823 and a former president of St Patrick's College, Maynooth. Not having sufficient Latin or Greek, the young man was sent to Tralee to study. Once he reached proficiency in these two subjects, he would be allowed to enter the seminary at Maynooth.[57]

St Patrick's College at Maynooth was opened in the autumn of 1795, a direct consequence of an act of parliament which allowed the endowment of seminaries in Ireland. Previously, the necessity of attending college in France or Spain ensured that most priests came from a high social stratum.[58] The college contended that the majority of its students came from middle class backgrounds, but the rolls list most students as farmers, an occupation covering many classes and incomes.[59]

The training available at Maynooth does not appear to have been drastically different from that on offer at other educational institutions. It is widely held, however, that a Maynooth education was narrower, more functional and 'calculated to foster severe moral attitudes and a puritanical outlook on human life in general'.[60] Students spent between six and seven years at Maynooth, during which time their education and lifestyle was imbued with monastic discipline.[61]

In 1827 O'Connell wrote to Mary of his hopes that Charles Connor be 'priested' so that he might remain a curate in Tralee where he could attend to his siblings. A curate could begin his career making around £50 annually, a salary equivalent to that of starting army ensigns, doctors and lawyers. A parish priest could make from £200 to £500 per year, and a bishop from £500 to £1000.[62] Whether Charles was ready to be ordained in 1827 or O'Connell was merely planning ahead is not clear. In 1830 Mary's nephew became chaplain at Derrynane Abbey for the summer. As students generally spent about six years in training, it can be assumed that Derrynane was Charles's first assignment.[63] He later served as curate of Sandyford and Glencullen in County Dublin. Charles Connor died in 1861 at the age of sixty, having served as a priest for at least thirty-one years.

Religion permeated the lives and actions of Irish Catholics on more than just the occasions of the sacraments discussed above. The nineteenth century was characterized by a particular religious zeal within both the Catholic and Protestant Churches.[64] Politics and nationalism aside, for the O'Connells, like most Irish Catholics, continued religious education, prayers, devotions and Lenten obligations were all a part of everyday life. Moreover, the O'Connells actively encouraged others to join their religion; and they consciously surrounded themselves with those sharing the same beliefs.

Formal institutions for catechetical education were only beginning to be developed at the beginning of the nineteenth century. By 1820 improvement in catechetical instruction became a main objective of the Catholic Church and evidence suggests that the Irish were fairly well-educated with regard to their religion. Priests taught through their sermons or held Sunday schools; pay schools gave religious instruction; and, of course, children learned the catechism at home.[65]

Religious education in the home naturally requires a strong influence on the part of the mother. For most religious women, motherhood was viewed as a 'project in salvation'. A mother's role was to educate her offspring in the ways of the Church in the hopes of gaining their eternal salvation. The methods of teaching involved not only familiarizing the child with the rules and laws of the religious faith but setting a living example which they could follow. In 1813, for instance, Mary O'Connell kept her children home from school on St Patrick's Day in keeping with a strict observance of the holy days. As a result, Maurice did not receive his usual high marks for his schoolwork that week. The incident demonstrates Mary's belief that the children's religious development took precedence over their secular education.[66]

Catechism was taught in the O'Connell home and covered a large span of years during the child's upbringing. In 1816 Mary writes of John learning his catechism very well.[67] In addition to religious education in the home, the O'Connell boys were subject to formal religious training at Clongowes Wood College. Alongside history, geography, philosophy, languages, mathematics and science, the college claimed that 'Unceasing care is taken to convey to the minds of the pupils solid instructions on the principles of religion, and to engage their hearts to the observance of its precepts.'[68]

As Mary strove to educate her children in the ways of their religion, she also chose to enrich her own knowledge through continued education and prayer under the guidance of a religious director. Seán Connolly writes that during the early nineteenth century complaints abounded regarding the actions of many Catholic priests who 'neglected basic pastoral duties, failing to preach regularly, to provide … religious instructions … or to ensure that their parishioners fulfilled their obligatory religious duties'.[69] The O'Connell correspondence, however, reveals no such laxity: both Mary and Daniel held their directors in the highest of esteem. Mary frequently met with Rev. L'Estrange in Dublin and also had a religious director during her time in France.

It is also clear from the correspondence that Mary kept her own books on catechetical instruction. In addition, her regular attendance at mass allowed her the benefit of religious instruction in the form of the priest's sermons. She wrote to O'Connell of one such sermon at Townsend Street Chapel, describing the 'beautiful panegyric' given on St Patrick by 'a young gentleman of the name of McCabe' who 'at the same time gave the

Education Society a great dressing. He called upon the rich and the middling classes to lose no time in uniting to do away the danger that was abroad. Proselytism was the Bible hawkers' view and not the religious education of the poor of Ireland.'[70] Ten days later, at the Church Street Chapel, she listened as Rev. Michael Bernard Keogh, a popular preacher and parish priest of Howth, 'gave the Bible *hawkers* and the Education Society a great dressing'.[71]

Most likely Mary was referring to the Society for Promoting the Education of the Poor in Ireland, usually known as the Kildare Place Society. Founded in 1811 by an interdenominational committee, the society's goal was to form schools 'divested of all sectarian distinctions in Christianity'. In reality, according to D.H. Akenson, these 'religiously neutral' schools, formed by Anglican clergy and landlords who received funding from the society, 'inevitably had a strong Anglican flavour'. Although originally open to the idea, Roman Catholics gradually came to see these schools as proselytizing institutions. In the 1820s especially, O'Connell (formerly a Society member) and the Catholic clergy led the campaign against these schools.[72] The sermons mentioned by Mary were an obvious attack on the Society as well as the evangelical movement which came to dominate the Church of Ireland during this period. The evangelicals worked to convert Catholics to their faith through the formation of societies and the distribution of bibles. This, of course, only heightened the strain between the two Churches and their followers.[73] Furthermore, it provoked the spirit of reform that characterized the Catholic Church in early nineteenth-century Ireland. As a result of these reforms and women's efforts to continue their own education and to instruct their husbands and children, Mary and her family made up part of what was perhaps the most religiously well-educated generation of Catholics in Irish history.[74]

During the nineteenth century the Church placed an increasing emphasis on the emotional side of religion. Private prayers, or devotions, were encouraged, and communal services carried strong, moving themes. Devotions, consisting of acts of piety, generally prayers, were believed to give a physical expression of one's will to serve God. As a member of this 'devotional revolution', Mary, in carrying out her religious faith, relied heavily on private prayer, and she regularly attended services where she participated in public devotions.[75]

Concern for her soul and those of her loved ones was a prime motivation for Mary's prayer and spirituality. She worried lest her prayers were not worthy of answer. As Morgan set off on his first military assignment she prayed for his safety, confiding in O'Connell, 'I wish I was as deserving of the favour of Providence as you think me however if truest affection and I may add adoration of a husband and children entitle me I do indeed merit the protection of Heaven.'[76] If conflict arose between Mary and her children, she turned to prayer to resolve it. On one occasion when Betsey, then fourteen, was being particularly difficult, Mary found it useless to talk to the young girl. She instead found solace in prayer.[77]

Weather permitting, Mary attended prayer services outside the home.[78] Yet she also prayed at home and encouraged her family to follow suit. From early ages the young O'Connell children said their prayers, either to the governess or to their mother at bedtime.[79] Special intentions for family members filled the family's prayers. O'Connell often asked for inclusion in his wife's prayers. During Lent in 1816, O'Connell's first Lent upon his full return to practising Catholicism, he asked his wife to pray for him. He begged the favour again when the family departed for France in 1822.[80] Any family problem or difficulty was an occasion for prayer. As stated earlier, Morgan's departure with the military was a cause for much family prayer as was O'Connell's trial in 1831 and the return of any family member in the parliamentary elections.[81]

Most obviously, prayer served to console the family in times of sickness. Even when he considered himself a deist, O'Connell believed in the benefits and comforts of a strong faith when a loved one fell ill. 'If I were a religionist', he wrote to Mary, who was suffering from a serious pregnancy-related illness, 'I should spend every moment in praying for you—and this miserable philosophy which I have taken up and been proud of—in the room of religion, affords me now no consolation in my misery.'[82] Mary, on the other hand, willingly placed her trust in God when illness plagued her or a family member. When her brother Edward fell ill in 1808, the family expected that his end was near. 'May God restore him to us,' Mary told her husband, 'On his divine Will I place all my confidence, and for the worst I am prepared.'[83] As O'Connell's faith grew stronger, he too placed his trust in God in times of sickness. Discussing the illness of his uncle Hunting Cap with Mary, O'Connell wrote, 'May the great God bestow on him eternal happiness.'[84]

Symbolic acts of sacrifice were another way in which the O'Connell family carried out their religious convictions. Lent, for example, with its rules and fasting, became a topic in the correspondence between Mary and Daniel every spring. To fast involved taking but one full meal a day; to abstain was to refrain from a certain kind of food. The *Catholic Directory* for 1836, the first published, listed the days of fasting on one meal as: Fridays and Saturdays in Advent; quarter tense, or Ember Days; Days of Lent, except Sundays; Vigils of Nativity and Pentecost; Vigil of Saints Peter and Paul; the feast of the Assumption and All Saints Day. Days of abstinence from meat were all Saturdays and Sundays in Lent and the Feast of Saint Mark.[85] Many believed that some kind of moral leeway was granted to those who fasted and prayed regularly.[86]

Although Mary encouraged her family to hold to their Lenten obligations, she sometimes became worried at O'Connell's zealous keeping of the fast. Her letters frequently scolded him for his too strict observance. 'At all events,' she wrote to him on one occasion,

> while on circuit, I think you ought to relax in some degree. Wednesday, Friday and Saturday would be quite sufficient for you to fast from breakfast. To be from nine o'clock in the morning to perhaps ten at night without eating a morsel in a cold court-house is more than any constitution (however good) will be able to bear.

She begged him to promise that he would give up fasting should he find it disagreed with him. O'Connell assured her in his reply that though fasting 'fatigues me sometimes a little ... it agrees perfectly with me'.[87] Indeed O'Connell continued through the years to observe the Lenten rules of fasting and always found that 'it is actually of use to my health'.[88] Mary's persistent concern led O'Connell to accuse teasingly in 1824, 'there is leave for meat this Lent in Dublin and I suspect that a certain cocknosed woman of my acquaintance ... wrote to a priest at Townsend Street Chapel'.[89] O'Connell's suspicions were correct. Mary had in fact written to Patrick Coleman requesting a dispensation for her husband, which was readily agreed to by the priest.

> The lines you lately sent me needed no apology. Every attention has been and shall continue to be paid to your request. I agree with you that our Friend's health is of too much importance not merely to his Family, but as you say to his Country and I shall add to Religion, that his Constitution should be trifled with.[90]

The rules of Lenten obligation varied, depending on where one lived. Generally, the use of eggs or meat was not allowed except on Sundays. Mary noted that the rules in Cork were stricter than those in Dublin. For Maurice, at Clongowes in the Diocese of Kildare, meat was never allowed even on Sundays.[91] Sometimes dispensations were given. 'Hard labour, travelling, long journeys, decrepit old age, extreme poverty, infirmity, pregnancy and after birth, exempt persons from the obligation of fasting, but they should abstain,' the *Catholic Directory* advised. Dispensations were not to be granted by anyone other than a confessor or pastor.[92] In 1818 Mary allowed her daughter Ellen and her niece Ricarda to eat meat only 'with the leave of their Directors'. She herself would abstain that week. In 1820, leave was granted in Dublin for the consumption of meat every day but Wednesday. O'Connell told Mary he would consult his physician and fast only as directed. During Lent in 1824 O'Connell assured his wife that he was suffering no inconvenience at all as his director, Rev. Coleman, encouraged him to take milk in his tea. Coupled with a large quantity of dry toast every morning, O'Connell 'felt no kind of effect whatsoever from the Lent save continuing to grow fat'.[93]

Still, most were happy when Lent was over. Easter brought relief from the harsh regimen of fasting and abstinence. A dinner with family and friends marked the celebration of Easter Sunday and the end of the Lenten obligations. The festivities included indulging in previously forbidden delights such as meat and sweets, as well as congratulating each other on the successful fulfilment of the fast and penance.[94]

The successful completion of Lent required the fulfilment of the Easter duty as well. This was especially important to Mary, who frequently reminded her children and husband of their obligation.[95] Easter duty involved confessing and receiving communion at least once annually, usually at or around the time of Easter. After 1816 O'Connell joined Mary in keeping a careful vigil over their children's performance of this important task. Though they did not seem to force the children to carry out their obligation, they made references to the matter in their letters. This constant surveillance perhaps propelled the O'Connell children into attending confession and communion.[96]

The sacraments, religious education, prayer and ritual all permeated the lives of the O'Connell family. Faith brought solace in times of need and promised redemption in the hereafter. As time passed, O'Connell grew more religious than any other member of the family. While Mary and the children were away in France it was O'Connell's turn to remind them to take communion regularly.[97]

On at least one occasion, he and Mary attempted to counsel a Protestant woman considering converting to Catholicism. Mary first wrote to her husband on the subject in early May 1823 while in Tours. The woman, the wife of a naval captain, was 'making a great noise amongst the Prodestants [*sic*] in consequence of her constant attendance during Lent to the Sermons preached in the Cathedral'. The woman's husband forbade her to go there anymore but Mary, her confidante, was 'convinced the time is not very distant when she will declare her sentiments very freely'. The woman revealed that she firmly believed in the doctrine of the Catholic faith and requested books of instruction from Mary, which Mary eagerly agreed to lend. Mary also promised to introduce the woman to her religious director for, as she told O'Connell, 'he is of all others the best qualified for the instruction of a Convert'. Obviously Mary spoke of O'Connell frequently and fervently to the woman and, delighted to inform O'Connell of this new friendship, she wrote, 'I give you this intelligence Darling knowing how you will rejoice at the return of even one strayed sheep to the fold. Mrs. Thorton ... wishes much to know you not more for your Patriotism than for your piety.'[98] O'Connell responded enthusiastically to Mary's report regarding her new Protestant friend. He advised Mary to tell the woman:

> ... the best way to be a Catholic is to excel in the performance of every duty. Mildness and attention towards everybody. Her husband should perceive by a thousand little attentions and those manners which sweeten life that his wife was rendered the better woman by embracing a better religion. There are a thousand cares in a family which may be performed in the spirit of the most perfect Christian charity and would go farther to soften down all opposition to the public profession of the Catholic faith than anything else.[99]

O'Connell encouraged his wife to cultivate the woman's confidence. He instructed her to use his 'hints ... discreetly or not at all as you think fit'. He continued:

> As you are in her confidence you will do right to suggest this as the most easy mode to overcome opposition and perhaps to have the still greater happiness of getting her husband to think more seriously of the Catholic religion when he sees its mild and gentle precept making the performance of every duty more light and cheerful.

O'Connell assured his wife that the woman was in his prayers.[100] Although there is no other mention in the correspondence between Mary and O'Connell of attempts to convert others to Catholicism, the enthusiasm with which they greeted the task in the above incident is striking.

The O'Connells also expressed their religious beliefs in their attempts to surround themselves with those of the same faith. The proximity of other Catholics was an important consideration to O'Connell in choosing a location where Mary and the children might reside while the family attempted to economize. Exeter, for example, was one spot that appealed to O'Connell, for 'There will be no difficulty in becoming acquainted with any Catholics of that vicinity we please … There are many Catholics there as I understand.'[101] Hiring Catholic labourers was also preferable to Mary and O'Connell. When screening painters for work on the house in Merrion Square, Mary provided two names to O'Connell and asserted that both were of the Catholic faith.[102] Moreover, it was important to O'Connell that his children marry Catholics. As he told Mary in one letter in reaction to a potential suitor for his daughter Kate, he did not want his grandchildren 'doomed' to a fate other than Catholicism. He insisted that they should be raised in the Catholic faith and any would-be suitor necessarily must be Catholic.[103]

According to Seán Connolly, many Irish Catholics fell short of performing the minimum obligatory religious practices. Though most Catholics performed their Easter duty, 'it appears to have been unusual to confess or receive communion more than two or three times a year at most. Large numbers reached adulthood without having been confirmed.'[104] Connolly further reports that in pre-Famine Ireland,

> religion was something which intruded on their [i.e. the majority of Irish Catholics'] lives with considerably less frequency than was to be the case in later decades. When it did so, furthermore, it was generally in circum-

stances which did little to inspire in them that awe and reverence by which religion, or its representative, could hope to intimidate and persuade.[105]

Were the O'Connells unusual? Does their careful attention to religious duty reflect an urban influence. A higher income bracket? Perhaps it reflects both. In County Tipperary in the eighteenth and nineteenth centuries, Kevin Whelan has found, deep class-based differences existed in the ways in which Irish Catholics carried out their religious beliefs.[106] As outside influences gained strength throughout Ireland and the standard of living improved, attachment to traditional attitudes and customs regarding religion began to change. Based in Dublin, moving in politically enlightened circles, with a rising income and growing prestige, the O'Connell family sought all avenues of respectability, including distancing themselves from a more primitive and traditional religious past.

The purchase of private seating in Catholic chapels was one means families used to demonstrate these differences. Separate seating for 'quality' was common. The money used to purchase these seats went toward the upkeep of the chapel or the building of a new one. As early as 1806 the O'Connells were purchasing seats in their chapel in Kerry. By 1817, when Mary was in Clifton, it appeared to be common practice for the family. 'I returned the priest's visit on Tuesday. He is rather a gentlemanly man, reserved in his manner and very handsome. I am to pay by the month for our accommodation at the chapel.' Furthermore, the prospect of a new chapel being built on Pembroke Street in 1824 pleased Mary because of its convenient location and the opportunity such a place would provide for 'a pew all to ourselves'.[107] The issue of private seating reveals that despite the seemingly united front which emerged amongst Catholics during the struggle for Emancipation and Repeal, social divisions did exist within the ranks.[108]

The modernizing influence of the Catholic Church was not felt in all regions of the country at the same time, nor in all classes. The diffusion of reform practices and new educational techniques first affected only the core areas of Irish Catholicism—namely the south-east region and the urban centres. In more remote areas, especially the Gaelic-speaking communities, a vernacular religion in the form of wakes, patterns and other festivals continued to resist the modernization process. These traditional practices were common occurrences for many years in County Kerry and O'Connell was often in attendance. Yet by and large, the family—most specifically its female members—participated in none of the traditional or 'superstitious' rituals of the Gaelic peasantry. Instead, as part of the growing Catholic middle class apparent in towns throughout the country, the O'Connells were part of the modernization of the Catholic Church in Ireland.[109] And Mary, as the keeper of the hearth by which most of the family's religious rituals and practices took place, played a key role in that effort.

Afterword

M ary O'Connell is not a traditional biographical subject. She was not a feminist, a radical, a writer, or a visionary. Her marriage to Daniel O'Connell made her political only insofar as she espoused the political ideals of her husband. She did not write or speak out on any political topic except in private letters to her family. Her political influence on her husband was, at best, minimal. Mary's prime functions in life were in the domestic sphere. Childbearing, child-rearing, and housekeeping activities were her main occupations. She embraced the patriarchal assumptions of her day regarding her 'place'. Most importantly, she valued her role as mother and wife.

This is the role that most Irish women filled during the early nineteenth century, but the story of Mary O'Connell can in no way be considered representative of women in Ireland during this time. As a member of the middle class, her lifestyle and experience was certainly far different from that of the majority of Irish women. The stories of the women of the lower classes remain relatively unstudied due to a lack of source material. The women who wrote, who kept diaries and who corresponded diligently, were generally the women of the middle and upper classes.

If the lives of peasant women have been almost entirely ignored by historians, women of the middle class have fared only marginally better. Existing historiography concerning Catholic women revolves primarily around the experiences of those with religious vocations. Other scholarship in Irish women's history has delved into such issues as philanthropy, gender, education, piracy, industry, prostitution, infanticide, domestic service, agriculture, housework, immigration, widowhood, spinsterhood, food preparation, labour and unions, divorce, arts and crafts, crime, legislation, insanity, rape, domestic violence, poverty, childbirth, medicine, folklore, property, inheritance, marriage and feminism.[1] Little research has been conducted on the personal lives of women. Existing studies on marriage, for example, tend to focus on inheritance law and the legal rights of the participants rather than the actual experiences of the parties involved—their perceptions, expectations, disappointments.

There is hope, however. The study of women's history in Ireland is, in the words of Maria Luddy, in a 'stage of recovery'.[2] Maryann Gialanella Valiulis and Mary O'Dowd agree that historians have 'entered a different phase in women's history'. The field has advanced 'from the emphasis on great women to the "add women and stir" model where the broad historical outlines remain the same except that women's participation is noted'. Valiulis and O'Dowd argue that historians must move beyond this stage in order to find 'the true revolutionary potential to challenge what we think is historically important, what we consider the defining moments in history, and the time frame which we use in writing the historical narrative'.[3]

It is through the individual stories of women that these defining moments will emerge. This account of the world of Mary O'Connell is only one attempt to identify and explore the themes central to one woman's life. Until further research is carried out in relation to these themes—marriage, mothering, domesticity, worship, and others—our understanding of the history of women in Ireland cannot evolve. Source material is still 'out there'. The letters of Mary O'Connell were overlooked for years. Their only value was thought to be in their political content and their insights into the mind of the Liberator. Yet Mary's letters reveal a virtually unexplored world in the history of nineteenth-century Ireland. This is a world in need of much scholarly attention.

Notes

INTRODUCTION

1   The bulk of the collection is housed at the National Library of Ireland, Dublin. A smaller collection of papers is located in the University College Dublin Archives.

2   W.J. Fitzpatrick, ed., *The Correspondence of Daniel O'Connell*, 2 vols (London, 1888).

3   M.R. O'Connell, ed., *The Correspondence of Daniel O'Connell*, vol. 1, 1792–1814 (Shannon, 1972), p. viii.

4   Edwards, *Daniel O'Connell and His World* (London, 1975), pp. 22, 60.

5   M. MacDonagh, *The Life of Daniel O'Connell* (London, 1903), p. 118.

6   O'Ferrall, *Daniel O'Connell* (Dublin, 1981), pp. 22, 76–7.

7   Helen Mulvey, 'The Correspondence of Daniel and Mary O'Connell', in *The Correspondence of Daniel O'Connell*, vol. 1, ed. M.R. O'Connell , p. xx.

8   See O. MacDonagh, *O'Connell: The Life of Daniel O'Connell, 1775–1847* (London, 1991).

9   Edith Gelles' biography of Abigail Adams provided me with an excellent model on which to pattern my own work. See *Portia: The World of Abigail Adams* (Bloomington, Indiana, 1992).

10 See Maryann Gialanella Valiulis and Mary O'Dowd, eds, *Women and Irish History* (Dublin, 1997).

11 Dorothea Herbert, *Retrospections of Dorothea Herbert, 1770–1806*, with commentary by L.M. Cullen (Dublin, 1988); L.A. Clarkson, 'Love, Labour and Life: Women in Carrick-on-Suir in the Late Eighteenth Century', *Irish Economic and Social History* 20 (1993): 18–24; Stella Tillyard, *Aristocrats: Caroline, Emily, Louisa and Sarah Lennox 1740–1832* (London, 1994); Kevin O'Neill, '"Almost a Gentlewoman": Gender and Adolescence in the Diary of Mary Shackleton', in *Chattel, Servant or Citizen: Women's Status in Church, State and Society*, eds Mary O'Dowd and Sabine Wichert (Belfast, 1995); Mary McNeill, *The Life and Times of Mary Ann McCracken 1770–1866* (Dublin, 1960, rpr. Belfast, 1988); Marie-Louise Legg, ed., *The Synge Letters: Bishop Edward Synge to His Daughter Alicia, Roscommon to Dublin, 1746–1752* (Dublin, 1996).

12 See Daniel Corkery, *The Hidden Ireland: The Gaelic Poetry of Eighteenth-Century Munster* (Dublin, 1925, rpr. 1967). See also L.M. Cullen, *The Hidden Ireland: Reassessment of a Concept* (Dublin, 1988).

13 S.J. Connolly, 'Approaches to the History of Irish Popular Culture', *Bullán* 2/2 (Winter/Spring 1996): 90.

14 Ibid., pp. 89, 90. See also Peter Burke, *Popular Culture in Early Modern Europe* (London, 1978).

15 Kevin Whelan, *The Tree of Liberty: Radicalism, Catholicism and the Construction of Irish Identity, 1760–1830* (Cork, 1996), p. 3. See also David Dickson's essay 'Middlemen' in *Penal Era and Golden Age: Essays in Irish History, 1690–1800*, eds Thomas Bartlett and D.W. Hayton (Belfast, 1979), pp. 162–85.

16 O. MacDonagh, *O'Connell*, p. 4.

17 Ibid., p. 6; Whelan, *Tree of Liberty*, p. 7.

18 Whelan, *Tree of Liberty*, pp. 15–17.

19 O. MacDonagh, *O'Connell*, p. 3.

20 Connolly, 'Popular Culture', p. 94.

21 W.J. O'Neill Daunt, *Personal Recollections of Daniel O'Connell*, vol. 1 (London, 1848), pp. 14–15, quoted in Gerard Murphy, 'The Gaelic Background', in *Daniel O'Connell: Nine Centenary Essays*, ed. Michael Tierney (Dublin, 1949), pp. 2–4.

22 Murphy, 'Gaelic Background', p. 6.

23 These laws effectively banned Catholics from participation in almost all forms of public or civic life. Property and inheritance rights for Catholics were also limited and, after 1729, the right to vote was effectively taken away from Catholic freeholders. As a result, by 1800 Catholics, making up three quarters of the population, owned only 14 per cent of Irish land. Though often loosely enforced, the Penal Laws remained a constant source of friction between the Catholic majority and the ruling Protestant minority.

24 Murphy, 'Gaelic Background', pp. 15, 18.

25 Mary E. Daly, *Social and Economic History of Ireland since 1800* (Dublin, 1981), p. 111; D. George Boyce, *Nineteenth-Century Ireland* (Dublin, 1990), pp. 11, 15.

26 O. MacDonagh, *O'Connell*, pp. 85–7, 188.

27 Mary to O'Connell, 12 August 1803, University College Dublin, O'Connell Papers, P12/B/1 (hereafter cited as UCD).

CHAPTER ONE

1 Russell McMorren, *Tralee: A Short History and Guide to Tralee and Environs* (n.p., 1980), pp. 17, 19, 21, 31.

2 Mary and O'Connell frequently referred to Hunting Cap by this appellation.

3 O'Connell to Mary, 26 December 1800, *O'Connell–FitzSimon Papers* microfilm 1620, National Library of Ireland, Dublin (hereafter cited as NLI, FS).

4 O'Connell to Mary, 28 November 1800, NLI, FS 1620.

5 Ibid.

6 Ibid., 24 January, 5 May, 13 June 1801.

7 Ibid., 6 February 1801.

8 Ibid., 21 April 1801.

9 Mary to O'Connell, 24 April 1801, *O'Connell Papers*, Ms. 13650 (1), National Library of Ireland, Dublin (hereafter cited as NLI, Ms.).

10   Ellen O'Connell to O'Connell, 12 June 1801, NLI, Ms. 13645 (3).

11   O'Connell to Mary, 20 June, 7 July 1801, NLI, FS 1620.

12   Ibid., 11 July 1801; Mary to O'Connell, 13 July 1801, UCD, P12/2B/211.

13   O'Connell to Mary, 16 July 1801, NLI, FS 1620.

14   Mary to O'Connell, 2 December 1801, NLI, Ms. 13650 (2).

15   O'Connell to Mary, 8 November 1801, NLI, FS 1620.

16   John O'Connell to O'Connell, [January 1803], NLI, Ms. 13645 (3).

17   Mary to O'Connell, 3 February 1803, NLI, Ms. 13650 (3).

18   O'Connell to Mary, 1 February 1803, NLI, FS 1620.

19   Ibid., 5 February 1803.

20   Mary to O'Connell, 6 February 1803, UCD P12/2B/213.

21   O'Connell to Mary, 8 February 1803, NLI, FS 1620.

22   Ibid., 3 December 1803.

23   John O'Connell to O'Connell, [January 1803], NLI, Ms. 13645 (3).

24   O'Connell to Mary, 3 February 1803, NLI, FS 1620.

25   O'Connell to Mary, [7 April 1803], NLI, FS 1622.

26   Mary to O'Connell, [12 August 1803], UCD P12/B/1.

27   O'Connell to Mary, 9 October 1903, NLI, FS 1620.

28   Mary to O'Connell, 16 April 1805, NLI, Ms. 13650 (9).

29   O'Connell to Mary, 30 November 1803, NLI, FS 1620.

30   Ellen O'Connell, *Ellen O'Connell Recounts Her Father's Life*, NLI, Ms. 1504.

31   Mary to O'Connell, 25 July 1805, NLI, Ms. 13650 (9).

32   Mary to O'Connell, 21 March 1808, UCD P12/2B/220.

33   O'Connell to Mary, 27 March 1808, NLI, FS 1620.

34   Mary to O'Connell, 18 April 1808, NLI, Ms. 13650 (15). See chapter 4 for a more detailed account of the housekeeper's illness.

35   J.L. McCracken, 'The Age of the Stage Coach', in *Travel and Transport in Ireland*, ed. Kevin Nowlan (Dublin, 1973), pp. 47–63; Constantia Maxwell, *Country and Town in Ireland Under the Georges* (Dundalk, 1949), pp. 283–4.

36   Mary to O'Connell, 30 July 1814, NLI 13650 (29); Mary to O'Connell, 1, 2 August 1814, NLI 13650 (30).

37   Maxwell, *Country and Town*, pp. 259–60; Mary to O'Connell, 23 September 1812, UCD P12/2B/225; Mary to O'Connell, 1 October 1812, NLI 13650 (loose).

38   Mary to O'Connell, 23 September 1812, P12/2B/225; 29 September 1812, NLI, Ms. 13650 (25); 1 October 1812, NLI, Ms. 13650 (loose).

39   Mary to O'Connell, 2 August 1814, NLI, Ms. 13650 (30).

40   Mary to O'Connell, 8 August 1814, NLI, Ms. 13650 (31).

41   Mary to O'Connell, 18 September 1809, NLI, Ms. 13650 (19).

42   O'Ferrall, *Daniel O'Connell*, p. 17; Donal McCartney, ed., 'The World of Daniel O'Connell', in *The World of Daniel O'Connell* (Dublin, 1980), pp. 2–3; Donal McCartney, *The Dawning of Democracy: Ireland 1800–1870* (Dublin, 1987), pp. 40–3, 49.

43   Mary E. Daly, 'Late Nineteenth and Early Twentieth Century Dublin', in *The Town in Ireland*, eds D.W. Harkness and M. O'Dowd (Belfast, 1981), pp. 221–2.

44   Peter Somerville-Large, *Dublin: The First Thousand Years* (Belfast, 1988), pp. 194–6, 227; R.B. McDowell, ed., *Social Life in Ireland 1800–1845* (Dublin, 1957), pp. 12, 13.

45   See chapter 3 regarding Mary's maternal health.

46   O. MacDonagh, *O'Connell*, pp. 108, 117.

47   Mary to O'Connell, 27 March 1824, NLI, Ms. 13651 (29).

48   Mary to O'Connell, 7 August 1812, in M.R. O'Connell, ed., *The Correspondence of Daniel O'Connell*, vol. I (Shannon, 1972), p. 304 (hereafter cited as *Correspondence*).

49   Mary to O'Connell, 3 December 1825, NLI, Ms. 13651 (32).

50   Ibid., 16 December 1825 (copy).

51   Mary to O'Connell, 23 March 1814, NLI, Ms. 13650 (29).

52   O'Connell to Mary, 3 February 1815, NLI, FS 1622.

53   O. MacDonagh, *O'Connell*, p. 138.

54   Mrs Morgan John O'Connell, *The Last Colonel of the Irish Brigade* (London, 1892), pp. 253–4.

55   O. MacDonagh, *O'Connell*, p. 143.

56   Ibid., p. 144.

57   See chapter 2 regarding the O'Connell family's financial woes.

58   Ellen O'Connell, *Narrative of a Residence in France*, NLI, FS 1623, vol. I, p. 4.

59   O'Connell to Mary, 3 May 1822, NLI, FS 1621.

60   Ibid., 15, 24 May 1822.

61   Ellen O'Connell, *Narrative*, I, pp. 7, 9, 10, 17.

62   Ibid., pp. 22–3.

63   Ibid., pp. 124, 127, 130.

64   Ibid., II, p. 4

65   Ibid., I, p. 158; O'Connell to James Sugrue, 7 October 1822, NLI, Ms. 5759.

66   Ellen O'Connell, *Narrative*, II, p. [13].

67   Mary to O'Connell, 23 December 1823, NLI, Ms. 13651 (25).

68   Mary to O'Connell, 23, 27 January 1824, NLI, Ms. 13651 (26).

69   Mary to O'Connell, 4 February 1824, NLI, Ms. 13651 (27).

70   Ibid.

71   James O'Connell to O'Connell, 5 February 1824, *Correspondence*, III, p. 22.

72   Mary to O'Connell, 16 September 1825, NLI, Ms. 13651 (30).

73   Mary to O'Connell, 15 April 1825, *Correspondence*, III, p. 146.

74   Ibid., 26 November 1825, p. 204.

75   Mary to O'Connell, 1 December 1825, NLI, Ms. 13651 (32).

76   O. MacDonagh, *O'Connell*, p. 287.

77   O'Connell to Mary, 4 May 1825, NLI, FS 1621.

78   Mary to O'Connell, 7 May 1825, *Correspondence*, I, p. 166.

79   Mary to O'Connell, 2 February 1830, NLI, Ms. 13651 (33); Mary to Daniel Jr, 1 May 1830, NLI, Ms. Accession 4705, box 3; 3 July [1830], NLI, FS 1622.

80   See chapter 3 regarding the settling of the O'Connell children.

81   O'Connell to Mary, 13 September 1825, *Correspondence*, V, p. 332; 30 May 1836, NLI, FS 1621; O'Connell to Richard Barrett, 4 September 1836, *Correspondence*, V, p. 393.

CHAPTER TWO

1   Judith Lewis, *In the Family Way: Childbearing in the British Aristocracy, 1750–1860* (New Brunswick, NJ, 1986), p. 18; S.J. Connolly, 'Family, Love and Marriage: Some Evidence from the Early Eighteenth Century', in *Women in Early Modern Ireland*, eds Mary O'Dowd and Margaret MacCurtain (Edinburgh, 1991), p. 279; Olwen Hufton, *The Prospect Before Her: A History of Women in Western Europe, Vol. 1, 1500–1800* (London, 1995), p. 63; A.P.W. Malcomson, *The Pursuit of the Heiress: Aristocratic Marriage in Ireland, 1750–1820* (Belfast, 1982), pp. 33–9.

2   Randolph Trumbach, *The Rise of the Egalitarian Family* (New York, 1978), p. 3; Lawrence Stone, *The Family, Sex and Marriage in England 1500–1800* (London, 1977), pp. 4, 7.

3   See L.A. Clarkson, 'Love, Labour and Life'; K.H. Connell, 'Marriage in Ireland after the Great Famine: The Diffusion of the Match', *Journal of the Statistical and Social Inquiry Society of Ireland*, XIX (1945–6), pp. 82–103; A.P.W. Malcomson, *The Pursuit of the Heiress*; Connolly, 'Family Love and Marriage', 276–90.

4   Edward Shorter, *The Making of the Modern Family* (London, 1976), p. 120; S.J. Connolly, *Priests and People in Pre-Famine Ireland, 1780–1845* (Dublin, 1982), pp. 194, 196, 199. See chapter 7 of the present work for a more detailed discussion of clandestine marriages.

5   Pat Jalland, *Women, Marriage and Politics 1860–1914* (Oxford, 1986), p. 21; Stone, *Family, Sex and Marriage*, p. 272.

6   Hufton, *Prospect Before Her*, p. 64; Trumbach, *Egalitarian Family*, p. 77; Clarkson, 'Love, Labour and Life', pp. 21–2.

7   Jalland, *Women, Marriage and Politics*, p. 68; O'Connell, *Last Colonel*, p. 243.

8   Stone, *Family, Sex and Marriage*, p. 271.

9   M.R. O'Connell, 'Income and Expenditure', in *Daniel O'Connell, The Man and His Politics* (Dublin, 1990), p. 25.

10   O'Connell to Mary, 24 January 1801, NLI, FS 1620.

11   See chapter 3 for the settling of the O'Connell children.

12   Mary to O'Connell, 12 August 1805, NLI, Ms. 13650 (10).

13   Mary to O'Connell, 11 March 1811, NLI, Ms. 13650 (28).

14   Mary to O'Connell, 16 March 1811, NLI, Ms. 13650 (22).

15   Mary to O'Connell, 28 November 1804, NLI, Ms. 13650 (7).

16   O'Connell to Mary, 23 August 1802, NLI, FS 1620.

17   O'Connell to Mary, 20 October 1802, NLI, Ms. 17070 (1) photocopy.

18   O'Connell to Mary, 28 August 1802, NLI, FS 1620.

19   Ibid., 23 August 1802.

20   O'Connell to Mary, 5 August 1802, NLI, Ms. Accession 4705, box 1.

21   O'Connell to Mary, 1 September 1802, NLI, FS 1622.

22   Mary to O'Connell, 27 August 1802, NLI, FS 1620.

23   O'Connell to Mary, 28 August 1802, NLI, FS 1620.

24   Ibid., 16 November 1802.

25   Ibid., 25 November 1802.

26   Ibid., 27 July 1802.

27   Ibid., 31 July 1802.

28   Ibid., 29 March 1809.

29   Ibid., 8 March 1815.

30   O'Connell to Mary, 1 January 1820, NLI, FS 1621.

31   Mary to O'Connell, 4 January 1820, NLI, Ms. 13651 (20).

32   O'Connell to Mary, 5 April 1810, NLI, FS 1620.

33   Ibid., 19 October 1815.

34   O'Connell to Mary, 20 August 1811, NLI, Ms. 5759; 22, 28 August, NLI, FS 1620.

35   O'Connell to Mary, 23 August 1819, NLI, FS 1621.

36   Mary to O'Connell, 26 August 1819, NLI, Ms. 13651 (18).

37   O'Connell to Mary, 28 August, 12 September 1819, NLI, FS 1621; Mary to O'Connell, 4, 10 September 1819, NLI, Ms. 13651 (19).

38   O. MacDonagh, *O'Connell*, p. 82.

39   Mary to O'Connell, 12 December 1804, NLI, Ms. 13650 (8).

40   Mary to O'Connell, 25 March 1803, UCD P12/2B/215.

41   O'Connell to Mary, 26 December 1822, NLI, FS 1622.

42   Mary to O'Connell, 4 August 1810, NLI, Ms. 13650 (21).

43   O'Connell to Mary, 5 April 1817, NLI, FS 1621.

44   Mary to O'Connell, 4 August 1810, NLI, Ms. 13650 (21).

45   Ibid., 8 September 1810.

46   Mary to O'Connell, 10 August 1814, NLI, Ms. 13650 (31).

47   Mary to O'Connell, 12 April 1816, NLI, Ms. 13651 (6).

48   O'Connell to Mary, 9 April 1817, NLI, FS 1621.

49   Mary to O'Connell, 30 January 1824, NLI, Ms. 13651 (26).

50   Mary to O'Connell, 19 April 1808, NLI, Ms. 13650 (15).

51   O'Connell to Mary, 21 April 1808, NLI, FS 1620.

52   Ibid., 28 March 1809.

53   O'Connell to Mary, 22, 28 May 1804, NLI, Ms. 5759.

54   Ibid., 29 November 1804.

55   O'Connell to Mary, 24 June 1817, NLI, FS 1621.

56   Mary to O'Connell, 22 March 1809, NLI, Ms. 13650 (18); 25 March 1818, NLI, Ms. 13651 (16).

57   Mulvey, 'Daniel and Mary O'Connell', p. xx.

58   See M.R. O'Connell, 'O'Connell and his Family', in *The World of Daniel O'Connell*, ed. Donal McCartney (Dublin, 1980), p. 22; Edwards, *Daniel O'Connell*, pp. 23–4.

59   S.J. Connolly, in his study of marriage in Ireland, writes that 'the [romantic] sentiments expressed in correspondence between spouses cannot always be taken literally', and that many couples paid only 'lip service' to a romantic ideal. Connolly, 'Family, Love and Marriage', p. 281.

60   Diarmaid Ó Muirithe, 'O'Connell in the Irish Folk Tradition', in *Daniel O'Connell: Political Pioneer*, ed. M.R. O'Connell (Dublin, 1991), p. 78.

61   J. J. Lee, 'Daniel O'Connell', in *Political Pioneer*, ed. M.R. O'Connell, pp. 2–3.

62   O'Ferrall, *Daniel O'Connell*, pp. 22–3; O. MacDonagh, *O'Connell*, pp. 641–2; M.R. O'Connell, 'O'Connell and His Family', p. 23.

63 Mary to O'Connell, 5 March 1812, in Fitzpatrick, *Correspondence*, I, pp. 19–20; O'Connell to Mary, 19, 20, 26 April 1825, NLI, FS 1621.

64 O'Connell to Mary, 24 March 1809, NLI, FS 1620.

65 O'Connell to Mary, 29 March, 6 April 1809, NLI, FS 1620.

66 Mary to O'Connell, 16 October 1816, NLI, Ms. 13651 (9). Mary was well aware of her husband's pre-marital dalliances and the monetary support he bestowed upon at least one of the women involved.

67 O'Connell to Mary, 3 August 1820, NLI, FS 1621.

68 O'Connell to Mary, 30 November 1823, *Correspondence*, II, p. 521.

69 O'Connell to Mary, 21 January 1824, NLI, FS 1621.

70 Ellen Courtenay, *A Narrative* (London, 1832), p. v. For a fuller discussion of the Courtenay affair and of the question of O'Connell's marital fidelity, see Erin I. Bishop, 'Was O'Connell Faithful? Ellen Courtenay Revisited', *Eire-Ireland* (Fall/Winter 1996): 58–75.

71 O'Connell to Leslie Grove Jones, 14 January 1832, *Correspondence*, IV, p. 399.

72 O. MacDonagh, *O'Connell*, p. 642; O'Ferrall, *Daniel O'Connell*, pp. 22–3; John J. Horgan, 'O'Connell—The Man', in *Daniel O'Connell: Nine Centenary Essays*, ed. Michael Tierney (Dublin, 1949), p. 276; Denis Gwynn, *Daniel O'Connell and Ellen Courtenay* (Oxford, 1930), pp. 10–11.

73 See Sean O'Faolain, *King of the Beggars* (London, 1938), p. 41.

74 The last mention of Ricarda in the correspondence is in October 1816. There is only one extant letter between November and February. When the correspondence between Mary and Daniel resumes in March 1817, no mention is made of Ricarda, although the antics of Daniel Jr are reported in detail (Mary to O'Connell, 16 October 1816, NLI 13651 (9); Mary to O'Connell, 13 March 1817, NLI 13651 (11)). In a letter dated 5 April 1817, Mary mentions all of the children except Ricarda (NLI 13651 (11)). On the same day O'Connell wrote to Mary regarding his distress over the illness of Daniel Jr. 'I could not indeed I could not bear to be *taken in* about another little darling,' he wrote, possibly referring to the loss of baby Ricarda (O'Connell to Mary, 5 April 1817, NLI, FS 1621).

75 James O'Connell to O'Connell, 18 May 1817, *Correspondence*, II, p. 144.

76 Mary to O'Connell, 12 June 1817, NLI, Ms. 13651 (12).

77 Ibid.

78 O'Connell to Mary, 11 July 1817, NLI, FS 1621.

79 Mulvey, 'Daniel and Mary O'Connell', p. xix.

80 O'Faolain, *King of the Beggars*, p. 228.

81 Fitzpatrick, *Correspondence*, I, p. 51.

82 As late as 1995, Maria Luddy published this excerpt from Mary's letter in a documentary history of women in Ireland under the heading 'A Wife Writes of Her Love to Her Husband'. She too presents only this small section of a lengthy and complex letter. Maria Luddy, *Women in Ireland 1800–1918, A Documentary History* (Cork, 1995), pp. 30–1.

83 Mary to O'Connell, 14 July 1817, NLI, Ms. 13651 (12).

84 O'Connell to Mary, 5 August 1817, *Correspondence*, II, p. 162.

85 Mary to O'Connell, 11 August 1817, NLI, Ms. 13651 (13).

86　See Gwynn, *Daniel O'Connell and Ellen Courtenay*, p. 21.

87　Mulvey, 'Daniel and Mary O'Connell', p. xxii. For a detailed account of O'Connell's financial woes, see M.R. O'Connell, 'Income and Expenditure', pp. 13-29.

88　M.R. O'Connell, 'Income and Expenditure', p. 15.

89　O'Connell to Mary, 23 August 1802, NLI, FS 1620.

90　O'Connell to Mary, 29 November 1804, NLI, Ms. 5759.

91　O'Connell to Mary, 26 March 1807, NLI, FS 1620.

92　Ibid., 12 March 1807.

93　Mary to O'Connell, 15 March 1809, NLI, Ms. 13650 (18); 4 April 1811, NLI, Ms. 13650 (23); 17 July 1815, NLI, Ms. 13651 (3); 29 March 1816, NLI, Ms. 13651 (4).

94　Mary to O'Connell, 19 September 1820, NLI, Ms. 13651 (22).

95　O'Connell to Mary, 1 April 1807, 1 August 1808, 29 March 1813, NLI, FS 1620.

96　M.R. O'Connell, 'Income and Expenditure', p. 16; O'Connell to Denis McCarthy, 20 January 1806, NLI, Ms. 5759.

97　Mary to O'Connell, 18 September 1809, NLI, Ms. 13650 (19).

98　M.R. O'Connell, 'Income and Expenditure', p. 26; O. MacDonagh, *O'Connell*, p. 155.

99　Kevin Whelan argues that the social pressures on old Catholic landed families to be hospitable were particularly intense. See Whelan, 'An Underground Gentry?', p. 21.

100　O'Connell to Mary, 31 March 1806, NLI, FS 1620; Mary to O'Connell, 2 April 1806, UCD P12/2B/216.

101　Throughout my research I have continually been told that Mary hated Kerry. To date I have found no source material that documents this disdain.

102　Mary to O'Connell, 1 April 1807, UCD P12/2B/219; 31 March 1808, NLI, Ms. 13650 (14); 5 April 1808, UCD P12/2B/222; 10 April 1808, UCD P12/2B/224. It is interesting to note that Mary's concern about her husband's tendency to squander money in Kerry virtually disappears from the correspondence after 1829, when receipt of a substantial monetary national testimonial freed O'Connell from all debt. Mary's letters to her son Daniel Jr during the years 1830–2 express delight and excitement at the vacation time spent at Derrynane. NLI, Ms. 13644.

103　Mary to O'Connell, 8 April 1813, NLI, Ms. 13650 (27).

104　Mary to O'Connell, 1 October 1814, NLI, Ms. 13650 (32).

105　O'Connell to Mary, 13 March 1815, NLI, FS 1620.

106　Mary to O'Connell, 14, 16 March 1815, NLI, Ms. 13651 (1); O'Connell to Mary, 17 March 1815, NLI, FS 1620.

107　M.R. O'Connell, 'Income and Expenditure', p. 19.

108　O'Connell to Mary, 26 March 1818, NLI, FS 1621.

109　Ibid., 22 January 1823.

110　M.R. O'Connell, 'Income and Expenditure', p. 25.

111　Mary to O'Connell, 15 October 1820, NLI, Ms. 13651 (23).

112　O'Connell to Mary, 22 March 1821, NLI, FS 1621.

113　Ibid., 5 April 1822.

114　Ibid., 5 April 1821; O'Connell to Ellen O'Connell, 16 October 1821, NLI, FS 1621.

115 James O'Connell to O'Connell, 28 March 1822, *Correspondence*, II, p. 363.

116 Mrs M.J. O'Connell, *Last Colonel*, pp. 261–2.

117 M.R. O'Connell, 'Income and Expenditure', p. 20; O'Connell to Mary, 17 March 1822, NLI, FS 1621.

118 O'Connell to Mary, 31 May 1822, 22 March 1824, NLI, FS 1621.

119 Ibid., 17 January 1823.

120 Ibid., 22 January, 2 April 1823.

121 Ibid., 26 January, 27 February 1824, 1 November 1825.

122 M.R. O'Connell, 'Income and Expenditure', p. 26.

123 O'Connell to Mary, 30 October 1827, NLI, FS 1621.

124 M.R. O'Connell, 'Income and Expenditure', p. 26.

125 Mulvey, 'Daniel and Mary O'Connell', p. xxi.

126 Ellen O'Connell, *Her Father's Life*, NLI, Ms. 1504.

127 O'Connell to Mary, 24 December 1827, NLI, FS 1621.

128 Ibid., 16 January 1824.

129 Ibid., 27 October 1827.

CHAPTER THREE

1 Edward Shorter, in *A History of Women's Bodies* (London, 1983), argues that 'before 1900 or so, femininity was basically a negative concept for most women … a burden with which God had saddled them' (p. xi). Shorter attributes the subordination of women at this time to the burden of childbearing, motherhood and sex-specific disease. Women were not only disadvantaged objectively, but 'subjectively they accepted their disadvantaged status as part of the natural order. They concurred in society's judgement that they were poisonous, diseased, and inferior' (pp. xii, 285). Moreover, they faced pregnancy and childbirth with 'a collective sense of fearfulness' (p. xi). Shorter and other scholars have placed much of the blame for this phenomenon on male obstetricians, who were gradually replacing the female midwife (see Porter and Porter, *Patients' Progress*, Barker-Benfield, *The Horrors of the Half-Known Life*, Smith-Rosenberg, *Disorderly Conduct*, and Douglass-Wood, 'Fashionable Diseases').

2 O'Connell to Mary, 11 November 1802, NLI, Ms. 5759.

3 O'Connell to Mary, 23 November 1802, NLI, FS 1620.

4 Ibid., 30 November 1802. Maurice Leyne, M.D. (d. 1833) was a Tralee physician, educated in Paris. The O'Connell family frequently called upon his services.

5 O'Connell to Mary, 4 December 1802, NLI, FS 1620.

6 Mary to O'Connell, 6 February 1803, UCD P12/2B/213.

7 O'Connell to Mary, 25 November 1802, Fitzpatrick, *Correspondence*, I, pp. 13–14.

8 O'Connell to Mary, 16 August 1804, NLI, Ms. 5759.

9 Mary wrote to O'Connell on 16 November 1804, arguing that she was well enough to travel as she had spent 'better than a month' in bed. Mary to O'Connell, NLI, Ms. 13650 (6).

10 O'Connell to Mary, 22 April 1805, NLI, FS 1620.

11 Lewis, *Family Way*, p. 149. Lewis adds, 'Since there was not much an accoucheur

could do to relieve these symptoms anyway, it was a splendid rationalization.'

12   Mary to O'Connell, 3, 20 August 1809, NLI, Ms. 13650 (16).

13   O'Connell to Mary, 7 March 1809, NLI, FS 1620.

14   Ibid., 9, 11 March 1809, NLI, FS 1620; Mary to O'Connell, 13, 14, March 1809, NLI, Ms. 13650 (17); 15 March 1809, NLI, Ms. 13650 (18). Judith Lewis cites prematurity as one of the prime causes of infant mortality. 'Generally, premature babies were those conceived rapidly after the births of one or more siblings, in which a succession of rapid birth intervals probably did not allow time for the buildup of sufficient maternal nutritional stores.' Lewis, 'Maternal Health', p. 102.

15   O'Connell to Mary, 20 August 1804, NLI, FS 1620.

16   Ibid., 24 March 1808.

17   Jo Murphy Lawless, 'The Silencing of Women in Childbirth or Let's Hear it for Bartholomew and the Boys', *Women's Studies International Forum* 6/4 (1988), pp. 124, 128.

18   O'Connell to Mary, 3 August 1806, 25 April 1808, NLI, FS 1620; Mary to O'Connell, 26 August 1806, NLI, Ms. 13650 (11); 28 March 1808, NLI, Ms. 13650 (14); 23 April 1808, NLI, Ms. 13650 (15); 1 October 1812, NLI, Ms. 13650 (loose).

19   Christopher FitzSimon to O'Connell, 13 August 1830, NLI, Ms. 13656 (5).

20   O'Connell to Mary, 3, 9, 14, 18 March 1807, NLI, FS 1620.

21   Mary to O'Connell, 15 August 1816, NLI, Ms. 13651 (8); O'Connell to Mary, 22 August 1816, NLI, Ms. Accession 4705, box 3.

22   O'Connell to Mary, 20, 26 November 1834, NLI, FS 1621.

23   O'Connell to Mary, 1, 2 December 1834, *Correspondence*, V, pp. 212–13.

24   Ibid., 13, 15, 17, 18 December 1834, NLI, FS 1621. During the eighteenth century, it was widely held that sex during pregnancy would somehow weaken the child and could even induce miscarriage. As the century progressed these taboos appear to have weakened, indicating that pregnancy gradually came to be viewed as a more natural state. Judith Lewis, in her work on childbearing in the English aristocracy, found several examples of children arriving as much as four months 'late'; she sees this as evidence of continued sexual relations amongst couples during periods of perceived pregnancy. Lewis, *Family Way*, pp. 167, 177–9.

25   O'Connell to Mary, 13 November 1804, NLI, Ms. 422; 7 August 1808, NLI, FS 1620.

26   Lewis, *Family Way*, p. 199.

27   Jalland, *Women, Marriage and Politics*, p. 152.

28   O'Connell to Mary, 8 November 1804, NLI, Ms. 5759.

29   Lewis, *Family Way*, pp. 171, 197. See also J. Jill Suitor, 'Husbands' Participation in Childbirth: A Nineteenth-Century Phenomenon', *Journal of Family History* 6/3 (Fall 1981): 278–93; and Jalland, *Women, Marriage and Politics*.

30   Stone, *Family, Sex and Marriage*, pp. 426–32; Valerie Fildes, *Breasts, Bottles and Babies: A History of Infant Feeding* (Edinburgh, 1985), p. 105; Hufton, *Prospect Before Her*, p. 194. Breast-feeding and wet-nursing have been the subject of lively historical debate. Randolph Trumbach and Lawrence Stone argue that by the 1780s maternal breast-feeding had become common practice. Judith Lewis chal-

lenges this view, claiming that while there may have been more mothers breast-feeding in this period than in earlier generations, the practice was far from universal. She cites short birth intervals amongst aristocratic women as proof that wet-nursing was still quite common. Yet Olwen Hufton argues that no more than 4 per cent of children were wet-nursed. These children were the offspring of aristocratic families and the few of the urban middle class who could afford to hire a nurse and who lived in the cities (which they regarded as unhealthy for a new-born infant). Regardless of the numbers who hired wet-nurses, historians generally have viewed the practice of wet-nursing as involving widespread neglect of children at the hands of 'mercenary' wet-nurses. Certainly, mortality rates for infants who were boarded out to wet-nurses were extremely high, especially in France where the practice was common. However, the charge of neglect on the part of all parents who opted for wet-nursing is unfounded. See Trumbach, *Rise of the Egalitarian Family*; Lewis, *Family Way*, pp. 209, 211; Hufton, *Prospect Before Her*, pp. 193–4. For the view of wet-nursing as neglectful, see Stone, as well as Shorter, *Modern Family*; deMause, ed., *History of Childhood;* and Flandrin, *Families in Former Times*. For a different view, see Sussman, 'The End of the Wet-Nursing Business in France'.

31 Mary to O'Connell, 12 August 1803, UCD P12/B/1. Mary makes reference to O'Connell's own foster experience. It would appear that the terms fostering and wet-nursing were used interchangeably throughout the O'Connell letters. O'Connell's purported time of fostering, until four years of age, generally believed to be a kind of apprenticeship in which he became immersed in the Gaelic traditions of his heritage, may in fact have been only the result of his being sent out to a wet-nurse.

32 See Lewis, *Family Way*, p. 163; Jalland, *Women, Marriage and Politics*, p. 143.

33 Mary to O'Connell, 9 November 1804, NLI, Ms. 13650 (5).

34 Mary to O'Connell, 16 November 1804, NLI, Ms. 13650 (6).

35 Ibid., 18 November 1804.

36 Ibid., 5 December 1804; 13 May 1805, NLI, Ms. 13650 (9). This scenario differs sharply from that presented by Edward Shorter in his work *The Making of the Modern Family*, in which he states, 'Once the infants had been boarded out, their parents seldom visited them … they would ascertain by mail every now and then that all was well … Neglect and indifference were the norm' (pp. 178, 180).

37 Mary to O'Connell, 26 August 1806, NLI, Ms. 13650 (11).

38 Mary to O'Connell, 16 March 1810, NLI, Ms. 13650 (20); O'Connell to Mary, 18 March 1810, NLI, FS 1620.

39 Mary to O'Connell, 2, 4 April 1811, NLI, Ms. 13650 (23).

40 Ibid., 16 March 1810, NLI, Ms. 13650 (20); Hufton, *Prospect Before Her*, p. 195.

41 Mary to O'Connell, 16 November 1804, NLI, Ms. 13650 (6).

42 Mary to O'Connell, 3, 20 August 1808, NLI, Ms. 13650 (16).

43 Hufton, *Prospect Before Her*, p. 201; Mary to O'Connell, 20 August 1808, NLI, Ms. 13650 (16).

44 Mary to O'Connell, 12 August 1805, NLI, Ms. 13650 (10).

45 Mary to O'Connell, 26 August 1806, NLI, Ms. 13650 (11).

46 Ibid.; O'Connell to Mary, 6 March 1807, NLI, FS 1620.

47 Mary to O'Connell, 6 August 1816, NLI, Ms. 13651 (7).

48 O'Connell to Mary, 9 March 1818, NLI, FS 1621.

49 Mary to Daniel Jr, [c. November 1831], NLI, Ms. 13644 (11).

50 Guy Williams, *The Age of Miracles* (London, 1981), p. 82.

51 Stone, *Family, Sex and Marriage*, pp. 651–2; Shorter, *Modern Family*, p. 168.

52 Linda A. Pollock, *Forgotten Children: Parent-Child Relations from 1500–1900* (Cambridge, 1983), p. 133; Roy Porter and Dorothy Porter, *In Sickness and in Health: The British Experience 1650–1850* (London, 1988), p. 78; Jalland, *Women, Marriage and Politics*, p. 181. Pollock offers the theory that perhaps a parent, fully aware of the tenuous grasp her child held on life, loved and pampered the baby that much more as a result.

53 O'Connell to Mary, 22 November 1804, NLI, Ms. 20,739.

54 O'Connell to Mary, 3 April 1810, NLI, FS 1620.

55 Edward O'Connell was born in July 1808 and died sometime around January 1809 (*Correspondence*, I, p. 181, n. 1). Daniel Stephen O'Connell was born on 29 December 1812 and died on 10 February 1814 (*Correspondence*, I, p. 318, n. 5). Gloriana is first noted in March 1813 and appears in four letters (Mary to O'Connell, 20, 27 March 1813, NLI, Ms. 13650 (26); O'Connell to Mary, 29 March, 12 September 1813, NLI, FS 1620). Mary is mentioned three times in April 1814 (O'Connell to Mary, 30 March, 6 April 1814, NLI, FS 1620; Mary to O'Connell, 4 April 1814, NLI, Ms. 13650 (29)). In May 1815 O'Connell writes that his wife is about to be confined and then Ricarda appears in the correspondence in June 1815 when O'Connell asks for news of his 'sweet little pet of a Ricarda … How my heart clings to the treasure of a doat' (O'Connell to Maurice O'Connell, 15 May 1815, *Correspondence*, II, p. 34; O'Connell to Mary, 10 June 1815 NLI, FS 1620; Mary to O'Connell, 17 July 1815, NLI, Ms. 13651 (3)). The seven O'Connell children who survived to adulthood are Maurice (27 January 1803 – 18 October 1853), Morgan (31 October 1804 – 1885), Ellen (12 November 1805 – 1885), Kate (18 March 1807 – 19 April 1891), Betsey (21 February 1810 – 3 February 1893), John (20 December 1810 – 1858), and Daniel Jr (22 August 1816 – 1897).

56 O'Connell to Mary, 8 November 1804, NLI, Ms. 5759.

57 Ibid., 10 July 1815, NLI, FS 1620; Mary to Daniel, 1 April 1816, NLI, Ms. 13,651 (5); 13 April 1816, NLI, Ms. 13,651 (1); 6 August 1816, NLI, Ms. 13,651 (7); 9 August 1816, NLI, Ms. 13,650 (3); 10 August 1816, NLI, Ms., 13,651 (1); 28 September, 16 October 1816, NLI, Ms. 13,651 (9).

58 O'Connell to Mary, 5 April 1817, NLI, FS 1621.

59 Mary to O'Connell, 4 April 1810, NLI, Ms. 13650 (20).

60 O'Connell to Mary, 26 August 1804, NLI, FS 1620.

61 Smith-Rosenberg, *Disorderly Conduct*, p. 71.

62 Mary to O'Connell, 16 April 1805, NLI, Ms. 13650 (9).

63 Pollock, *Forgotten Children*, p. 268; Lewis, *Family Way*, pp. 12–13.

64 Mary to O'Connell, 18 February 1825, NLI, Ms. 13651 (30); O'Connell to Mary, 19, 29 March 1809, NLI, FS 1620; 16 February, 19 August 1824, 20 April 1825, NLI, FS 1621; Mary to O'Connell, 14 November 1825, NLI, Ms. 13651 (31); Maurice O'Connell to O'Connell, 13 February 1816, UCD P12/3/66; Mary to

O'Connell, 16, 26 March 1816, NLI, Ms. 13651 (4); 1 April 1816, NLI, Ms. 13651 (5); Mary to Daniel Jr, 22 May 1830, NLI, Ms. Accession 4705, box 3.

65   Lewis, *Family Way*, pp. 58, 65.

66   Mary to O'Connell, 3 May 1805, NLI, Ms. 13650 (9).

67   Ibid., 23 July 1805.

68   Mary to O'Connell, 21 March 1808, UCD P12/2B/220; 27 March 1813, NLI, Ms. 13650 (26).

69   Mary to O'Connell, 5 December 1804, NLI, Ms. 13650 (6).

70   O'Connell to Mary, 1 May 1804, NLI, Ms. 5759. The basket to which O'Connell refers was a wicker walking frame. Generally children were not encouraged to crawl but were placed in these baskets as a direct transition to walking (Hufton, *Prospect Before Her*, p. 203).

71   O'Connell to Mary, 12 August 1805, NLI, Ms. 5759.

72   Mary to O'Connell, 12 August 1805, NLI, Ms. 13650 (10).

73   Ibid., 16 August 1805.

74   O'Connell to Mary, 4 December 1804, NLI, FS 1620.

75   Ibid., 10 November 1803, 1 March 1812; O'Connell to Mary, 19 March 1909, FS 1620; O'Connell to Maurice O'Connell, 29 May 1815, NLI 4705, box 3; O'Connell to John O'Connell, 1 April 1818, NLI 4705, Box 1; Mary to O'Connell, 4 April 1816, NLI 13651 (5), 1 April 1820, NLI 13651 (21).

76   Mary to O'Connell, 5 March 1812, Fitzpatrick, *Correspondence*, I, pp. 19–20.

77   Nancy F. Cott, *The Bonds of Womanhood: 'Woman's Sphere' in New England, 1780–1835* (New Haven, 1977), p. 91.

78   O'Connell to Mary, 19 November 1803, NLI, FS 1620.

79   Ibid., 24 September 1810.

80   Mary to O'Connell, 5 December 1803, NLI, Ms. 13650 (3).

81   Mary to O'Connell, 28 March 1809, NLI, Ms. 13645 (11).

82   Mary to O'Connell, 17, 19 August 1814, NLI, Ms. 13650 (31).

83   O'Connell to Mary, n.d., NLI, Ms. Accession 4705, box 1; 20 March 1811, *Correspondence*, I, p. 249.

84   O'Connell to Mary, 24 September, 8 October 1810, NLI, FS 1620.

85   O'Connell to John O'Connell, 1 April 1818, NLI, Ms. Accession 4705, box 1.

86   Maurice O'Connell to Mary, 27 June 1818, NLI, Ms. 13645 (1).

87   Mary to Daniel Jr, 19 January 1831, NLI, Ms. 13644 (9).

88   Ibid., [14 January 1831].

89   O'Connell to Mary, 15 April 1811, NLI, FS 1620.

90   Mary to O'Connell, 30 March 1811, NLI, Ms. 13650 (22).

91   O'Connell to Mary, 1 April 1811, NLI, FS 1620.

92   O'Connell to Mary, 1 April 1820, NLI, FS 1621.

93   Mary to O'Connell, 1 April 1820, NLI, Ms. 13651 (21).

94   Ellen O'Connell to O'Connell, 20 March 1820, NLI, Ms. 13645(6).

95   O'Connell to Mary, 12, 14 May 1825, NLI, FS 1621.

96   Mary to Daniel Jr, [c. November 1831], NLI, Ms. 13644 (11).

97   Mary to O'Connell, 1 April 1820, NLI, Ms. 13651 (21).

98   Trumbach, *Egalitarian Family*, p. 238, 252–4; Stone, *Family, Sex and Marriage*, p. 22.

99 Kate O'Connell to Daniel Jr, 26 January 1831, NLI, Ms. 13644 (4).

100 O'Connell to Daniel Jr, [6 January 1831], NLI, Ms. 13644 (5).

101 Mary to Daniel Jr, 29 [November] 1831, NLI, Ms. 13644 (9).

102 Maria Luddy, *Women in Ireland 1800–1918: A Documentary History* (Cork, 1995), pp. 89–90; Stone, *Family, Sex and Marriage*, p. 354–5.

103 Ellen O'Connell, *Her Father's Life*, NLI, Ms. 1504. Bishop and Wollstonecraft were sisters of Mary Wollstonecraft Godwin.

104 O'Connell to Mary, 3 April 1811, NLI, FS 1620.

105 Ellen O'Connell, *Her Father's Life*, NLI, Ms. 1504. See chapter 4 for a more detailed account of the women employed by the O'Connell family as governesses.

106 Mary to O'Connell, 12 August 1819, NLI, Ms. 13651 (18).

107 O'Connell to Mary, 5 May 1822, NLI, FS 1621.

108 Ellen O'Connell to O'Connell, 10 August 1819, NLI, Ms. 13645 (6); O'Connell to Mary, 16 February 1824, NLI, FS 1621.

109 Mary to O'Connell, 14, 19 November 1825, NLI, Ms. 13651 (31).

110 Trumbach, *Egalitarian Family*, p. 70.

111 Hufton, *Prospect Before Her*, p. 66; Malcomson, *Pursuit of the Heiress*, p. 4.

112 S.J. Connolly, 'Marriage in Pre-Famine Ireland', in Art Cosgrove, ed., *Marriage in Ireland* (Dublin, 1985), pp. 78–93; Maria Luddy, *Women in Ireland 1800–1918*, p. 5.

113 Cullen, *Hidden Ireland*, pp. 31–2.

114 Connolly, *Priests and People*, p. 195.

115 See Malcomson, *Pursuit of the Heiress*, for many examples of aristocratic marriages where dowries ranged anywhere between £10,000 and £50,000, and in some cases more.

116 M.R. O'Connell, *O'Connell*, p. 25; O. MacDonagh, *O'Connell*, p. 202.

117 Hufton, *Prospect Before Her*, p. 69.

118 Mary to O'Connell, 18 February 1825, NLI, Ms. 13651 (30).

119 O'Connell to Mary, 21 February 1825, *Correspondence*, III, p. 116.

120 Hufton, *Prospect Before Her*, p. 116.

121 O'Connell to Mary, 7, 17, 18 March 1825, NLI, FS 1621.

122 Mary to O'Connell, 6 February 1824, NLI, Ms. 13651 (27); O'Connell to Mary, 7 February 1824, NLI, FS 1621.

123 O'Connell to Mary, 18 February 1824, NLI, FS 1621.

124 Ibid., 1 November 1825.

125 Mary to O'Connell, 1 December 1825, NLI, Ms. 13651 (32).

126 Mary to O'Connell, 2 March 1830, NLI, Ms. 13651 (33).

127 O'Connell to Mary, 2 March 1831, NLI, FS 1621.

128 Mary to Daniel Jr, 8 March 1831, NLI, Ms. 13644 (9).

129 Ibid., 8, 19 March 1831.

130 Ibid.

131 Ibid., 23 March 1831.

132 O'Connell to Mary, 12 March 1809, NLI, FS 1620; Mary to O'Connell, 14 March 1809, NLI, Ms. 13650 (17).

133 Mary to O'Connell, 27 March 1810, NLI, Ms. 13650 (20).

134 O'Connell to Mary, 3, 7, 11 January, 10, 15, 18, 22 September 1820, NLI, FS 1621.

135 Ibid., 8 April 1823.

136 Mary to O'Connell, 20 April 1823, NLI, Ms. 13651 (25).

137 O'Connell to Mary, 22 May, 29 June 1823, NLI, FS 1621.

138 Ibid., 9 August 1827; Mary to O'Connell, 15 August 1827, NLI, Ms. 13651 (33).

139 O'Connell to Mary, 13 April 1829, *Correspondence*, IV, p. 44; 26 May 1831, NLI, FS 1621.

140 O'Connell to Mary, 20 December 1832, *Correspondence*, IV, p. 476; M.R. O'Connell, 'O'Connell and his Family', p. 23.

141 M.R. O'Connell, 'O'Connell and his Family', p. 23; Mary to O'Connell, 5 April 1808, UCD P12/2B/222; O'Connell to Mary, 26 March 1814, NLI, FS 1620.

142 Mary to O'Connell, 11 August 1817, NLI, Ms. 13651 (13).

143 Mary to O'Connell, 20 April 1823, NLI, Ms. 13651 (25).

144 M.R. O'Connell, 'O'Connell and his Family', p. 5.

145 O'Connell to Mary, 22 August 1833, NLI, FS 1621.

146 O'Connell to Mary, 2 October 1816, NLI, Ms. Accession 4705, box 3; 7 February 1824, NLI, FS 1621.

147 John O'Connell to O'Connell, 21 October 1826, NLI, Ms. 13645 (6).

148 M.R. O'Connell, 'O'Connell and his Family', p. 25.

149 Daniel O'Connell Jr, *Journal of Daniel O'Connell Jr*, NLI, Ms. 17882.

150 Ibid.

151 Mary to Daniel Jr, 25 [November 1831], NLI, Ms. 13644 (11); [15 December 1831], NLI, Ms. 13644 (9); 1 December [1831], NLI, Ms. 13644 (10); John O'Connell to Daniel Jr, 28 January 1832, NLI, Ms. 13644 (10).

152 M.R. O'Connell, 'O'Connell and his Family', p. 28.

CHAPTER FOUR

1 Jane Rendall, *The Origins of Modern Feminism: Women in Britain, France and the United States, 1780–1860* (Chicago, 1985), p. 31. For discussion of the rise of domesticity in Europe see also Stone, *Family, Sex and Marriage*; Trumbach, *Rise of the Egalitarian Family*; Shorter, *Making of the Modern Family*; and Susan Bell and Karen M. Offen, eds, *Women, the Family, and Freedom: The Debate in Documents, Vol. 1, 1750–1880* (Stanford, 1983).

2 Rendall, *Modern Feminism*, p. 207.

3 Shorter, *Modern Family*, p. 227.

4 Michael Anderson, *Approaches to the History of the Western Family 1500–1914* (London, 1980), p. 45; Barbara Welter, 'The Cult of True Womanhood: 1820–1860', *American Quarterly* 18/2 (Summer 1966), p. 152; Cott, *Bonds of Womanhood*, p. 64.

5 L.A. Clarkson, 'Love, Labour and Life', p. 29.

6 Mary to O'Connell, 14 April 1806, NLI, Ms. 13650 (12).

7 Mary to O'Connell, 13 April 1816, NLI, Ms. 13651 (1); 21 August 1816, NLI, Ms. 13651 (8); 2 April 1817, NLI, Ms. 13651 (11).

8 Mary to O'Connell, 19 May 1807, NLI, Ms. 13650 (13).

9   Mary to O'Connell, 25 April 1808, NLI, Ms. 13650 (15).
10   Mary to O'Connell, 16 September 1825, NLI, Ms. 13651 (30).
11   Mary to O'Connell, 13 August 1809, NLI, Ms. 13650 (19); 7 October 1810, NLI, Ms. 13650 (21); 8 March 1814, NLI, Ms. 13650 (29).
12   O'Connell to Mary, 2 April 1808, NLI, FS 1620; 20 July 1825, NLI, FS 1621.
13   Mary to O'Connell, 17 April 1806, NLI, Ms. 13650 (12).
14   O'Connell to Mary, 10 August 1808, *Correspondence*, I, p. 183.
15   O'Connell to Mary, 10 March 1812, NLI, FS 1620.
16   Mary to O'Connell, 16 March 1811, NLI, Ms. 13650 (22).
17   Ibid., 23 March 1811.
18   Ibid., 16 March 1811.
19   Mary to O'Connell, 13 March 1813, NLI, Ms. 13650 (26).
20   O'Connell to Mary, 19 March 1811, NLI, Ms. 5759; 20 March 1811, Fitzpatrick, *Correspondence*, I, p. 18; Mary to O'Connell, 2 April 1811, NLI, Ms. 13650 (23).
21   O'Connell to Mary, 29 September, 1 October 1813, NLI, FS 1620; Mary to O'Connell, 17 August 1814, NLI, Ms. 13650 (31); O'Connell to Mary, 9 March 1815, NLI, FS 1620.
22   Mary to O'Connell, 14 September 1819, NLI, Ms. 13651 (19).
23   O'Connell to Mary, 22, 27 October 1825, NLI, FS 1621; Mary to O'Connell, 14, 19 November 1825, NLI, Ms. 13651 (31); 22 November 1825, *Correspondence*, III, p. 202; 26 November 1825, *Correspondence*, III, p. 204; 28 November 1825, NLI, Ms. 13651 (31).
24   O'Connell to Mary, 9 March 1812, NLI, FS 1620.
25   Mary to O'Connell, 21 May 1807, NLI, Ms. 13650 (13).
26   Mary to O'Connell, 15 March 1811, NLI, Ms. 13650 (22); 31 March 1813, 13 April 1816, NLI, Ms. 13651 (1).
27   O'Connell to Mary, 30 October 1827, NLI, FS 1621.
28   Ibid., 17 August 1824, 16 March, 15 April, 23, 25 May, 20 July 1825, 22 March 1827, 8 April 1829.
29   Ibid., 11 March, 4, 11 April 1822.
30   Ibid., 21 March 1822.
31   Ibid., 22 March 1822.
32   Ibid., 3 May 1822.
33   Ibid., 14 May 1822.
34   Ellen O'Connell, *Narrative*, I, p. 132.
35   Ibid., pp. 135–6.
36   Ibid., pp. 136, 138.
37   Ibid., pp. 137, 150.
38   Ibid., pp. 152, 154, 156, 159, 173.
39   Mary to O'Connell, 10 February 1824, NLI, Ms. 13651 (27).
40   Mary to O'Connell, 19 May 1807, NLI, Ms. 13650 (13); 19, 25 April 1808, NLI, Ms. 13650 (15); 31 March 1813, NLI, Ms. 13650 (26).
41   Mary to O'Connell, 28 March 1815, NLI, Ms. 13651 (2).
42   Mary to O'Connell, 14 January 1809, NLI, Ms. 13650 (17).
43   Mary to O'Connell, 14 April 1806, NLI, Ms. 13650 (12).
44   Mary to O'Connell, 7 September 1819, NLI, Ms. 13651 (19).

45   Mary to O'Connell, 1 October 1812, NLI, Ms. 13650 (loose).

46   Mary to O'Connell, 19, 23 January 1824, NLI, Ms. 13651 (26).

47   Mary to O'Connell, 12 February 1824, NLI, Ms. 13651 (27).

48   O'Connell to Mary, 18 March 1826, Fitzpatrick, *Correspondence*, I, pp. 117–8; Mary to O'Connell, 17 March 1830, *Correspondence*, IV, p. 140.

49   Mary to Daniel Jr, 1 May 1830, NLI, Ms. Accession 4705, box 3.

50   Mary to O'Connell, 1 August 1814, NLI, Ms. 13650 (30); 26 March 1816, NLI, Ms. 13651 (4).

51   Mary to O'Connell, 4 February 1824, NLI, Ms. 13651 (27).

52   Mary to O'Connell, 2 August 1814, NLI, Ms. 13650 (30), 13 April 1816, NLI, Ms. 13651 (1).

53   O'Connell to Mary, 6 February 1801, NLI, FS 1620. The woman referred to remains unidentified.

54   O'Connell to Mary, 18 August 1819, NLI, FS 1621.

55   Mary to O'Connell, 16 August 1819, NLI, Ms. 13651 (18); O'Connell to Mary, 18 August 1819, NLI, FS 1621.

56   Mary to O'Connell, 7 September [1818], NLI, Ms. 13651 (17).

57   Mary to O'Connell, 23 December 1823, NLI, Ms. 13651 (25).

58   Lenore Davidoff, *The Best Circles: Society Etiquette and the Season* (London, 1973), p. 41.

59   Mary to O'Connell, 23 January 1824, NLI, Ms. 13651 (26).

60   Mary to O'Connell, 27 January, 10 February 1824, NLI, Ms. 13651 (27).

61   O'Connell to Mary, 22 March 1826, NLI, Ms. 5759.

62   Mary to O'Connell, 5 December 1830, *Correspondence*, IV, p. 242.

63   Ellen O'Connell, *Her Father's Life*, NLI, Ms. 1504.

64   Hufton, *Prospect Before Her*, p. 78.

65   Daly, *Social and Economic History*, p. 105; Hufton, *Prospect Before Her*, pp. 72, 77.

66   O'Connell to Mary, 22 January 1823, NLI, FS 1621.

67   *First Report of the Dublin Society, for the Improvement and Encouragement of Servants; from its institution, May 5 1825, to December 31, 1827* (Dublin, 1828), pp. 2, 4.

68   Mary to O'Connell, 6 March 1803, UCD P12/2B/214.

69   Mary to O'Connell, 8 March 1814, NLI, Ms. 13650 (29).

70   Ibid., 4 April 1814.

71   Mary to O'Connell, 10 August 1815, NLI, Ms. 13651 (1).

72   Lenore Davidoff and Catherine Hall, *Family Fortunes: Men and Women of the English Middle Class, 1780–1850* (London, 1992), p. 393.

73   Mary to O'Connell, 16 August 1819, NLI, Ms. 13651 (18).

74   O'Connell to Mary, 22 January 1823, NLI, FS 1621.

75   O'Connell to Mary, 27 October 1810, NLI, FS 1620.

76   Mary to O'Connell, 12 June 1817, NLI, Ms. 13651 (12).

77   O'Connell to Kate O'Connell, 24 May 1822, NLI, FS 1621.

78   O'Connell to Mary, 11 November 1823, NLI, FS 1621.

79   Ibid., 25 October 1827.

80   O'Connell to Mary, 13 November 1827, NLI, FS 1621.

81   Mary to Daniel Jr, [14 January 1831], [9 July 1831], NLI, Ms. 13644 (9); [January 1831], [February 1831], June [1831], [November 1831], 25 [November

1831], NLI, Ms. 13644 (11); Daniel Jr to Mary, 10 November [1831], NLI, Ms. 13645 (6).

82 Hufton, *Prospect Before Her*, p. 85.

83 Ellen O'Connell, *Her Father's Life*, NLI, Ms. 1504; O'Connell to Mary, 24 September 1810, NLI, FS 1620.

84 Ellen O'Connell, *Her Father's Life*, NLI, Ms. 1504; Mary to O'Connell, 16 September 1814, NLI, Ms. 13650 (31); O'Connell to Mary, 21 September 1814, NLI, Ms. Accession 4705, box 1.

85 Ellen O'Connell, *Her Father's Life*, NLI, Ms. 1504; O'Connell to Mary, 11 October 1810, NLI, FS 1620.

86 O'Connell to Mary, 3 April 1815, NLI, FS 1620.

87 Ibid., 10 July 1815.

88 Ellen O'Connell, *Her Father's Life*, NLI, Ms. 1504.

89 Mary to O'Connell, 17 July 1815, NLI, Ms. 13651 (3).

90 Mary to O'Connell, 6 March 1812, NLI, Ms. 13650 (24); 26 March 1816, NLI, Ms. 13651 (4).

91 Mary to O'Connell, 11 August 1817, NLI, Ms. 13651 (13).

92 Ellen O'Connell, *Narrative*, NLI, FS 1623, I, p. 4; Christopher FitzSimon to O'Connell, 28 August 1826, NLI, Ms. 13646.

93 Cott, *Bonds of Womanhood*, pp. 22, 71.

94 Mary to O'Connell, 6 November 1801, NLI, Ms. 13650 (2).

95 Mary to O'Connell, 2 April 1808, NLI, Ms. 13650 (15); 10 April 1808, UCD P12/2B/224.

96 Mary to O'Connell, 19 April 1808, NLI, Ms. 13650 (15).

97 Mary to O'Connell, 16 January 1809, UCD P12/2B/223.

98 See chapter 6, note 61.

99 O'Connell to Mary, 9 March 1818, NLI, FS 1621; Mary to O'Connell, 10 March 1818, NLI, Ms. 13651 (15).

100 Daly, *Social and Economic History*, p. 105.

101 Stone, *Family, Sex and Marriage*, p. 349.

CHAPTER FIVE

1 On kin work, see Micaela di Leonardo, 'The Female World of Cards and Holidays: Women, Families and the Work of Kinship', *Signs* 21 (1987): 442–3, 450; Smith-Rosenberg, *Disorderly Conduct*, pp. 61–2; Davidoff and Hall, *Family Fortunes*, pp. 32, 322.

2 Smith-Rosenberg, *Disorderly Conduct*, pp. 61, 62; Robert Adams Day, *Told in Letters* (Ann Arbor, Michigan, 1966), p. 49; Howard Anderson, Philip B. Daghlian and Irvin Ehrenpreis, eds, *The Familiar Letter in the Eighteenth Century* (Lawrence, Kansas, 1966), pp. 270, 272; David Fitzpatrick, *Oceans of Consolation: Personal Accounts of Irish Migration to Australia* (Cork, 1994), p. 492.

3 O'Connell to Mary, 7 March 1829, NLI, FS 1621; Mary to O'Connell, 6 March 1812, NLI, Ms. 13650 (24).

4 Mulvey, 'Daniel and Mary O'Connell', p. xx.

5   O'Connell to Mary, 3 April 1806, NLI, FS 1620.
6   Mary to O'Connell, 26 August 1806, NLI, Ms. 13650 (11); 20 August 1808, NLI, Ms. 13650 (16); 4 August 1809, NLI, Ms. 13650 (19).
7   Mary to O'Connell, 11 April 1827, UCD P12/2B/217.
8   O'Connell to Mary, 5 March 1807, NLI, Ms. 5759; Mary to O'Connell, 18 September 1809, NLI, Ms. 13650 (19).
9   Mary to O'Connell, 25 March 1803, UCD P12/2B/215.
10   O'Connell to Mary, 10 November 1803, NLI, FS 1620.
11   O'Connell to Mary, 6 March 1803, 29 November 1804, NLI, Ms. 5759; 17 July 1820, NLI, FS 1621.
12   Mary to O'Connell, 4 August 1810, NLI, Ms. 13650 (21); 6 March 1812, NLI, Ms. 13650 (24); 30 January 1824, NLI, Ms. 13651 (26).
13   O'Connell to Mary, 4 August 1810, NLI, FS 1620; 14 April 1825, NLI, FS 1621.
14   O'Connell to Mary, 5, 24 August, 22 October 1810, NLI, FS 1620.
15   Michael O'Dwyer, *Tralee, A Historical Guide*, p. 14; O'Connell to Mary, 12 September, 11 October 1820, NLI, FS 1621; 23 September 1823, NLI, Ms. Accession 4705, box 2.
16   O'Connell to Mary, 8 April 1807, 14 August 1814, NLI, FS 1620.
17   Mary to O'Connell, 2 December 1801, NLI, Ms. 13650 (2).
18   O'Connell to Mary, 2 August 1809, NLI, FS 1620.
19   Ibid., 3 October 1813.
20   Ibid., 23 August 1804; Mary to O'Connell, 14 November 1804, NLI, Ms. 13650 (6); 16 March 1811, NLI, Ms. 13650 (22).
21   Mary to O'Connell, 27 February 1824, NLI, Ms. 13651 (28); 2 March 1824, NLI, Ms. 13651 (29).
22   O'Connell to Mary, 28 July 1814, NLI, FS 1620.
23   Mary to O'Connell, 17 October 1816, NLI, Ms. 13651 (9).
24   O'Connell to Kate O'Connell, 24 May 1822, NLI, FS 1621.
25   O'Connell to Mary, 31 May 1822, NLI, FS 1621.
26   Ibid., 2 April 1823.
27   Ibid., 5 May 1822.
28   Ellen O'Connell to O'Connell, 22 June 1822, *Correspondence*, II, p. 401.
29   O'Connell to Kate O'Connell, 24 May 1822, NLI, FS 1621.
30   O'Connell to Mary, 3 April 1815, NLI, FS 1620; 13 April 1819, NLI, FS 1621; 28 July 1817, NLI, Ms. Accession 4705, box 1; Morgan O'Connell to O'Connell, 27 March 1818, NLI, Ms. 13645 (1).
31   Ellen O'Connell to O'Connell, 27 March 1817, NLI, Ms. Accession 4705, box 3.
32   Mary to O'Connell, 22 March 1806, NLI, Ms. 13650 (11); 2 April 1817, NLI, Ms. 13651 (11).
33   Mary to O'Connell, 25 March 1808, NLI, Ms. 13650 (14).
34   Ibid., 28 March 1808.
35   Mary to O'Connell, 25 March 1803, UCD P12/2B/215.
36   Mary to O'Connell, 21 March 1809, NLI, Ms. 13650 (18).
37   O'Connell to Mary, 29 March 1809, NLI, FS 1620.
38   Mary to O'Connell, 4, 7 September 1819, NLI, Ms. 13651 (19); O'Connell to Mary, 18 September 1819, NLI, FS 1621.

39 O'Connell to Mary, 22 February 1825, Fitzpatrick, *Correspondence*, I, pp. 99–100; 4 March 1825, Fitzpatrick, *Correspondence*, I, pp. 106–8; 27 April 1825, NLI, FS 1621; 10 February 1829, *Correspondence*, IV, p. 10; 5 March 1831, NLI, FS 1621.

40 O'Connell to Mary, 28 June 1826, Fitzpatrick, *Correspondence*, I, pp. 128–9.

41 Mary to O'Connell, 27 March 1824, NLI, Ms. 13651 (29).

42 O'Connell to Mary, 16 April 1822, NLI, FS 1621.

43 Ibid., 1 May 1825, 4 April 1832.

44 Mary to O'Connell, 27 January 1824, NLI, Ms. 13651 (26).

45 O'Connell to Mary, 18 January 1810, NLI, FS 1620.

46 Max Gluckman, 'Gossip and Scandal', *Current Anthropology* 4 (1963): 307–8.

47 Ibid., 13 September 1814, Fitzpatrick, *Correspondence*, I, p. 24.

48 Mary to O'Connell, 6 February 1803, UCD P12/2B/213.

49 Mary to O'Connell, 21 March 1815, NLI, Ms. 13651 (2). The two letters referred to remain unidentified within the extant O'Connell correspondence.

50 Robert Paine, 'What is Gossip About? An Alternative Hypothesis', *Man* 2 (1967), p. 279; Elizabeth Bott, *Family and Social Network* (London, 1957), p. 67.

51 Hufton, *Prospect Before Her*, p. 117.

52 O'Connell to Mary, 9 August 1827, NLI, FS 1621.

53 Catherine O'Connell to O'Connell, 18 November 1802, *Correspondence*, I, p. 82.

54 Paine, 'What is Gossip About?', pp. 278–83.

55 Mary to O'Connell, 24 April 1801, NLI, Ms. 13650 (1); O'Connell to Mary, 28 April 1801, NLI, FS 1620.

56 O'Connell to Mary, 14 April 1814, NLI, FS 1620.

57 Gelles, *Portia*, p. 79.

58 O'Connell to Mary, 7, 11 December 1823, NLI, FS 1621.

59 Stone, *Family, Sex and Marriage*, p. 8.

60 Lewis, *Family Way*, p. 13. Edward Shorter's analysis of the making of the modern family differs slightly from Stone's regarding kin relations. Shorter cites two characteristics that transformed the traditional family: 'The couple's almost complete withdrawal from routine community life, and the corresponding strengthening of their ties to parents and close relatives.' Shorter goes on to say that 'whereas in traditional society the kin group counted for relatively little in emotional terms, being primarily a reservoir of material support in emergencies, nowadays it's chiefly the parents of the married couple—and the gaggle of uncles, aunts, and cousins the couple might well find about them—who breach the walls of the nuclear family.' Shorter, *Modern Family*, p. 234.

61 Trumbach, *Egalitarian Family*, pp. 41, 61.

62 Lewis, *Family Way*, p. 48.

63 Ellen Connor to O'Connell, 12 June 1819, NLI, Ms. 13645 (3).

64 O'Connell to Mary, 15 April 1822, NLI, FS 1621.

65 Mary to O'Connell, 1 April 1820, NLI, Ms. 13651 (21).

66 Mary to O'Connell, 15 October 1820, NLI, Ms. 13651 (23).

67 O'Connell to Mary, 16 October 1820, NLI, FS 1621; Mary to O'Connell, 15 October 1820, NLI, Ms. 13651 (23).

68 O'Connell to Mary, 2 April 1821, *Correspondence*, II, p. 312; James O'Connell to O'Connell, 26 May 1821, *Correspondence*, II, p. 324. The story of Ellen Connor is

an striking example of how gossip functioned in society, especially in relation to the choosing of a suitable marriage partner. Ellen's suitor was apparently drawn to her in part by the rumour that she would get a substantial settlement from her uncle, O'Connell.

69   Mary to Daniel Jr, [31 May 1830], NLI, FS 1622.

70   James O'Connell to O'Connell, 28 March 1822, *Correspondence*, II, p. 363.

71   Mary to O'Connell, 7, 14 September 1819, NLI, Ms. 13651 (19).

72   Mary to O'Connell, 19 November 1825, NLI, Ms. 13651 (31); O'Connell to Mary, 15 April 1822, NLI, FS 1621.

73   Mary to Daniel Jr, [6 June 1831], NLI, Ms. 13644 (5).

74   See chapter 7.

75   O'Connell to Mary, 7 December 1823, NLI, FS 1621.

76   Ibid., 19 November 1827.

77   Carroll Smith-Rosenberg argues that within the framework of domesticity there developed 'a specifically female world … built around a generic and unself-conscious pattern of single-sex or homosocial networks'. These networks were further supported by the institutionalization of rituals that would accompany every rite of passage in a woman's life. Although Davidoff and Hall, in their work on the English middle class, 'uncovered little evidence of an exclusively female culture in practice', they do, however, agree that 'in a society dominated by institutions framed to give men power, authority and rewards, women continued to find ways of expressing their needs and desires, often in terms of their claim for a separate sphere'. Smith-Rosenberg, *Disorderly Conduct,* p. 60–1, 64; Davidoff and Hall, *Family Fortunes*, p. 32; see also Bott, *Family and Social Network,* p. 136–7.

78   Smith-Rosenberg, *Disorderly Conduct*, p. 32.

79   Kate O'Connell to Daniel Jr, 26 January 1831, NLI, Ms. 13644 (4).

80   Davidoff and Hall, *Family Fortunes*, p. 341.

81   O'Connell to Mary, 23 March 1818, 9, 14 October 1820, NLI, FS 1621; Mary to O'Connell, 15 October 1820, NLI, Ms. 13651 (23).

82   Mary to O'Connell, 14 March 1809, NLI, Ms. 13650 (17).

83   O'Connell to Mary, 20, 26 November 1834, NLI, FS, 1621; 1, 2 December 1834, *Correspondence*, V, pp. 212–13; 13, 15, 17, 18 December 1834, NLI, FS 1621.

84   A notebook of Kate O'Connell's, located in the National Library of Ireland (Ms. 16694), documents the births and baptisms of her children. In nearly every instance the child's sponsor is a close female family member.

85   Mary to O'Connell, 2 August 1814, NLI, Ms. 13650 (30); O'Connell to Mary, 13 June 1817, NLI, FS 1621.

86   Betsey O'Connell to O'Connell, 9 October 1844, NLI, Ms. 13645 (6).

87   Mary habitually closed letters to Daniel by naming all the current members of the household who united with her in wishing their love to her husband. Likewise, in his letters, O'Connell nearly always sent his regards to any house guests.

88   Mary to O'Connell, 15 August 1816, NLI, Ms. 13651 (8).

89   Mary to O'Connell, 2 August 1814, NLI, Ms. 13650 (30).

90   O'Connell to Mary, 18 August 1814, NLI, FS 1620.

91   O'Connell to Mary, 19 August 1824, NLI, FS 1621.

92   O'Connell to Mary, 30 September 1810, NLI, FS 1620.

93   Mary to O'Connell, 31 March 1808, NLI, Ms. 13650 (14); 18 April 1808, NLI, Ms. 13650 (15).

94   Mary to O'Connell, 23 March 1814, NLI, Ms. 13651 (29).

95   Mary to O'Connell, 28 November 1825, NLI, Ms. 13651 (31); O'Connell to Mary, 8 November 1827, 30 March 1832, NLI, FS 1621.

96   Mary to O'Connell, 28 March 1815, NLI, Ms. 13651 (2).

97   Bott, *Family and Social Network*, p. xv.

98   B.N. Adams, 'The Social Significance of Kinship: 2', in *Sociology of the Family*, ed. Michael Anderson (Harmondsworth, 1971), pp. 132–3.

CHAPTER SIX

1   Porter, *In Sickness*, p. 102.

2   Mary to O'Connell, 25 March 1808, NLI, Ms. 13650 (14); 2 April 1816, NLI, Ms. 13651 (5); O'Connell to Mary, 31 January 1810, NLI, Ms. 5759; 22 April 1805, 18 October 1813, NLI, FS 1620.

3   Mary to O'Connell, 20 August 1808, NLI, Ms. 13650 (16).

4   Mary to O'Connell, 4 August 1809, NLI, Ms. 13650 (19).

5   O'Connell to Mary, 28 July 1814, NLI, FS 1620.

6   O'Connell to Mary, 3 October 1813, n.d., NLI, FS 1622.

7   O'Connell to Mary, 16 August 1814, NLI, FS 1620; 11 July 1820, 10 June 1817, NLI, FS 1621.

8   O'Connell to Mary, 20 November 1834, NLI, FS 1621.

9   Mary to O'Connell, 5 December 1804, NLI, Ms. 13650 (8); O'Connell to Mary, 16 July 1801, NLI, FS 1620.

10   Mary to O'Connell, 28 March 1808, NLI, Ms. 13650 (14).

11   O'Connell to Mary, 1 November 1825, NLI, FS 1621; 18 August 1814, NLI, FS 1620.

12   O'Connell to Mary, 10 Mary 1806, NLI, FS 1620.

13   O'Connell to Mary, 30 December 1800, NLI, FS 1620.

14   Máiréad Dunlevy, *Dress in Ireland* (London, 1989), pp. 131–2.

15   J.E. Schmidt, *Medical Discoveries, Who and When* (Springfield, Illinois, 1959), pp. 113, 446, 525.

16   Inoculation involved lancing the skin on one or both arms and placing a small amount of infected smallpox matter into the wound. See Porter, *In Sickness*, p. 159; William Buchan, *Domestic Medicine, or a Treatise on the Prevention and Cure of Diseases by Regimen and Simple Medicines*, 9th ed. (Dublin, 1784), p. 185; Pollock, *Forgotten Children*, p. 231; Mary to O'Connell, 2 April 1811, NLI, Ms. 13650 (23); 13 April 1816, NLI, Ms. 13651 (1).

17   O'Connell to Mary, 3 February 1803, NLI, FS 1620.

18   Ibid., 24 November 1803.

19   Mary to O'Connell, 25 March 1808, NLI, Ms. 13650 (14); 26 March 1808, UCD P12/2B/221; 28 March 1808, NLI, Ms. 13650 (14).

20   O'Connell to Mary, n.d., NLI, Ms. 24923.

21   O'Connell to Mary, 1 August 1814, NLI, FS 1620.

22   Ibid., 29 May 1807.

23   Porter, *In Sickness*, pp. 134, 168; O'Connell to Mary, 24 January 1801, NLI, FS 1620.

24   O'Connell to Mary, 14, 16, 18 August 1816, NLI, FS 1620.

25   See Fitzpatrick, *Oceans of Consolation*, p. 505.

26   Mary to O'Connell, 14, 16 November 1804, NLI, Ms. 13650 (6); 18 November 1804, NLI, Ms. 13650 (15).

27   O'Connell to Mary, 22 November 1804, NLI, Ms. 20,739.

28   Mary to O'Connell, 21, 23, 25 November 1804, NLI, Ms. 13650 (7).

29   O'Connell to Mary, 17 November 1804, NLI, FS 1620; Mary to O'Connell, 9, 16 November 1804, NLI, Ms. 13650 (6).

30   Mary to O'Connell, 18 November 1804, NLI, Ms. 13650 (6).

31   O'Connell to Mary, 17 November 1804, NLI, FS 1620; Mary to O'Connell, 21 November 1804, NLI, Ms. 13650 (6).

32   Mary to O'Connell, 31 November 1804, NLI, Ms. 13650 (7).

33   O'Connell to Mary, 4, 8 December 1804, NLI, FS 1620.

34   Mary to O'Connell, 12 June 1817, NLI, Ms. 13651 (12).

35   O'Connell to Mary, 10 March 1823, NLI, FS 1621.

36   Porter, *In Sickness*, p. 64; O'Connell to Mary, 5 March 1807, NLI, Ms. 5759.

37   O'Connell to Mary, 3 February 1803, NLI, FS 1620; Mary to O'Connell, 6 February 1803, UCD P12/2B/213; O'Connell to Mary, 27 March 1808, NLI, FS 1620.

38   Mary to O'Connell, 28 March 1815, NLI, Ms. 13,651 (2); O'Connell to Mary, 25 August 1810, NLI, Ms. 5759; 24 August 1810, NLI, FS 1620.

39   O'Connell to Mary, 23 March 1809, NLI, FS 1620.

40   O'Connell to Mary, 23 August 1804; 30 May 1823, NLI, FS 1621.

41   O'Connell to Mary, 25 June 1826, *Correspondence*, III, p. 252; Porter, *In Sickness*, p. 140; S. Solomon, *Guide and Health, or Advice to Both Sexes in a Variety of Complaints*, 2nd ed. (Stockport, 1800), p. 59.

42   O'Connell to Mary, 29 June 1823, NLI FS 1621

43   Mary to O'Connell, 30 August 1805, NLI, Ms. 13650 (10).

44   O'Connell to Mary, 20 November 1834, NLI, FS 1621.

45   Porter, *In Sickness*, p. 47.

46   Mary to O'Connell, 6 August 1816, NLI, Ms. 13651 (7); 27 March 1810, NLI, Ms. 13650 (20).

47   Porter, *In Sickness*, pp. 105–6, 143; Laurel Thatcher Ulrich, *A Midwife's Tale: The Life of Martha Ballard, Based on Her Diary, 1785–1812* (New York, 1990), p. 54.

48   Buchan, *Domestic Medicine*, p. 155.

49   Ulrich, *Midwife's Tale*, pp. 55–6.

50   Buchan, *Domestic Medicine*, p. 453.

51   O'Connell to Mary, 25 September 1816, NLI, FS 1620.

52   Buchan, *Domestic Medicine*, p. 254.

53   G.B. Risse, *Hospital Life in Enlightenment Scotland* (Cambridge, 1986), p. 199.

54   O'Connell to Mary, 3 October 1813, NLI, FS 1620; Mary to O'Connell, 2 March 1824, NLI, Ms. 13651 (29).

55   O'Connell to Mary, 24, 25 November 1834, NLI, FS 1621.

56 J. Worth Estes, *Dictionary of Protopharmacology, Therapeutic Practices, 1700–1850* (Massachusetts, 1990), p. 99; Leonard Goldwater, *Mercury: A History of Quicksilver* (Baltimore, Maryland, 1972), p. 216.

57 O'Connell to Mary, 31 August 1809, NLI, Ms. 5759; Mary to O'Connell, 8 April 1816, NLI, Ms. 13651 (5); O'Connell to Mary, 5, 27 February 1824, NLI, FS 1621.

58 O'Connell to Mary, 3 March 1815, NLI, FS 1620; Mary to O'Connell, 13 March 1815, NLI, Ms. 13651; Buchan, *Domestic Medicine*, p. 294.

59 O'Connell to Mary, 5, 9 March 1918, NLI, FS 1621; Estes, *Therapeutic Practices*, p. 33.

60 O'Connell to Mary, 3 March 1807, NLI, FS 1620.

61 Dr O'Riordon (sometimes spelled O'Reardon), family physician to the O'Connells, was a first cousin of Daniel O'Connell, his mother Joan Sugrue being the sister of O'Connell's father, Morgan. Entering Maynooth in 1797, O'Riordon first studied theology but a 'pause' in his speaking voice forced him to make a change in his career choice. He became a physician in 1802. He studied in various Paris hospitals and published a Latin medical dissertation. In 1814 he returned to Ireland, and became best known for his work at the Cork Street Fever Hospital. He died in 1866 (O'Connell, *Last Colonel*, pp. 244–6).

62 Porter, *Patients' Progress*, p. 80.

63 Buchan, *Domestic Medicine*, p. 255.

64 Ellen O'Connell, *Her Father's Life*, NLI, Ms. 1504; Mary to O'Connell, 13 March 1815, NLI, Ms. 13651.

65 John Richard Elmore, M.D. (d. 26 August 1860) was a native of England but lived many years in Clonakilty, Co. Cork. It is unclear if he was a personal friend of the O'Connells or merely their family doctor in England. In any event it would appear that he treated Mary as well as Daniel Jr.

66 O'Connell to Mary, 2, 5, 8, 9, 17 December 1834, NLI, FS 1621. Quote from O'Connell to Mary, 13 December 1834, NLI, FS 1621.

67 O'Connell to Mary, 3 December 1803, NLI, FS 1620.

68 Porter, *In Sickness*, p. 68.

69 Lord Brain, *Doctors Past and Present* (Springfield, Illinois, 1964), pp. 9–10. Galen, born *c.*AD 129, is known as the 'father of experimental physiology'. His importance to and influence on medicine is second only to that of Hippocrates.

70 G. F. Drinka, *The Birth of Neurosis: Myth, Malady, and the Victorians* (New York, 1985), p. 33.

71 Ibid., p. 34.

72 Ibid., p. 35.

73 Ibid., p. 33.

74 Mary to O'Connell, 13 July 1801, UCD P12/2B/211; 5 March 1818, NLI, Ms. 13,651 (14).

75 Buchan, *Domestic Medicine*, pp. 151–4.

76 Solomon, *Guide and Health*, p. 112.

77 Porter, *In Sickness*, p. 83.

78 O'Connell to Mary, 30 March 1814, NLI, FS 1620. See chapter 3 for a fuller account of Maurice's 'fidgets'.

79 Porter, *In Sickness*, p. 156.

80 Ibid., pp. 36, 158.

81 Mary to O'Connell, 2 August 1814, NLI, Ms. 13650 (30).

82 O'Connell to Mary, 19 August 1824, NLI, FS 1621.

83 Buchan, *Domestic Medicine*, pp. 59–64; Mary to O'Connell, 13 March 1815, NLI, Ms. 13651.

84 O'Connell to Mary, 13 September 1814, NLI, Ms. 13645; Mary to O'Connell, 2 August 1814, NLI, Ms. 13650 (30).

85 O'Connell to Mary, 18 August 1814, NLI, FS 1620.

86 Mary to O'Connell, 22 March 1814, NLI, Ms. 13650 (29).

87 Mary to O'Connell, 7 September 1819, NLI, Ms. 13651 (19).

88 Mary to O'Connell, 26 November 1825, *Correspondence*, III, p. 204.

89 Solomon, *Guide and Health*, p. 275.

90 Ibid., pp. 257, 260, 262–4, 270.

91 Ibid., p. 260; O'Connell to Mary, 20 August 1811, NLI, Ms. 5759; 22 August 1811, NLI, FS 1620.

92 O'Connell to Mary, 28 August 1810, NLI, FS 1620.

93 O'Connell to Mary, 1, 4 September 1819, NLI, FS 1621; Mary to O'Connell 7 September 1819, NLI, Ms. 13651 (19).

94 Solomon, *Guide and Health*, p. 288.

95 Ibid., pp. 288–9.

96 Michael Durey, *The Return of the Plague: British Society and the Cholera, 1831–32* (Dublin, 1979), p. 2.

97 S.J. Connolly, 'The "blessed turf": cholera and popular panic in Ireland, June 1832', *Irish Historical Studies* 23/91 (May, 1983), p. 215.

98 Mary to Daniel Jr, 14 November 1831, NLI, Ms. 13644 (9).

99 Porter, *In Sickness*, pp. 118, 188, 192.

100 O'Connell to Mary, 2 April 1823, NLI, FS 1621.

CHAPTER SEVEN

1 P.J. Corish, 'Women and Religious Practices', in *Women in Early Modern Ireland*, eds Mary O'Dowd and Margaret MacCurtain (Edinburgh, 1991), p. 213.

2 Hufton, *Prospect Before Her*, pp. 395–6.

3 O. MacDonagh, *O'Connell*, p. 101.

4 Mary to O'Connell, 21 March 1809, NLI, Ms. 13650 (18).

5 O. MacDonagh, *O'Connell*, p. 27.

6 Arthur Houston, *Daniel O'Connell: His Early Life and Journal, 1795–1802* (London, 1906), p. 118.

7 Ibid., p. 116.

8 O. MacDonagh, *O'Connell*, p. 44.

9 Mary to O'Connell, 21 March 1809, NLI, Ms. 13650 (18).

10 Mary to O'Connell, 1 April 1816, NLI, Ms. 13651 (5).

11 Mary to O'Connell, 26 March 1816, NLI, Ms. 13651 (4).

12 O'Connell to Mary, 13 January 1816, *Correspondence*, II, p. 79.

13   Mary to O'Connell, 11 August 1817, NLI, Ms. 13651 (13).

14   O'Connell to Mary, 1 April 1820, NLI, FS 1621.

15   O'Connell to John O'Connell, 6 February 1824, NLI, Ms. Accession 4705, box 3.

16   O'Connell to Mary, 18 March 1824, NLI, FS 1621. Rev. Patrick Coleman (d. 1838) was the curate of Townsend Street chapel for many years and O'Connell's spiritual director. He also served as parish priest of St Paul's, Dublin, 1825–8, St Michan's, Dublin, 1828–38, and sometimes as the vicar-general of the Dublin archdiocese.

17   Born in Dublin but educated and ordained on the Continent, Rev. William L'Estrange O.D.C. (d. 6 December 1833) was provincial of the Irish Carmelites and prior of St Teresa's, Clarendon Street, Dublin. He served for many years as Mary's spiritual director.

18   Mary to O'Connell, 28 March 1815, NLI, Ms. 13651 (1).

19   See chapter 2 for a fuller account of the affair.

20   Mary's pregnancy and confinement are mentioned in the correspondence between Mary and O'Connell on several occasions in the spring of 1815. News of the birth of a baby girl filled O'Connell's letter to his sons, Maurice and Morgan, then at school at Clongowes, in May 1815. The child was baptized on 4 June, and in July O'Connell first writes of his 'sweet little pet of a Ricarda'. (Mary to O'Connell, 28 March 1815, NLI, Ms. 13651 (2); O'Connell to Maurice O'Connell, 15 May 1815, NLI, Ms. Accession 4705, box 3; O'Connell to Mary, 10 July 1815, NLI, FS 1620.)

21   Mary to O'Connell, 3 March 1816, NLI, Ms. 13651 (4); 1, 2 April 1816, NLI, Ms. 13651 (5); O'Connell to Mary, 4 August 1816, NLI, Ms. Accession 4705, box 3; Mary to O'Connell, 10 August 1816, NLI, Ms. 13651 (1); 13 August 1816, NLI, Ms. 13651 (7).

22   Mary to O'Connell, 10 August 1816, NLI, Ms. 13651 (1).

23   O'Connell to Mary, 11 August 1816, NLI, Ms. Accession, 4705, box 3.

24   Mary to O'Connell, 3 September 1816, NLI, Ms. 13645 (6).

25   O'Connell to Mary, 1 September 1816, NLI, Ms. Accession 4705, box 3.

26   S.J. Connolly, *Religion and Society in Nineteenth-Century Ireland* (Dublin, 1985), p. 49.

27   O'Connell to Maurice O'Connell, 2 June 1815, NLI, Ms. 13645 (26); O'Connell to Mary, 12, 19 December 1834, NLI, FS 1621.

28   Mary to O'Connell, 28 March 1808, NLI, Ms. 13650 (14).

29   Mary to Daniel Jr, [c. 1831], NLI, Ms. 13644 (11).

30   O'Connell to Mary, 22 March 1826, NLI, Ms. 5759.

31   O'Connell to Mary, 25 October, 6 December 1827, NLI, FS 1621.

32   Mary to Daniel Jr, 22 May, 4 June, 3 July 1830, NLI, Ms. Accession 4705, box 3.

33   Mary to O'Connell, 3 December 1825, NLI, Ms. 13651 (32).

34   O'Connell to Mary, 3 August 1820, NLI, FS 1621.

35   Mary to O'Connell, 30 January 1824, NLI, Ms. 13651 (26).

36   Connolly, *Priests and People*, pp. 95–6.

37   Kevin Whelan, 'The Catholic Parish, the Catholic Chapel and Village Development in Ireland', *Irish Geography* 16 (1983), p. 5.

38   Mary to O'Connell, 27 January 1824, NLI, Ms. 13651 (26).

39   The Penal Laws restricted the construction of Catholic churches. Steeples and
      bells, for example, were prohibited. The few churches that did exist often dou-
      bled as a schools or markets. With Emancipation in 1829 came the freedom to
      build large churches and cathedrals. See R.F. Foster, *Modern Ireland 1600–1972*
      (New York, 1988), pp. 209, 338–9.
40   O'Connell to Mary, 22 November 1834, NLI, FS 1621.
41   Whelan, 'Catholic Parish', p. 3.
42   Mary to O'Connell, 21 September 1820, NLI, Ms. 13651 (22); 30 July 1814, NLI,
      Ms. 13650 (29); 16 September 1825, NLI, Ms. 13651 (30); 15 August 1827, NLI,
      Ms. 13651 (33).
43   O'Connell to Mary, 9 August 1827, NLI, FS 1621.
44   Mary to O'Connell, 31 May 1830, NLI, FS 1622; W. J. Battersby, ed., *A Complete
      Catholic Directory, Registry, and Almanac, 1836* (Dublin, 1836), p. 126.
45   Desmond Keenan, *The Catholic Church in Nineteenth-Century Ireland: A Socio-
      logical Study* (Dublin, 1983), p. 94.
46   Davidoff, *Best Circles*, p. 51.
47   Ellen O'Connell to O'Connell, 10 March 1815, NLI, Ms. 13645 (6).
48   Mary to O'Connell, 13 March 1821, NLI, Ms. 13651 (24) copy. Location of orig-
      inal is unknown.
49   Connolly, *Priests and People*, pp. 194, 196, 199.
50   Hufton, *Prospect Before Her*, p. 60.
51   P. J. Corish, 'Catholic Marriage Under the Penal Code', in *Marriage in Ireland*,
      ed. Art Cosgrove (Dublin, 1985), p. 70; Connolly, *Priests and People*, pp. 200–1.
52   Mary to O'Connell, 28 December 1823, NLI, Ms. 13651 (25).
53   Mary to O'Connell, 19 January 1824, NLI, Ms. 13651 (26).
54   Ibid., 23, 30 January 1824.
55   Ibid., 30 January 1824.
56   O'Connell to Mary, 5 February 1824, NLI, FS 1621.
57   Ibid., 11 March 1824. A meeting of the Trustees of the Royal College of
      Maynooth, held on 26 June 1821, had resolved, 'That after the expiration of two
      years from this date, no scholar shall be admitted … who shall not be found
      capable of answering in the Latin and Greek authors' (Battersby, *Catholic Direc-
      tory*, p. 150). Charles Connor was one year shy of the June 1823 deadline for
      admittance without knowledge of Latin and Greek.
58   The cost of attending Maynooth was estimated at £50 for the first year and at
      least £12 per year after if one had a scholarship. A pensioner was likely to pay
      £70 for the first year and around £33 per year after. While less expensive than a
      continental education, Maynooth was still very expensive and unquestionably
      out of the reach of the lower classes (Keenan, *Catholic Church*, pp. 62–3).
59   Connolly, *Priests and People*, pp. 35, 39.
60   Ibid., p. 47.
61   For a detailed history of Maynooth College see, J. Healy, *Maynooth College,
      1795–1895* (Dublin, 1895) and P.J. Corish, *Maynooth College, 1795–1995*
      (Dublin, 1995).
62   Keenan, *Catholic Church*, p. 63.
63   Mary to Daniel Jr, 31 May 1830, NLI, Ms. Accession 4705, box 3.

64   Daly, *Social and Economic History*, p. 127.

65   Keenan, *Catholic Church*, pp. 89, 90; Kevin Whelan, 'The Regional Impact of Irish Catholicism, 1700–1850', in *Common Ground: Essays on the Historical Geography of Ireland*, eds William J. Smyth and Kevin Whelan (Cork, 1988), p. 266.

66   Mary to O'Connell, 20 March 1813, NLI, Ms. 13650 (26).

67   Mary to O'Connell, 28 September 1816, NLI, Ms. 13651 (9); O'Connell to Mary, 23 May 1823, NLI, FS 1621.

68   Battersby, *Catholic Directory*, p. 151.

69   Connolly, *Religion and Society*, p. 10.

70   Mary to O'Connell, 7 May 1823, NLI, Ms. 13651 (25); 18 March 1820, NLI, Ms. Accession 4705, box 3.

71   Mary to O'Connell, 28 March 1820, NLI, Ms. 13651 (20).

72   D.H. Akenson, *The Church of Ireland: Ecclesiastical Reform and Revolution, 1800–1885* (New Haven, 1971), p. 141.

73   Daly, *Social and Economic History*, p. 114.

74   Connolly, *Priests and People*, p. 85; Whelan, 'Irish Catholicism', p. 266.

75   Keenan, *Catholic Church*, p. 148; Catholic University of America, *New Catholic Encyclopædia, Vol. IV*, p. 833; O'Connell to Mary, 19 December 1822, NLI, FS 1621.

76   Mary to O'Connell, 4 April 1820, NLI, Ms. 13651 (21).

77   Mary to O'Connell, 25 February 1824, NLI, Ms. 13651 (28).

78   Mary to O'Connell, 16 September 1814, NLI, Ms. 13650 (31); 8 April 1816, NLI, Ms. 13651 (5); 12 April 1816, NLI, Ms. 13651 (6).

79   Mary to O'Connell, 2 April 1808, NLI, Ms. 13650 (15); 7 September 1819, NLI, Ms. 13651 (19).

80   O'Connell to Mary, 4 April 1816, NLI, Ms. Accession 4705, box 3; 15 May 1822, NLI, FS 1621.

81   Mary to O'Connell, 18 March 1820, NLI, Ms. Accession 4705, box 3; O'Connell to Mary, 2 April 1820, NLI, FS 1621; Mary to Daniel Jr, 1 January 1831, NLI, Ms. 13644 (11); 19 January, 23 March 1831, NLI, Ms. 13644 (9).

82   O'Connell to Mary, 1 February 1803, NLI, FS 1620.

83   Mary to O'Connell, 7 March 1807, UCD P12/2B/218; 10 April 1808, UCD P12/2B/224.

84   O'Connell to Mary, 5 February 1824, NLI, FS 1621.

85   Battersby, *Catholic Directory*, p. 85.

86   Keenan, *Catholic Church*, p. 23.

87   Mary to O'Connell, 11, 16 March 1816, NLI, Ms. 13651 (4); O'Connell to Mary, 20 March 1816, NLI, Ms. Accession 4705, box 3.

88   O'Connell to Mary, 28 March 1816, NLI, Ms. Accession 4705, box 3; 10, 26 March 1823, NLI, FS 1621.

89   O'Connell to Mary, 27 February 1824, NLI, FS 1621.

90   P. Coleman to Mary, 4 March 1824, NLI, Ms. 13645 (7).

91   Mary to O'Connell, 4 April 1816, NLI, Ms. 13651 (5); 13 April 1816, NLI, Ms. 13651 (1).

92   Battersby, *Catholic Directory*, p. 86.

93   Mary to O'Connell, 17 March 1818, NLI, Ms. 13651 (15); O'Connell to Mary, 5 February 1823, 11 March, 10 April 1824, NLI, FS 1621.

94   Mary to O'Connell, 13 April 1816, NLI, Ms. 13651 (1); 16 April 1816, NLI, Ms. 13651 (6); 5 April 1817, NLI, Ms. 13651 (11).
95   Mary to O'Connell, 10 April 1811, NLI, Ms. 13650 (23).
96   O'Connell to Mary, 29 June, 13 July 1823, 19 April 1825, NLI, FS 1621.
97   Ibid., 10 March 1823.
98   Mary to O'Connell, 7 May 1823, NLI, Ms. 13651 (25).
99   O'Connell to Mary, 22 May 1823, NLI, FS 1621.
100 Ibid., 22, 23 May 1823.
101 Ibid., 2 April 1823.
102 Mary to O'Connell, 27 February 1824, NLI, Ms. 13651 (28).
103 O'Connell to Mary, 18 April, 7 December 1823, NLI, FS 1621.
104 Connolly, *Religion and Society*, p. 47–8.
105 Ibid., p. 99.
106 Kevin Whelan, 'The Catholic Church in County Tipperary 1700–1900', in *Tipperary: History and Society*, ed. William Nolan (Dublin, 1985), p. 242.
107 Mary to O'Connell, 26 August 1806, NLI, Ms. 13650 (11); 12 June 1817, NLI, Ms. 13651 (12); 19 February 1824, NLI, Ms. 13651 (28).
108 Connolly, *Priests and People*, p. 30.
109 Connolly, *Religion and Society*, p. 52; Whelan, 'The Catholic Parish', p. 2; Whelan, 'Irish Catholicism', pp. 266–7, 271.

CONCLUSION

1   For an excellent bibliography of sources in women's history see Maria Luddy, *Women in Ireland, 1800–1918: A Documentary History* (Cork, 1995).
2   Luddy, *Women in Ireland*, p. xxvi
3   Maryann Gialanella Valiulis and Mary O'Dowd, eds, *Women and Irish History: Essays in Honour of Margaret MacCurtain* (Dublin, 1997), p. 9.

Bibliography

PRIMARY SOURCES

MANUSCRIPTS

O'Connell Papers. National Library of Ireland, Dublin.
O'Connell Papers. University College Dublin Archives, Dublin.
O'Connell-FitzSimon Papers. Microfilm. National Library of Ireland, Dublin

PUBLISHED DOCUMENTS AND LETTERS

Fitzpatrick, W. J., ed. *The Correspondence of Daniel O'Connell.* 2 vols, London, 1888.
Houston, Arthur. *Daniel O'Connell: His Early Life, and Journal, 1795–1802.* London, 1906.
O'Connell, M.R., ed. *The Correspondence of Daniel O'Connell.* 8 vols, Shannon, 1972.

CONTEMPORARY BOOKS AND PAMPHLETS

Annual Register, a record of World Events, 1836. London, 1837.
First Report of the Dublin Society, for the Improvement and Encouragement of Servants; from its institution, 5 May 1825, to December 31, 1827. Dublin, 1828.
Battersby, W. J., ed. *A Complete Catholic Directory, Almanack, and Registry.* Dublin, 1836.
Buchan, William. *Domestic Medicine, or a Treatise on the Prevention and Cure of Diseases by Regimen and Simple Medicines.* 9th ed. Dublin, 1784.
Courtenay, Ellen. *A Narrative by Miss Ellen Courtenay, of Most Extraordinary Cruelty, Perfidy & Depravity, Perpetrated Against Her by Daniel O'Connell, Esq. (M.P. for Kerry): and also A Faithful History of Many of the Circumstance of her Eventful Life, Which such Outrage immediately, collaterally or remotely influenced.* London, 1832.
O'Connell, Mrs. Morgan John (Mary Anne). *The Last Colonel of the Irish Brigade.* London, 1892.
O'Neill Daunt, W. J. *Personal Recollections of Daniel O'Connell,* vol. 1. London, 1848.

Plumtre, Anne. *Narrative of a Residence in Ireland, 1814–1815*. London, 1817.

Solomon, S. *Guide and Health, or Advice to Both Sexes in a Variety of Complaints*. 2nd ed. Stockport, 1800.

SECONDARY SOURCES

BOOKS

Akenson, D.H. *The Church of Ireland: Ecclesiastical Reform and Revolution, 1800–1885*. New Haven, Connecticut, 1971.

Anderson, Howard, Philip B. Daghlian and Irvin Ehrenpreis, eds. *The Familiar Letter in the Eighteenth Century*. Lawrence, Kansas, 1966.

Anderson, Michael. *Approaches to the History of the Western Family 1500–1914*. London, 1980.

Ariès, Philippe. *Centuries of Childhood*. Translated by Robert Baldick. London, 1973.

Barker-Benfield, G.J. *The Horrors of the Half-Known Life: Male Attitudes toward Women and Sexuality in Nineteenth-Century America*. New York, 1976.

Bell, Susan Groag, and Karen M. Offen, eds. *Women, the Family, and Freedom: The Debate in Documents, Vol. I, 1750–1880*. Stanford, California, 1983.

Bossy, John. *The English Catholic Community 1570–1850*. London, 1975.

Bott, Elizabeth. *Family and Social Network*. London, 1957.

Boyce, D. George. *Nineteenth-Century Ireland: The Search for Stability*. Dublin, 1990.

Bradley, Ian. *The English Middle Classes are Alive and Kicking*. London, 1982.

Brain, Lord. *Doctors Past and Present*. Springfield, Illinois, 1964.

Browne, Alan, ed. *Masters, Midwives and Ladies-in-Waiting: The Rotunda Hospital 1745–1995*. Dublin, 1995.

Burke, Peter. *Popular Culture in Early Modern Europe*. London, 1978.

Catholic University of America. *New Catholic Encyclopaedia*. New York, 1967.

Connolly, S. J. *Priests and People in Pre-Famine Ireland, 1780–1845*. Dublin, 1982.

——. *Religion and Society in Nineteenth-Century Ireland*. Dublin, 1985.

Corish, P.J. *Maynooth College, 1795–1995*. Dublin, 1995.

Corkery, Daniel. *The Hidden Ireland: The Gaelic Poetry of Eighteenth-Century Munster*. Dublin, 1925, repr. 1967.

Cott, Nancy F. *The Bonds of Womanhood: 'Woman's Sphere' in New England, 1780–1835*. New Haven, Connecticut, 1977.

Cullen, L.M. *The Emergence of Modern Ireland, 1600–1900*. New York, 1981.

——. *The Hidden Ireland: Reassessment of a Concept*. Dublin, 1988.

Daly, Mary E. *Social and Economic History of Ireland since 1800*. Dublin, 1981.

Davidoff, Lenore. *The Best Circles: Society Etiquette and the Season*. London, 1973.

Davidoff, Lenore, and Catherine Hall. *Family Fortunes: Men and Women of the English Middle Class, 1780–1850*. London, 1992.

Day, Robert Adams. *Told in Letters*. Ann Arbor, Michigan, 1966.

deMause, Lloyd, ed. *The History of Childhood*. New York, 1974.

Drinka, G.F. *The Birth of Neurosis: Myth, Malady, and the Victorians*. New York, 1985.

Dunlevy, Máiréad. *Dress in Ireland*. London, 1989.

Durey, Michael. *The Return of the Plague: British Society and the Cholera, 1831–32.* Dublin, 1979.

Ehrenreich, B., and D. English. *Complaints and Disorders: The Sexual Politics of Sickness*. New York, 1973.

Edwards, R. Dudley. *Daniel O'Connell and his World*. London, 1975.

Estes, J. Worth. *Dictionary of Protopharmacology, Therapeutic Practices, 1700–1850.* Massachusetts, 1990.

Fildes, Valerie. *Breasts, Bottles and Babies: A History of Infant Feeding*. Edinburgh, 1985.

Fitzpatrick, David. *Oceans of Consolation: Personal Accounts of Irish Migration to Australia*. Cork, 1994.

Fleetwood, John. *History of Medicine in Ireland*. Dublin, 1951.

Gelles, Edith. *Portia: The World of Abigail Adams*. Bloomington, Indiana, 1992.

Goldwater, Leonard J. *Mercury: A History of Quicksilver*. Baltimore, Maryland, 1972.

Gwynn, Denis. *Daniel O'Connell and Ellen Courtenay*. Oxford, 1930.

Healy, J. *Maynooth College, 1795–1895*. Dublin, 1895.

Heilbrun, Carolyn. *Writing a Woman's Life*. n.p., 1988.

Herbert, Dorothea. *Restrospections of Dorothea Herbert*, 'Women's History', 1770–1806. With accompanying commentary by L.M. Cullen. Dublin, 1988.

Hufton, Olwen. *The Prospect Before Her: A History of Women in Western Europe, Vol. 1, 1500–1800*. London, 1995

Jalland, Pat. *Women, Marriage and Politics 1860–1914*. Oxford, 1986.

Keenan, Desmond. *The Catholic Church in Nineteenth-Century Ireland: A Sociological Study*. Dublin, 1983.

Legg, Marie-Louise, ed. *The Synge Letters: Bishop Edward Synge to His Daughter Alicia, Roscommon to Dublin, 1746–1752*. Dublin, 1996.

Lerner, Gerda. *The Majority Finds Its Past: Placing Women in History*. Oxford, 1979.

——. *The Creation of Feminist Consciousness*. New York, 1993.

Lewis, Judith. *In the Family Way: Childbearing in the British Aristocracy, 1750–1860*. New Brunswick, New Jersey, 1986.

McCartney, Donal. *The Dawning of Democracy: Ireland 1800–1870*. Dublin, 1987.

MacCurtain, Margaret, and Donnchadh Ó Corráin, eds. *Women in Irish Society: The Historical Dimension*. Dublin, 1978.

MacDonagh, Michael. *The Life of Daniel O'Connell*. London, 1903.

MacDonagh, Oliver. *O'Connell: The Life of Daniel O'Connell, 1775–1847*. London, 1991.

McDowell, R.B., ed. *Social Life in Ireland 1800–1845*. Dublin, 1957.

McFarlane, A. *Marriage and Love in England 1300–1840*. New York, 1986.

McMorran, Russell. *Tralee: A Short History and Guide to Tralee and Environs*. n.p., 1980.

Malcomson, A.P.W. *The Pursuit of the Heiress: Aristocratic Marriage in Ireland, 1750–1820*. n.p., 1982.

Maxwell, Constantia. *Country and Town in Ireland under the Georges*. Dundalk, 1949.

O'Connell, M.R. *Daniel O'Connell: The Man and his Politics*. Dublin, 1990.

O'Connor, Sir James. *History of Ireland, 1798–1924, Vol. I*. London, 1925.

O'Dwyer, Michael. *Tralee, A Historical Guide*. n.p., n.d.

O'Faolain, Sean. *King of the Beggars*. London, 1938.

O'Ferrall, Fergus. *Daniel O'Connell and His World*. Dublin, 1981.

Offen, Karen, Ruth Roach Pierson and Jane Rendall, eds. *Writing Women's History: International Perspectives*. London, 1991.

Pinchbeck, Ivy, and Margaret Hewitt. *Children in English Society*. London, 1973.

Pollock, Linda A. *Forgotten Children: Parent-Child Relations from 1500–1900*. Cambridge, 1983.

Porter, Dorothy, and Roy Porter. *Patients' Progress: Doctors and Doctoring in Eighteenth Century England*. Cambridge, 1989.

Porter, Roy, ed. *Patients and Practitioners. Lay Perceptions of Medicine in Pre-Industrial Society*. Cambridge, 1985.

Porter, Roy, and Dorothy Porter. *In Sickness and in Health: The British Experience 1650–1850*. London, 1988.

Quinlan, M.J. *Victorian Prelude: A History of English Manners 1700–1830*. London, 1941.

Rendall, Jane. *The Origins of Modern Feminism: Women in Britain, France and the United States, 1780–1860*. Chicago, 1985.

Risse, G.B. *Hospital Life in Enlightenment Scotland*. Cambridge, 1986.

Robins, Joseph. *The Lost Children: A Study of Charity Children in Ireland, 1700–1900*. Dublin, 1980.

Schmidt, J.E. *Medical Discoveries, Who and When*. Springfield, Illinois, 1959.

Shorter, Edward. *The Making of the Modern Family*. London, 1976.

——. *A History of Women's Bodies*. London, 1983.

Smith-Rosenberg, Carroll. *Disorderly Conduct: Visions of Gender in Victorian America*. New York, 1986.

Somerville-Large, Peter. *Dublin: The First Thousand Years*. Belfast, 1988.

Stone, Lawrence. *The Family, Sex and Marriage in England 1500–1800*. London, 1977.

Sussman, George. *Selling Mother's Milk: The Wet-Nursing Business in France, 1715–1914*. Illinois, 1982.

Tillyard, Stella. *Aristocrats: Caroline, Emily, Louisa and Sarah Lennox 1740–1832*. London, 1994.

Trumbach, Randolph. *The Rise of the Egalitarian Family*. New York, 1978.

Ulrich, Laurel Thatcher. *A Midwife's Tale: The Life of Martha Ballard, Based on Her Diary, 1785–1812*. New York, 1990.

Valiulis, Maryann Gialanella, and Mary O'Dowd, eds. *Women and Irish History: Essays in Honour of Margaret MacCurtain*. Dublin, 1997.

Whelan, Kevin. *The Tree of Liberty: Radicalism, Catholicism and the Construction of Irish Identity, 1760–1830*. Cork, 1996.

Williams, Guy. *The Age of Miracles*. London, 1981.

ARTICLES

Adams, B.N. 'The Social Significance of Kinship: 2.' In *Sociology of the Family*, edited by Michael Anderson. Harmondsworth, 1971.

Barker-Benfield, B. 'The Spermatic Economy: A Nineteenth-Century View of Sexuality.' *Feminist Studies* 1 (1973): 45–56.

Chevigny, Bell Gale. 'Daughters Writing: Toward a Theory of Women's Biography.' *Feminist Studies* 9/1 (Spring 1983): 79–102.

Clarkson, L.A. 'Love, Labour and Life: Women in Carrick-on-Suir in the Late Eighteenth Century.' *Irish Economic and Social History* 20 (1993): 18–24.

Connell, K.H. 'Marriage in Ireland after the Great Famine: The Diffusion of the Match'. *Journal of the Statistical and Social Inquiry Society of Ireland* XIX (1945–6): 82–103.

Connolly, S.J. 'The "blessed turf": cholera and popular panic in Ireland, June 1832.' *Irish Historical Studies* 23/91 (May 1983): 214–32.

———. 'Marriage in Pre-Famine Ireland.' In *Marriage in Ireland*, edited by Art Cosgrove. Dublin, 1985.

———. 'Approaches to the History of Irish Popular Culture.' *Bullán* 2/2 (Winter/Spring 1988): 83–100.

———. 'Family, Love and Marriage: Some Evidence from the Early Eighteenth Century.' In *Women in Early Modern Ireland*, edited by Mary O'Dowd and Margaret MacCurtain. Edinburgh, 1991.

Corish, P.J. 'The Catholic Community in the Nineteenth Century.' *Archivium Hibernicum* 38 (1983): 26–33.

———. 'Catholic Marriage Under the Penal Code.' In *Marriage in Ireland*, edited by Art Cosgrove. Dublin, 1985.

———. 'Women and Religious Practices.' In *Women in Early Modern Ireland*, edited by Mary O'Dowd and Margaret MacCurtain. Edinburgh, 1991.

Cott, Nancy F. 'Passionless: An Interpretation of Victorian Sexual Ideology, 1790–1850.' *Signs* 4 (1978): 219–36.

Daly, Mary. 'Feminist Research Methodology: The Case of Ireland.' Paper presented to the Third International Interdisciplinary Congress on Women, Dublin, July 6–10, 1987.

Daly, Mary E. 'Late Nineteenth and Early Twentieth-Century Dublin.' In *The Town in Ireland*, edited by D.W. Harkness and M. O'Dowd. Belfast, 1981.

Davis, Natalie Zemon. '"Women's History" in Transition: The European Case.' *Feminist Studies* 3/3–4 (Spring–Summer 1976): 83–103.

Degler, Carl N. 'What Ought To Be and What Was: Women's Sexuality in the Nineteenth Century.' *American Historical Review* 79/5 (December 1974): 1467–90.

di Leonardo, Micaela. 'The Female World of Cards and Holidays: Women, Families and the Work of Kinship.' *Signs* 21 (1987): 440–53.

Dickson, David. 'Middlemen.' In *Penal Era and Golden Age: Essays in Irish History, 1690–1800*, edited by Thomas Bartlett and D.W. Hayton. Belfast, 1979.

Figlio, K. 'Chlorosis and Chronic Disease in Nineteenth-Century Britain: The Social Constitution of Somatic Illness in a Capitalist Society.' *Social History* 3 (1978): 167–97.

Fitzpatrick, David. 'Women, Gender, and the Writing of Irish History.' *Irish Historical Studies* 27/107 (May 1991): 267–73.

Gluckman, Max. 'Gossip and Scandal.' *Current Anthropology* 4 (1963): 307–16.

Handelman, Dan. 'Gossip in Encounters: The Transmission of Information in a Bounded Society.' *Man* 8 (1973): 210–27.

Horgan, John J. 'O'Connell—The Man.' In *Daniel O'Connell: Nine Centenary Essays*, edited by Michael Tierney. Dublin, 1949.

BIBLIOGRAPHY

Kelly-Gadol, Joan. 'The Social Relation of the Sexes: Methodological Implications of Women's History.' *Signs* 1/4 (Summer 1976): 809–24.

——. 'The Doubled Vision of Feminist Theory: A Postscript to the "Women and Power" Conference.' *Feminist Studies* 5 (1979): 216–27.

Kiely, Benedict. 'The House at Derrynane.' *Capuchin Annual* (1946): 393–407.

Lawless, Jo Murphy. 'The Silencing of Women in Childbirth or Let's Hear it for Bartholomew and the Boys.' *Women's Studies International Forum* 6/4 (1988): 293–8.

Lee, J.J. 'Daniel O'Connell.' In *Daniel O'Connell: Political Pioneer*, edited by M.R. O'Connell. Dublin, 1991.

L'Esperance, Jean. 'Doctors and Women in Nineteenth-Century Society: Sexuality and Role.' In *Healthcare and Popular Medicine in Nineteenth-Century England: Essays in the Social History of Medicine*, edited by J. Woodward and D. Richards. London, 1977.

Lewis, Judith. 'Maternal Health in English Aristocracy: Myth and Realities, 1790–1840.' *Journal of Social History* 17/1 (Fall 1983): 97–114.

McCracken, J.L. 'The Age of the Stage Coach.' In *Travel and Transport in Ireland*, edited by Kevin Nowlan. Dublin, 1973.

Mulvey, Helen. 'The Correspondence of Daniel and Mary O'Connell.' In *The Correspondence of Daniel O'Connell*, vol. 1, edited by M.R. O'Connell. Shannon, 1972.

Murphy, Gerard. 'The Gaelic Background.' In *Daniel O'Connell: Nine Centenary Essays*, edited by Michael Tierney. Dublin, 1949.

O'Connell, Maurice R. 'Income and Expenditure.' In *Daniel O'Connell, The Man and His Politics*. Dublin, 1990.

——. 'O'Connell and his Family.' In *The World of Daniel O'Connell*, edited by Donal McCartney. Dublin, 1980.

Ó Danachair, Caoimhín. 'Marriage in Irish Folk Tradition.' In *Marriage in Ireland*, edited by Art Cosgrove. Dublin, 1985.

Ó Muirithe, Diarmaid. 'O'Connell in Irish Folk Tradition.' In *Daniel O'Connell: Political Pioneer*, edited by M.R. O'Connell. Dublin, 1991.

O'Neill, Kevin. '"Almost a Gentlewoman": Gender and Adolescence in the Diary of Mary Shackleton.' In *Chattel, Servant or Citizen: Women's Status in Church, State and Society*, edited by Mary O'Dowd and Sabine Wichert. Belfast, 1995.

Ó Tuathaigh, Gearóid. 'The Folk-hero and Tradition.' In *The World of Daniel O'Connell*, edited by Donal McCartney. Dublin, 1980.

Offen, Karen. 'Defining Feminism: A Comparative Historical Approach.' *Signs* 14/1 (1988): 119–57.

Paine, Robert. 'What is Gossip About? An Alternative Hypothesis.' *Man* 2 (1967): 278–85.

Quilligan, Maureen. 'Rewriting History: The Difference of Feminist Biography.' *The Yale Review* (Winter 1988): 259–86.

Rapp, R., E. Ross and R. Brindenthal. 'Examining Family History.' *Feminist Studies* V (1979): 174–200.

Scott, Joan W. 'Women's History: The Modern Period.' *Past and Present* 101 (1983): 141–57.

——. 'Gender, A Useful Category of Historical Analysis.' *American Historical Review* 91/4 (October 1986): 1053–75.

Scott, Joan W. and Louise A. Tilly. 'Women's Work and the Family in Nineteenth-Century Europe.' *Comparative Studies in Society and History* 17 (1975): 36–64.

Shorter, Edward. 'Female Emancipation, Birth Control, and Fertility in European History.' *American Historical Review* 78 (1973): 605–40.

Smith-Rosenberg, Carroll. 'The Hysterical Woman: Sex Roles and Role Conflict in Nineteenth-Century America.' *Social Research* 39 (1972): 652–78.

——. 'Puberty to Menopause: The Cycle of Femininity in Nineteenth-Century America.' *Feminist Studies* 1/3–4 (Winter–Spring 1973): 58–72.

——. 'The Female World of Love and Ritual: Relations between Women in Nineteenth Century America.' *Signs* 1 (Autumn 1975): 1–29.

Smith-Rosenberg, Carroll, et al. 'Politics and Culture in Women's History: A Symposium.' *Feminist Studies* 6 (Spring 1980): 55–64.

Suitor, J. Jill. 'Husbands' Participation in Childbirth: A Nineteenth-Century Phenomenon.' *Journal of Family History* 6/3 (Fall 1981): 278–93.

Sussman, G. D. 'The End of the Wet-Nursing Business in France 1874–1914.' *Journal of Family History* 2/3 (1977): 237–58.

Welter, Barbara. 'The Cult of True Womanhood: 1820–1860.' *American Quarterly* 18/2 (Summer 1966): 151–74.

Whelan, Kevin. 'The Catholic Parish, the Catholic Chapel and Village Development in Ireland.' *Irish Geography* 16 (1983): 1–15

——. 'The Catholic Church in County Tipperary, 1700–1900.' In *Tipperary: History and Society*, edited by William Nolan. Dublin, 1985.

——. 'The Regional Impact of Irish Catholicism 1700–1850.' In *Common Ground: Essays on the Historical Geography of Ireland*, edited by William J. Smyth and Kevin Whelan. Cork, 1988.

——. 'An Underground Gentry? Catholic Middlemen in Eighteenth-Century Ireland.' In *The Tree of Liberty: Radicalism, Catholicism and the Construction of Irish Identity, 1760–1830*. Cork, 1996.

Wickes, Ian G. 'A History of Infant Feeding, Part III: Eighteenth and Nineteenth-Century Writers.' *Archives of Disease in Childhood* 28 (1953): 332–40.

——. 'A History of Infant Feeding, Part IV: Nineteenth Century Continued.' *Archives of Disease in Childhood* 28 (1953): 416–502.

Wood, Ann Douglass. 'The Fashionable Diseases: Women's Complaints and their Treatment in Nineteenth-Century America.' *Journal of Interdisciplinary History* 4 (Summer 1973): 25–52.

Index